Gone to Another Meeting

Judaic Studies Series
Leon J. Weinberger, General Editor

Gone to Another Meeting

THE NATIONAL COUNCIL OF JEWISH WOMEN,
1893–1993

FAITH ROGOW

With a Foreword by Joan Bronk

The University of Alabama Press

Tuscaloosa and London

Copyright © 1993
The University of Alabama Press
Tuscaloosa, Alabama 35487–0380
All rights reserved
Manufactured in the United States of America

designed by zig zeigler

∞

The paper on which this book is printed meets the minimum
requirements of American National Standard for Information
Science-Permanence of Paper for Printed Library Materials,
ANSI Z39.48–1984.

Library of Congress Cataloging-in-Publication Data

Rogow, Faith, 1958–
    Gone to another meeting : the National Council of Jewish Women,
1893–1993 / Faith Rogow.
        p.   cm. — (Judaic studies series)
    Includes bibliographical references and index.
    ISBN 0-8173-0671-4
    1. National Council of Jewish Women—History.   2. Women, Jewish—
United States—Societies and clubs—History.   I. Title.
II. Series: Judaic studies series (Unnumbered)
HQ1904.R65   1993
305.48′696—dc20   92-24721

British Library Cataloguing-in-Publication Data available

If we could see the fabric of our lives spread out
What a wonderful weaving it might show;
Many a thread that we thought lost would re-appear
And form strange patterns of cause and effect.

(excerpt from poem by Theresa G. Lesem
appearing on dedication page of Hannah
G. Solomon's autobiography, *Fabric of
My Life*)

Contents

Foreword

EJECTED by the Jewish men's groups of the day, threatened by the missionary aspects of predominantly Christian social reform groups, and attacked by some Jewish religious leaders as well as the Jewish press, the fledgling National Council of Jewish Women emerged from its nest of home and family at the turn of the century. As NCJW grew to its present-day stature, it fulfilled its founders' vision of a vast national Jewish women's organization addressing human needs.

As Faith Rogow has detailed in these pages, however, the organization experienced several awkward periods. NCJW sought to address social welfare problems in the Jewish *and* general communities. Serving both populations was a massive undertaking. Even today, it is rare to find a Jewish organization that bridges both worlds.

Early NCJW leaders also were faced with accommodating differences of opinion within the membership. That the organization survived secessions and other crises is due in no small part to the skillful abilities of its founders and their judicious use of compromise. Stretching resources to the limit, the young NCJW met the demands of other organizations to coalesce around important projects, responded to the requests of the federal and local governments, and promoted new methods of advancing social welfare. Quite a tightrope act, as Rogow has commented.

The analysis of NCJW's first hundred years is absorbing reading; its second hundred are proving to be fascinating in the planning. As always, the NCJW is rapidly evolving.

During the interval that has elapsed since the author completed this work, the organization has placed increased emphasis on protection of women's reproductive rights—with an ongoing public education campaign, initiated in 1989. Pouring its resources into this campaign, NCJW today is the leading Jewish organization working on this issue. Balanced with this attention to women's issues is NCJW's traditional concern for the needs of families now translated into innovative national programs.

NCJW is particularly devoted to determining the nature and causes of problems as part of its continuing agenda to *prevent* as well as resolve social ills. Toward these goals, NCJW incorporates two research institutions: the Center for the Child housed at national headquarters in New York City; and the NCJW Research Institute for Innovation in Education at The Hebrew University of Jerusalem. These institutes provide invaluable data leading to NCJW advocacy and community service action on issues concerning children and their families.

At heart, the organization retains its original principles. Among them are a devotion to providing Jewish women with a national forum; a dedication to fulfilling its mission within the ethical context of Judaism; and a bedrock commitment to moral action regardless of fashion or public opinion.

Hannah Solomon wrote of her thoughts before NCJW's founding: "Should we have a [women's] congress; . . . would it have permanence, or would it be a brief bright tale in which was written, 'they met and parted.' In a flash, my thoughts crystallized to decision: we will have a congress out of which must grow a permanent organization!"

One hundred years later, there is no doubt that the National Council of Jewish Women is here to stay.

JOAN BRONK
National President
National Council of Jewish Women
New York City

Preface

HIS STUDY begins
with the assumption that rigid separation of gender roles in the
Jewish community led Jewish women and men to experience the
world differently. Rather than assume that American Jewish culture
was shaped largely by men with occasional help from women, I
have attempted to examine why and where men and women differed in their beliefs and practices, seeing this evaluation as a first
step toward a more complete understanding of an American Jewish
community that is the fusion of both male and female experience.
The National Council of Jewish Women is a productive starting
point for exploring that fusion because during its one-hundred-year
history it has functioned as an important conduit through which
Jewish women's voices have come to be heard.

Because in the past Jewish women's voices have so often been
ignored or silenced, this study attempts to let its subjects speak for
themselves as much as possible. In addition to extensive quotes, I
have omitted the definite article before references to NCJW or
Council and used "triennial" rather than "triennial convention" to
refer to NCJW's regular national conventions. This reflects the
speech patterns of Council members and therefore seems to give a
more authentic tone to the descriptions of their activities. Also,
when describing the years prior to World War I, the term "Jewish

community" refers to the community with which most Council women identified—the German Jewish community. It does not refer to the Eastern European immigrant Jewish community except where noted. I have also tried to quote as many different Council members as possible, and while Council's top leadership is inevitably overrepresented, the reader will find a diversity of voices that I believe accurately reflects the diversity within the organization itself.

Readers will also note that Council's post–World War II efforts are treated in a more general way than those of its formative years. In part this treatment is because details of Council's founding were necessary to demonstrate how Council's early decisions effected the formulation of policy in subsequent decades. In addition, the lack of detail for later time periods reflects a real decline in Council's influence in the Jewish community over the last half-century.

No study is undertaken in a vacuum; nor can a work such as this be completed without a great deal of support. My initial thanks goes to Rabbi Sue Elwell, who first brought NCJW to my attention and whose willingness to share her own research made the biographical sections of this study possible. I am also indebted to the State University of New York at Binghamton for its financial support and for the extraordinary encouragement and high quality of critical guidance I received from my thesis committee, Paula Hyman, Elizabeth Fox-Genovese, Kathryn Kish Sklar, Lance Sussman, and Deborah Britzman. A special thanks goes to Ellen Umansky, who was gracious enough to read the manuscript in its entirety, and whose insightful comments helped me clarify many issues.

The awarding of a Harvey B. Franklin Memorial Fellowship by the American Jewish Archives enabled me to complete the bulk of my research. Archives Associate Director Abraham J. Peck and Archivist Fanny Zelcer made my sojourn in Cincinnati both productive and pleasant. Paul Ledvina, Senior Manuscript Librarian at the Library of Congress, was also very helpful in guiding me to available sources. Without the support of these research institutions and their staffs, this study would not have come to fruition.

I also received essential cooperation from the national office of the National Council of Jewish Women. Assistant to the Executive Director Helen Powers answered all my queries with speed and spirit. She opened significant doors by arranging for me to interview Council leaders. Thanks are also due Council's 1987 national board members, who graciously agreed to share with me their perceptions about their organization, both positive and negative. Their frank and open assessments were an unusual and welcome departure from the tendency of leaders to paint their organizations in rosy hues. Their sincerity and devotion to Council were unmistakable, and I hope I have thanked them by presenting their organization with respect and fairness.

Finally, my deepest gratitude goes to my life partner Del Brown. Without her creative spirit, well-timed hugs, and willingness to support me this book would not exist.

Gone to Another Meeting

Introduction

*C*OMMENTING on her busy schedule, turn-of-the-century Chicago Council member Sara Hart quipped that if she were writing her own epitaph, her tombstone would read, "Gone To Another Meeting."[1] Her joke reflected the lifestyle of most early National Council of Jewish Women members. Like Hart, who served on more than twenty-five committees in a variety of Progressive social reform organizations, Council women considered volunteer work their special vocation. Council founder Hannah G. Solomon declared, "I was born a clubwoman, just as I was born . . . a Jew."[2] The pride inherent in this remark exposes the faultiness of common depictions of club "ladies" as incompetent, flighty, and shallow. To the contrary, club-women recognized their power to influence their communities through their organizations and consequently took their work quite seriously. Though outwardly they may have promoted themselves as genteel ladies, Council Board members were important community leaders.

Modeled after secular women's clubs, NCJW's organizational heritage was a combination of nineteenth-century women's clubs and Progressive social reform efforts. In some arenas, such as the fight against the white slave trade, the development of settlement

1

houses, and the aid of female immigrants, NCJW served as the Jewish component of a broader effort. As such, Council supplied both a Jewish voice in the world of women's clubs and a way to Americanize without sacrificing Jewish identity. NCJW was popular with Hart, Solomon, and their peers largely because it provided this point of intersection for otherwise scattered (and sometimes conflicting) facets of their identities as women, as Americans, and as Jews. The organization succeeded primarily because it was able to furnish its members a means by which to acculturate without losing ethnic identity or challenging the limited definitions of gender roles dominant in the United States.

An exemplary though not ideologically innovative Progressive social reform organization, Council made a distinctive contribution, which came as much from its ability to transfer social reform ideology to the Jewish community as from its role as the Jewish component of a broad American movement. Likewise, though NCJW enabled its members to bring their Jewish identity into the world of women's clubs, Council also provided a means by which Jewish women could adapt women's clubs' ideology of gender to the Jewish community. Founded in 1893, NCJW was the offspring of the economic and social success achieved by German Jewish immigrants in the United States. As this community of German Jews matured and stabilized, it faced the same challenge to gender role definitions that had accompanied Jacksonian democracy a half century earlier. That is, in light of their reverence for popular democracy and its promise of equal rights for every individual, how could the community justify continuing a double standard that granted men rights not given to women?[3]

The popular American answer to that dilemma was to define male and female natures (and therefore needs) as intrinsically different. Victorian notions of womanhood prevailed, limiting woman's arena to her home and her emotions. To men fell the public worlds of work and politics, as well as the tools of intellectual pursuit that would advance those areas. This division of gender roles left middle- and upper-class American women in an ironic position. On one hand, they enjoyed the prosperity brought by their husbands' labor, they believed in American democracy as the best guarantor of that prosperity, and they saw America's continued technological and commercial progress ease the burdens of caring for home and children. On the other hand, women found themselves excluded from any direct exercise of power in American society and prevented by social convention and law from taking advantage of the growing opportunities available to men.

By the mid-nineteenth century, many of these women had solved their conflict by transforming themselves from dutiful helpmates to domestic scientists and clubwomen. Participation in clubs took women beyond the confines of the home into the community, giving them what historian Theodora Penny Martin has termed a "semi-public" voice.[4] That is, women's clubs never seriously competed with men for public power, but they provided women with a piece of the "male" public pie by fostering self-education, public socializing, and charity work.

Council's role in American debates over attempts to modernize Jewish practice exemplified this "semi-public" club experience. Coming from communities to which they believed they could never return, German Jews had developed a uniquely American form of Reform Judaism as a way of adapting to American life without losing their religious identity. Reform's emphasis on modernization and acceptance of pragmatic changes in ritual would be an important precondition for NCJW's expansion of the traditional boundaries of Jewish womanhood, but it also invited late nineteenth-century challenges from traditionalists upset by Reform's apparent devaluation of Jewish law and custom. By 1893, movements promoting radical Reform and those insisting on a more moderate approach had coalesced. As these groups of predominantly German Jews battled for hegemony over the American Jewish community, their positions began to solidify. Prior to Council, women largely had been excluded from this debate. NCJW provided Study Circles where women could familiarize themselves with the texts and issues under discussion. Its conventions and publications, as well as invitations its leaders received from other Jewish groups to represent Jewish women, provided forums through which women could enter the deliberations. As the *American Hebrew* recognized, unlike the scattered or fraternal Jewish women's organizations that had preceded it, Council was "a potent factor" in the Jewish community with which people of this generation (1895) "must seriously reckon when [they] consider the elements that make up the religious condition of Israel in America."[5] Most importantly, as a women's club, NCJW allowed its members to enter religious debates without breaking "proper" gender roles, thus providing a means through which Jewish women could publicly influence the future of their community without confronting such difficult and potentially divisive issues as acceptance of women as rabbis or scholars.

In fact, though NCJW's success in finding a way to express American gender roles in a Jewish context contributed decisively to creating a unique American Jewish womanhood, Council would in no way initiate radical change in the Jewish community. Like other clubwomen faced with the need to justify public activities in light of their adherence to the precepts of "True Womanhood," Council adopted what scholars have dubbed "domestic feminism." In her study of the General Federation of Women's Clubs, an umbrella organization with which NCJW eventually affiliated, Karen Blair explains that clubs were successful because they used accepted notions of womanhood to justify their activities.[6] The term "domestic feminism" was coined by historian Daniel Scott Smith, who theorized about how nineteenth-century women asserted power in the home. His research documented a declining American birthrate in an era when birth control was not widely available. He concluded that women used prevailing notions of womanhood, which depicted proper ladies as pure and chaste, to justify limiting sexual contact with their husbands.[7] Blair notes that this pattern of justification went well beyond the bedroom. For example, clubwomen insisted that social welfare work was simply an extension of motherhood, thus justifying an expansion of woman's sphere beyond the home by using the very ideology that seemingly confined her to the hearth. This pattern of justification was the core of "domestic feminism." Rather than redefining the "ideal lady," as Blair has suggested, domestic feminism simply recast women's tasks. In Hannah G. Solomon's words, "Through it all women have not changed, but their opportunities have."[8] Council, especially, placed motherhood at the core of its definition of what it meant to be a Jewish woman, even as it demanded service outside the home from its members.

Council's pattern of conservatism was not unique to the Jewish community. As Ann Douglas has demonstrated, because women's clubs were created as a way for women to "fit in" to the male scheme of things rather than challenge society's sexist ideology, they tended to foster the preservation of the status quo.[9] Douglas cites the glorification of motherhood as one example of this conservative influence. She argues that as production moved out of the home while women remained confined behind its thresholds, women in mid nineteenth-century America lost their ability to be productive. America tried to compensate by "establishing a perpetual Mother's Day."[10] Thus, Council's glorification of motherhood reflected popular American sentiment as well as traditional Jewish notions of the "Eyshet Hayil" (Woman of Valor—a passage from Proverbs that extols the virtues of an ideal wife). This fusion of American and Jewish notions of womanhood was NCJW's primary raison d'être.

Council's ability to alter significantly women's position in the Jewish community was limited, not enhanced by its acceptance of the notion of complementary gender roles and the resulting equation of womanhood with motherhood. NCJW argued that gender roles had been Divinely designed to remain separate and that women's oppression came not from the denial of rights, but from the withholding of respect. In this spirit, NCJW did not support the ordination of women as rabbis until the 1970s, viewing such ordination as an infringement of the Divine Order. Instead it elevated woman's traditional role as mother to the status previously reserved for the most respected scholars. Thus, while NCJW insisted that women's opinions be accorded the attention due a dignitary, they provided women with no direct means to gain power in the Jewish community.

Furthermore, although it developed an elaborate social and philanthropic network based on women's unique experience of life in America, the separation of gender roles which created that unique perspective resulted from male constructions of womanhood. That is, Jewish women's culture, though distinctly different from the world as experienced by Jewish men, was not created in a vacuum. It was the result of the fusion of American values and Jewish tradition, both defined almost exclusively by men. NCJW's womanhood thus reaffirmed men's power rather than challenged it. Thus, though Council seemed to carve substantial inroads to equal representation for women in Jewish communal institutions, those gains

were temporary. By the 1950s almost no women held major posi-
tions in synagogues or (nonwomen's) Jewish communal institu-
tions. Not until the rise of modern feminism in the 1970s would
Jewish women again protest their exclusion from these positions.
Despite their efforts and the groundwork laid by organizations like
NCJW, parity has not yet been achieved.

Still, Council women certainly believed that their work advanced
the interests of women, and NCJW indisputably opened up new
paths to Jewish women. The great diversity among Council Sections and shifts in its ideology of womanhood since the 1960s make
NCJW difficult to place neatly in the scheme of American feminism or the development of the women's movement. If one accepts
historian Nancy Cott's general threefold definition of feminism as
opposition to a hierarchy that posits one sex as superior to the other,
the perception of women as a social as well as biological grouping,
and the recognition that woman's condition is socially but not divinely constructed, then NCJW was only partially feminist.[11] It
adopted Cott's first two conditions but steadfastly clung to the primacy of motherhood as woman's divinely assigned role.

Writing about the General Federation of Women's Clubs, historian Karen Blair has argued that despite adherence to such traditional
conceptions of womanhood, the public activities of clubwomen
"rendered obsolete the notion that 'woman's place is in the home,'
and thereby made a significant contribution to women's struggle for
autonomy."[12] In fact, Blair has argued that domestic feminism's
moderate approach to effecting change in women's roles was more
successful than was the militant feminism of many suffragists because
it was able to attract more adherents and because it brought real
change while appearing to be nonthreatening.[13] Council member
and Barnard founder Annie Nathan Meyer expressed a similar idea
when, commenting on turn-of-the-century struggles for women's
rights she wrote, "to put any radical scheme across, it must be done in
the most conservative manner possible."[14] Council's role in the
Jewish community contradicts both Nathan and Blair.

Though Council's expression of Jewish womanhood would not
bring radical change to the Jewish community, it did contribute a
distinctive voice. The fact that Council worked from a specifically
female perspective resulted in the development of programs that

were often different from those implemented by comparable male-run organizations. Among other things, this female perspective provided the impetus for NCJW's instrumental role in carving out a Jewish niche in the social reform movement.

Yet, Council was not founded because Jewish women were excluded from non-Jewish social reform efforts. Most Council members felt quite comfortable in the world of women's clubs and social reform organizations, as is attested by their tendency to affiliate with such organizations even while committed to NCJW (see Appendix A, Chart 20). Though Council founders occasionally encountered some prejudice in these groups, they prided themselves on their successful acculturation to life in America, and class interests shared with club sisters outweighed ethnic divisions. More detailed comparative studies must be done to ascertain whether Gentile clubwomen shared this attitude or whether Council women romanticized their acceptance into women's clubs because to do otherwise would have been to admit that either their efforts to acculturate had failed or the United States was not the panacea for Jews they believed it to be. In any case, Council founders never named anti-Semitism[15] as a justification for creating their own organization. They formed NCJW to give Jewish women a stronger voice in the women's world, not to back away from participation in an anti-Semitic environment.

In many ways, NCJW represents the intersection of several crossroads within the American Jewish community. Though founded and dominated by German Jews, Council's philanthropic work would immerse its members in the newer Eastern European immigrant Jewish community. Engaged in a religious revival, the organization would be caught in the power struggle between the Reform movement and more traditional interpretations of Judaism. Immersed in the debates of the turn-of-the-century women's movement, Council would come to represent both the modernization of and the renewal of Jewish womanhood. Council's uniqueness lay in its ability to make a cloth of these varied threads. Its intricate weave of American and Jewish cultures, as well as its longevity, make it an ideal starting point for the study of the development of modern Jewish womanhood.

This study of NCJW will remain incomplete, however, until scholars have examined all facets of the development of American Jewish womanhood. Though Council provides an example of how American definitions of religion as feminine influenced the Jewish community to alter its vision of womanhood, the resulting religious character attributed to Jewish women is here reported only through Council eyes. Before we can claim to understand American Jewish womanhood, we must trace the influence of America's connection of womanhood and religion on all facets of the Jewish community. The absence of such studies makes this examination of NCJW a starting point. Its gaps are an invitation to include gender analysis in future studies of the American Jewish experience.

1.

The Founding

F HARD WORK earned
Hannah Greenebaum Solomon the honor of being named NCJW's
first president, she became its founder by being in the right place at
the right time. In 1890, Chicago's elites were excitedly beginning to
plan various facets of the forthcoming World's Fair. The Fair was
designed to provide an international showcase for American industrial leadership. Organized into congresses planned and run by
appropriate experts, the Fair highlighted the best of America's technological and social advances. For practical reasons, residents of
Chicago did much of the preparation for the Exhibition. Tasks were
assigned to committees, and committees were divided by gender. The
most important of the women's committees was the Board of Lady
Managers of the Exposition, formed in 1891.[1]

The Board, headed by Bertha Honoré Palmer, was responsible
for providing exhibit staff and for organizing much of the women's
programming, both in and out of the proposed Woman's Building.
Palmer quickly recruited friends from the elite Chicago Women's
Club to aid in the planning, including Ellen M. Henrotin, whom
she appointed vice-president of the Board of Lady Managers.
Henrotin's duties included chairing the women's branch of the
General Committee on Religious Parliament. The responsibilities

of this position required her to appoint chairs for the women's committees representing each major religious denomination. Thus, Henrotin came to consider possible candidates for the Jewish Women's Committee. Unable to find Jewish female clergy or nationally known Jewish suffragists, Henrotin turned to her friends in Chicago.

Thirty-three-year-old Hannah Solomon was an obvious choice. Fifteen years earlier, Solomon and her sister, Henrietta Frank, were the first Jews invited to join the prestigious Chicago Women's Club. Solomon's father was a prominent merchant, and her family members had been active in several civic organizations since the 1850s. As a Woman's Club member Solomon had demonstrated she was "properly" cultured as well as an ardent and effective social reformer. She was a self-proclaimed suffragist but disavowed radical tactics. She was also involved in Chicago's most prominent Jewish organizations. She belonged to the radical Reform Temple Sinai, but her relatives helped found all five of Chicago's original Reform synagogues, providing her with connections to several leading rabbis as well as to a wide range of Chicago's Jewish community.[2] In short, Solomon was the perfect chair: a consummate clubwoman and a dedicated Jew from a respected family.

Ellen Henrotin invited her friend Hannah to convene the Jewish Women's Committee "under whatever division or divisions of the Exposition she thought best."[3] Solomon accepted with idealistic hopes that the Exposition would inspire international unity and that, for the first time in recorded history, it would give the Jewish community a showcase "on an equal footing with Christianity, not to defend itself but to tell the world what are its tenets and its deeds."[4]

Solomon viewed the Exposition as a golden opportunity for the Jewish community to prove its worth, and she assumed her role with a grave sense of responsibility and unbounded energy. Sources indicate that she did much of the early work alone.[5] Her first major decision was to organize the Jewish Woman's Congress under the auspices of the World Parliament of Religions rather than as part of the events being housed at the Woman's Building, where programs were dominated by a women's rights agenda. Deborah Grand Golomb has explained this decision as choosing allegiance to Jews over allegiance to women, a choice she claims manifested itself in later NCJW policy.[6] Solomon, however, had no reason to view the two groups as mutually exclusive. Many prominent advocates of women's rights participated in the Parliament of Religions, including Elizabeth Cady Stanton and Frances Willard.[7] In fact, Solomon explained that she chose the Parliament because she "felt that in the Parliament of Religions, where women of all creeds were represented, the Jewish woman should have a place."[8]

Moreover, though Solomon generally favored positions of the women's rights activists planning the Woman's Building programs, she had reason to wonder whether Jewish women, as Jews, would be welcomed there. Particularly troubling was the feminist debate over the role of western religion in the subjection of women. Like much of the Jewish press, Solomon reacted negatively to the book around which much of that debate centered, Elizabeth Cady Stanton's *Woman's Bible*.[9] Stanton's critique of Christianity included the accusation that Judaism was ultimately at fault for women's oppression. She explained: "The dogmas incorporated in the religious creeds derived from Judaism, teaching that woman was an afterthought in creation, her sex a misfortune. . . . These dogmas are an insidious poison."[10] Solomon may have believed that this debate would be continued in any religious programming done through the Woman's Building, and feeling uncomfortable with those women who backed Stanton's position, she chose to avoid them or at least to deny them a public forum that could have conceivably obscured Jewish women's contributions with anti-Jewish rhetoric.

More important, while Solomon was certain that Judaism promoted rather than precluded rights for women, she knew that Jewish women were not yet ready to substantiate that position. Unlike their Christian sisters, some of whom were ordained clergy, most of whom were well versed in the Bible, and all of whom had been debating these religious issues for at least forty years, most Jewish women barely possessed even elementary knowledge of the fine points of Jewish learning. Jewish tradition held that formal religious education was extraneous to women's duties in the home, and American religious schools were too few in number and too poor in material resources and teachers to provide a quality education, so few Jewish women had seriously studied the texts around which the feminist debate centered. Moreover, neither American culture nor Judaism approved of a public religious leadership role for women, so few Jewish women had experience speaking in public. At the time of the Exposition there were no Jewish women's organizations anywhere in the world that publicly discussed religious issues. Solomon even commented that many of the women who spoke at the Jewish Women's Congress were speaking in public for the first time in their lives.[11] Finally, Jewish women were relatively new to America. Most had been in the United States for a generation or less, and as immigrants fighting for acceptance, Jewish women were reluctant to enter any public debate, especially one that had so aroused emotions nationwide.

Solomon did not want to avoid the debate completely. In fact, she believed that defending Judaism was a primary responsibility of every Jew, especially those in the public eye as those who spoke at the Congress would surely be. As the first Jew in the Chicago Woman's Club, Solomon was familiar with the role of being the representative Jew in a non-Jewish context. She knew that many of her co-members based their opinion of Jews on their opinion of her. She was naturally concerned that these women know enough of Judaism to understand why it differed from Christianity without resorting to that difference as a basis for discrimination. She expressed her concern in 1892 by daring to break an unspoken Club ban on formal discussions of religion.[12] The paper she delivered, "Our Debt to Judaism," was an attempt to demonstrate that the Christian society of the clubwomen sprang from Jewish roots. One of Solomon's major hopes for the Congress was to publicize this positive view of Judaism by providing the groundwork for Jewish women's entrance into the discussion of religion's role in women's lives. Later that hope would be expressed in her insistence that a large portion of NCJW's energy be directed toward educating Jewish women about Judaism. In Solomon's mind, the only way to ensure that this discussion could begin in a nonthreatening environment was to place it in the Jewish context of the Parliament of Religions' Jewish Congress rather than the feminist environment in the Woman's Building.

Solomon also knew that in many of the Congresses, particularly those planned by Woman's Building organizers, women and men were preparing to square off as enemies. Solomon believed that Jewish men and women could bring their reputed cooperation in the home to the public sphere as a shining example to the women's movement that cooperation was more effective in advancing women's rights than setting men up as opponents.[13]

Solomon recruited a planning committee sympathetic with this view that "on an occasion when men and women of all creeds are realizing that the ties that bind us are stronger than the differences that separate, that when the world is giving to Israel the liberty, long withheld, of taking its place among all religions to teach the truths it holds for the benefit of man and the glory of the Creator, the place of the Jewish woman would not be vacant."[14] The likeminded committee Solomon secured was carefully selected from a pool of Jewish women with whom Solomon had already worked, including members of the Chicago Women's Aid Society, the South Side Sewing Society, Chicago's Reform synagogues, and her own family.[15]

According to Solomon, "At the first meeting of the Jewish Women's Committee, it was decided to work along the lines adopted by other committees. The committee also decided to collect and publish the traditional melodies of the Jews as a souvenir of the occasion." To sell the hymnbook and to advertise the Congress, the committee issued notices "to all Jewish publications, inviting the cooperation of all persons interested."[16] The committee naturally wanted to prepare the souvenir with the expertise befitting the occasion, and knowing of no capable women, they arranged for the Reverend William Sparger and Cantor Alois Kaiser to write the text and Dr. Cyrus Adler the introduction. They found a willing publisher in Mr. T. Rubovits, and the committee's first task was quickly completed.

In addition to publicizing the Congress in Jewish publications, the committee began to correspond with the few Jewish women authors and clubwomen they knew in other cities seeking potential speakers for the occasion. They also wrote to rabbis asking for suggestions of names to include in the program.[17] Solomon, alone, wrote ninety letters by hand.

Early in this process the committee happened upon two important discoveries. First, the correspondence indicated that "dozens of

Jewesses disclaim affiliation" and "hundreds proclaim indifference and confess absolute ignorance of Jewish history and literature."[18] Second, it was difficult to track down those women who were still committed to Judaism and might be qualified to speak or be interested in attending.[19] These two discoveries were the seeds from which NCJW sprang.

The committee was deeply committed to the survival of Judaism in the United States and adhered to the traditional notion that religious practice in the home was the key to such survival. Custom also held that women were responsible for such religious observance. If Jewish women were too ignorant or too apathetic to keep a Jewish home, then the committee could only conclude that the next generation would be lost and Judaism in the United States would succumb to assimilation. These women had grown up in an age that embraced the Enlightenment (and popular women's club) idea that education would be the great equalizer and that public education would produce a country of responsible citizens who would solve the nation's problems with their new-found knowledge. The committee members had found that many of the women they contacted were almost Jewishly illiterate, so they idealistically concluded that they could save Judaism simply by informing Jewish women of their religious duties. This notion would become a cornerstone of NCJW policy.

The decision to work toward this goal by creating a formal organization had its source in more practical considerations. Solomon explained, "The difficulty we experienced in reaching Jewish women for organized effort made it apparent that a national organization was necessary to obviate such difficulties in the future."[20] The committee recognized that, as a much publicized national gathering, the Jewish Women's Congress was an ideal place to reach potential members, and the founding of a national Jewish women's organization became "an integral part of the plan of the Congress . . . at one of [the committee's] earliest meetings."[21]

Never in history had Jewish women convened a national organization devoted to promoting Jewish religious activity, so the committee tentatively sought approval for this idea from the general Woman's Board of the Parliament of Religions. Solomon reported: "Organizing womankind was a popular theme among those who were working in the Woman's Congresses of the World's Fair, and the projected organization of the Jewish women . . . created much interest among the women attending the World's Congress of Representative Women."[22] The committee received particular encouragement from their friend and chair of the Woman's Board, Ellen M. Henrotin, who, no doubt, recognized that such a historic event would enhance the prestige of the Parliament.

Bolstered by support from such high places, Solomon's committee launched fullscale efforts to organize the Congress. Previous attempts to identify individual Jewish women interested in the Congress had revealed a great deal of apathy. In the new effort, "Circular letters were sent to larger cities, asking Jewish women to hold mass meetings to elect delegates. This measure was more successful than had been anticipated, twenty-nine cities being represented by ninety-three delegates." The committee's search for participants spanned the Jewish communities of England and the United States, entailing the exchange of "no less than two thousand letters."[23] All correspondence mentioned that "An attempt would be made to effect permanent organization."[24] In the appeal for delegates published throughout the Jewish community, the committee described their vision for "a National and International organization of Jewish women, which shall hold annual meetings and thus bring together thinking Jewish women, who have the advancement of Judaism and Jewish interests at heart and shall give them the opportunity of learning to know each other and each other's work."[25] The names of women who responded to the publicity became NCJW's first mailing list.

In addition to seeking delegates, the committee began its search for women qualified to present papers at the general parliament as representatives of all Jewish women, and at the Jewish Women's Congress itself. The committee obtained names and topics from a variety of sources and ultimately "found that every section of the country could be represented." To choose between all the possibilities was "no easy task," but eventually "Two representatives were chosen to present papers in the general parliament."[26] The first was Henrietta Szold, daughter of the widely respected Rabbi Benjamin Szold, his protégé, and a guiding force of the Jewish Publication Society. Szold had worked with many of the top Jewish scholars in the United States and had proved herself quite capable of holding her own with them. Twenty years later she would found what would become the world's largest Jewish women's organization, Hadassah. Szold would address the topic "What Judaism Has Done For Women." The second representative was nationally known author, Josephine Lazarus, sister of poet Emma. Lazarus presented a paper entitled "The Outlook of Judaism."

As news of the proposed Congress spread, the committee became aware that not everyone would be as supportive of these efforts as advocates such as Ellen M. Henrotin. In October 1892 Chicago's leading Jewish publication, the *Reform Advocate*, questioned the necessity of a separate Jewish women's event at the World's Fair, stating bluntly, "As far as we can understand, Jewish women, as women, are not different from other women. There is nothing specifically Jewish in their progres [sic]."[27] This view must have been particularly disconcerting to Solomon because it came from a rabbi she considered a personal supporter, the controversial publisher of the *Reform Advocate* and spiritual leader of Sinai Congregation, Emil G. Hirsch.

Perhaps Hirsch's influence led the committee planning the Fair's Jewish men's Congress to issue Solomon an invitation to attend one of their meetings, ostensibly to discuss cooperation between the two groups. Solomon's account of the meeting suggests that the men had no intention of giving the women a voice and may have been trying to convince them to abandon their plans. Solomon, on the other hand, came ready to participate as an equal with but one demand—that the men find a place on their program for papers delivered by women. In her memoirs, Solomon recalled the committee's response:

"Mrs. Solomon, will you cooperate with our sessions?"

"Well," I replied, "our plans are already far advanced and assignments have been given our representatives in the general Parliament. We will, however, be very glad to join with you if you will accord us active participation in your programs."

The program committee then retired to deliberate, and when they returned, lo and behold! not a single woman's name appeared in the recommendations!

"Mr. Chairman," I inquired, "just where on your program are the women to be placed?"

"Well," hemmed and hawed the chairman, "the program seems complete just as it stands."

"Very well," I replied, "under these circumstances we do not care to cooperate with you, and I request that the fact of our presence at this meeting be expunged from the records."[28]

Another source reported that Solomon's request for women's participation was answered with "Yes, Mrs. Solomon, you can be hostess."[29] The women's committee responded by including the following statement in subsequent publicity: "In most of the Religious Congresses the men's and women's committees have acted together and will hold one Congress. But the rabbis refuse to give the women adequate time, place or representation, so they were compelled to hold a separate Congress."[30]

Solomon's drastic and confident reply indicates that the committee had expected a less than warm welcome and had already decided on their course of action. In addition to the editorial comment in the *Reform Advocate*, the committee knew before the meeting that much of the the men's committee believed that Jewish women were not educated enough to deserve a place beside them in a scholarly forum. Recounting the incident Solomon wrote, "Our rabbis were aware of [Jewish women's ignorance], for although they invited us to assist in arranging their congress . . . the only part of the program they wished us to fill was the chairs." Though Solomon was frustrated by the rabbis' refusal to allow any women to deliver papers, she tempered her anger with the acknowledgment that her own experience to some extent affirmed the rabbis' position, "for when in some cities we called for a show of hands of those who owned Bibles, the number was very small, and it is safe to presume that the average of those who ever saw anything but the covers was still smaller."[31]

Solomon knew that many Jewish men still believed public display of religion, especially in leadership roles, to be the exclusive province of men and any attempt by women to enter that arena was not only inappropriate but sacrilegious. Given that the committee had more than enough reason to believe that the men would be uncooperative, it is fair to ask what motives were so compelling that they sought collaboration anyway. The possibilities are multifold.

First, while traditional Judaism stressed that public religious practice was properly the sphere of men, prevailing American notions taught that religion was emotional and therefore its public expression was naturally woman's proper pursuit. Prominent Jewish leaders as diverse as eighteenth-century traditionalist Isaac Leeser and turn-of-the-century radical Reformer Emil Hirsch had echoed the new American attitude, giving Solomon's committee reason to believe that the men might welcome women's effort, particularly in the progressive context of the World's Fair. [32]

Like many of these leading rabbis, Solomon saw the American attitude as a sign of modernity and believed the only way for Judaism to enter the modern world was to combine it with the traditional Jewish view to create a public religion shared by both genders. Responding to remarks by a renowned Jewish scholar suggesting that women were religiously superior to men and therefore it was up to women to ensure Judaism's survival, Solomon said, "He speaks of the power of the Jewish woman. He said that without Jewish women Judaism could not exist; but if Judaism must exist for the women alone, we do not want it. No social life, no church life, no club life, is complete, no civic life is right, where men and women do not work together." She emphasized the sureness of her position by rooting it in Jewish tradition, pointing out that "Even Paradise was not complete without a woman, and no paradise on earth can be perfectly complete unless we have men and women." [33] To Solomon, men were not oppressors, but partners. She in no way challenged the clear separation of gender roles inherent in Jewish law and thought, but rather accepted the traditional Jewish argument that female and male roles were complementary and equal. This belief that Judaism existed only through the partnership between men and women was bolstered by her personal life. Unlike many men, Solomon's husband, Henry, had always been supportive of her activities outside the home and her participation in public religious life. She described her marriage as "years of perfect companionship and harmony." [34] Solomon approached the Jewish men's committee with the hope that they would be as supportive as her husband but also with the expectation that such support was not yet so common as to be a certainty. She and her committee would have preferred cooperation, but they were prepared to proceed without it.

For two years Solomon and her committee arranged their program and publicized their efforts. By 4 September 1893, when the Jewish Women's Congress opened, almost all affiliated Jews were aware of the event and eagerly awaited reports of the proceedings. The saga of how the Congress began had been recorded in both the Jewish and the secular press. As the women constantly reminded those following the story, never before had Jewish women attempted such a gathering. That no one knew exactly what to expect added to the great sense of anticipation surrounding the event. Yet, even the committee's grandest dreams could not have included the excitement the Congress generated.

The *American Israelite* began its coverage with a description of the hall as people gathered for the first session:

> Women elbowed, trod on each others toes, and did everything else they could without violating the proprieties to gain the privilege of standing edgewise in a hall heavy with the fragrance of roses yesterday morning. They filled all the seats some time before the opening of the Jewish Women's Congress. By ten o'clock all the aisles were filled; ten minutes later there was an impassable jam at the doors that reached far down the corridor. Few men were present. They were thrust into the background into the remotest corners. They had no place on the program and seemed to look at themselves as interlopers. But the ladies did not consider them so: they did not consider them at all. [35]

Another publication, the *Jewish South*, noted that the Jewish men's Congress, supposedly the gathering of Judaism's foremost thinkers, was characterized by poor attendance and lack of interest. In contrast, the Jewish Women's Congress was "as enthusiastic as the other was cheerless." [36]

For four days, predominantly obscure speakers addressed overflowing halls. The audience, obviously not drawn by famous names, was captivated by a series of papers on subjects never before discussed in such a broad public forum, especially by women, and by jarring images. Most Jewish women had never seen a woman (other than a bride during the marriage ceremony) on a pulpit. How astounding it must have been for them to see the Congress opened with a benediction from Ray Frank, an extraordinary twenty-seven-year-old who had recently gained fame for inspiring Jews in Portland, Oregon, to organize a synagogue with her stunning oratory skills:

> Almighty God, Creator and Ruler of the universe, through Whose justice and mercy this first convention of Jewish women has been permitted to assemble, accept our thanks, and hearken, O Lord, to our prayer.
>
> In times past, when storms of cruel persecution drove us towards the reefs of adversity, seemingly overwhelmed by misfortune, we had Faith in Thee and Thy works, ever trusting and believing that Thou ordainest all things well. Because of this faith, we feel that Thou hast, in the course of events, caused this glorious congress to convene, that it may give expression to that which shall broadcast a knowledge of Thee and Thy deeds. . . . Grant, then, Thy blessing upon those assembled, and upon the object of their meeting. . . . Grant, we beseech Thee, that this convention may be productive of that which is in accordance with Thy will.[37]

The startling experience of hearing a Jewish woman preach was followed by Ellen Henrotin's brief greeting and her introduction of the hero of the day, Hannah Solomon, who delivered the welcoming address. Solomon acknowledged that the turnout exceeded her "fondest expectations" and set the tone of the conference as serious but tentative. She informed her audience that the papers they were about to hear were "not intended to startle the world as literary efforts," but they were intended to establish women as co-workers alongside men in the struggle for a better world.[38] So excited was the audience about the proceedings, that Miriam Del Banco, who recited a poem before any of the scheduled papers were read, received a standing ovation.[39] The audience remained captivated as speakers discussed woman's place in and responsibility to the Jewish community. Some traced women's role in Jewish history. About half the papers were in the field of social work, most encouraging Jewish women to become more involved. Ada Chapman, a delegate from Dallas married to a leading rabbi in that city, was typical of these speakers. After extolling the achievements of Biblical women, she exhorted the listeners not only to remember their foremothers but also to emulate them: "we women of Israel must not forget that a great part of this religious task lies in our hands, and we, conscious of our responsibility, ought to make it our pride to follow the example of our mothers in the wilderness, who worked with enthusiasm to build the Tabernacle. Let our sanctuary be our homes, and let us beautify them with the undoubted, holy influence of our beloved faith."[40]

The atmosphere was optimistic. The message was that Jewish women had the power to make the world a better place for their children but had not yet harnessed that power. The solution to that shortcoming would be presented eloquently in the final paper, Sadie American's call to establish the first national religious Jewish women's organization in history.

If Hannah Solomon typified the married clubwoman volunteer, American represented the other major constituency involved in the Congress—social welfare workers. Thirty-one years old and single, American was a club leader at Chicago's Maxwell Street Settlement and a teacher at Temple Sinai's religious school. Her speech was surprising and revealing. It was much longer than other papers presented, and its tone was markedly defensive. The committee had chosen American to make the call to organize because they hoped her own enthusiasm for the project would be transmitted to the audience. Instead, American took the opportunity to answer the detractors the committee had faced in their two-year preparation for this moment. She began as if to "butter up" the women assembled by recounting the good works of local Jewish women's groups. She continued with a detailed explanation of how a national organization would be more effective than scattered local efforts. She then launched into a series of defenses of the organizational structure she had just mapped out. She described how it could preserve the voice of the individual without chaos, how it could be exclusively Jewish without being clannish, and how it could be a strictly women's organization without offending men.

These remarks could hardly have been intended for the women present in the hall, who had already demonstrated clear support for the endeavor with their enthusiastic participation in the Congress. Perhaps American had not anticipated such support when she prepared the speech. More likely, her message was meant for the Jewish community at large. Whether her perception of opposition from American Jewish leaders was accurate is another matter.

Not until the end of the speech did American display the fervor that characterized her work on behalf of Council. She began her call,

> Friends, a great opportunity is ours. Let us understand it. Let us live up to it. Others have died for Judaism; let us live for it—a harder task. There is indifference in our ranks, there is narrowness, there is ignorance within and without them. Let us apply the torch of knowledge and enthusiasm to them. We may encounter opposition, tradition will plant itself in our path, apathy will drag our feet. Let them be burned away by our ardor. On the wings of a mighty purpose let us soar above and beyond them all and every obstacle. The Congress has clarified for us things that were dull or blurred. Let it not be like a meteor in the sky, leaving no trace behind. . . . Let us be the first to do and to dare.[41]

Before the applause died down, Solomon took the podium and officially transformed the assembly into a business meeting. With a flourish of Robert's Rules of Order, she gave the floor to renowned educator Julia Richman, who proposed the following resolution:

> Whereas, It is desirable that the zeal, energy, and loyalty to the cause of Judaism which have been evinced by the Jewish women of America in the preparations for and the discharge of the duties connected with this Congress be turned to permanent good; and
>
> Whereas, This is an opportune time to establish closer bonds to draw together the Jewish women of America; therefore be it
>
> Resolved, That this Congress resolve itself into a permanent organization to be known as the Jewish Women's Union, for the purpose of teaching all Jewish women their obligations to the Jewish religion.

The obligatory discussion following the resolution was anti-climactic. Pauline Rosenberg of Pittsburgh, who would become Council's second president, thought the organization should be called the "Columbian Union" after the name of the Exposition.

Others criticized the proposal as too narrow. When the vote was finally taken, the resolution lost, not because the women opposed creating the organization, but because they could not agree on the wording of the proposal.

Not about to let parliamentary bickering defeat her dreams, Sadie American stood and offered a substitute resolution: "Resolved, That we, Jewish women, sincerely believing that a closer fellowship will be encouraged, a closer unity of thought and sympathy and purpose, and a nobler accomplishment will result from a widespread organization, do therefore band ourselves together in a union of workers to further the best and highest interests of Judaism and humanity, and do call ourselves the 'National Council of Jewish Women.'"

The name had been suggested in an earlier conversation by Julia Felsenthal, daughter of Rabbi Bernard Felsenthal and, like American, a settlement house worker and religious school teacher. The principles American outlined reflected the visions of the planning committee. Though this new resolution passed easily, the delegates thought that it was still too ambiguous. Solomon, acting as chair, appointed a team, including Minnie D. Louis (a widow from New York City and leading social reformer and educator) and original Congress planning committee members Sadie American, Henrietta Frank, and Esther Witkowski, to adjourn and quickly draw up brief resolutions defining the goals of the new Council.

While the committee deliberated, letters of greeting and encouragement from well-wishers were read to the convention, including messages from Sabato Morais, Nina Morais Cohen, Pauline Steinem, and Bertha Honoré Palmer. When the committee returned to the floor, they presented the words that would shape the character of Council:

> Resolved, That the National Council of Jewish Women shall (1) seek to unite in closer relation women interested in the work of Religion, Philanthropy and Education and shall consider practical means of solving problems in these fields; shall (2) organize and encourage the study of the underlying principles of Judaism; the history, literature and customs of the Jews, and their bearing on their own and the world's history; shall (3) apply knowledge gained in this

study to the improvement of the Sabbath Schools, and in the work of social reform; shall (4) secure the interest and aid of influential persons in arousing general sentiment against religious persecutions, wherever, whenever, and against whomever shown, and in finding means to prevent such persecutions.

Though this new resolution was far from detailed, it defined women's "obligations to the Jewish religion" as becoming Jewishly educated, fighting anti-Semitism and assimilation, and solving society's problems through social reform work. It further assumed that participation in this work would bring Jewish women together, transforming division into harmony. No one publicly questioned whether or not the organization could actually achieve such ambitious objectives, and the resolution was adopted without discussion.

The next step was to elect officers. The first candidate nominated was Hannah Solomon. The entire hall stood in approval as they elected their first president by acclamation in a rising vote. Election of officers and a board of directors followed. In an impressive show of unity, candidates withdrew from the contest in favor of opponents so each vote was by acclamation. The new leaders were charged with drafting Council's constitution, and the business meeting ended in an atmosphere of cooperation, triumph, and hope for the future.

Reflecting on the enormity of the accomplishment, one woman noted: "At the time the Council was founded, participation by women in public life was still a new thing." The resulting excitement gave her "a heady sense of independence, a thrill, a feeling that one was taking part in the best kind of revolution, even if it involved nothing more at the moment than parliamentary debates about hot soup and recreation for school children."[42]

The Congress ended as it had begun, with a prayer from Ray Frank. Delegates returned home filled with the spirit of unlimited possibilities. In Sadie American's words, "For woman this was an epoch making day; to her it accorded for the first time the recognition of her individuality, her independence of thought, and of her right to represent these herself and not by proxy."[43] Just as American women who were excluded from leadership by the social conventions of the mid-nineteenth century built clubs over which they could exercise exclusive control, Jewish women founded NCJW to find their own voice.[44] Congress participants were left to reflect on how they would express their new independence and to struggle with how to transmit the messages of the Congress to their families and communities. Most importantly, many participants would become master recruiters, convincing friends and acquaintances to join them in Council activities.

The First Convention

Delegates did not delay in translating the energy from the Jewish Women's Congress into forming local Council Sections. Chicago, the site of Council's founding, was predictably the first city to organize. Led by Hannah Solomon, organizers secured the gratis use of the large meeting hall at Sinai Congregation, the synagogue to which Solomon belonged. This setting, a bastion of classical Reform, lent credibility to their efforts and reflected Council's desire to include itself in the mainstream of the Jewish community rather than working as a renegade feminist group.

The well-publicized meeting was headlined by Emil Hirsch and by four other local rabbis.[45] The presence of so many rabbis communicated broad-based (though not Orthodox) support both to potential Council members and to potential opposition.[46] Synagogue sisterhoods had not yet emerged as regular features of American synagogues, so the rabbis saw the meeting primarily as an opportunity to encourage women to return to Judaism and to exert influence over which interpretation of Judaism would dominate that return. They also may have donated the use of synagogue facilities hoping to regain power for the synagogue lost to fraternal organizations like B'nai B'rith earlier in the century.[47] Still confronting a lack of respect for the American rabbinate,[48] and also facing the growing numbers, monies, and influence of synagogues founded by traditional immigrants,[49] these rabbis saw the opportunity to house Council meetings as a way to make the synagogue more central in American Jewish life. They hoped that as synagogues housed increasingly diverse activities, they would attract more members.

More members meant more funds under the control of synagogue leaders and more secure jobs for synagogue rabbis. As the centrality of synagogues increased, so, too, did the power and prestige of the institution and its leaders.

The Chicago meeting attracted 300 women, and other cities soon followed Chicago's lead.[50] In smaller towns, the organizational meetings often convened in the home of a prominent community member. Wherever they went, organizers sought support from the local rabbi, but excitement for the creation of a Council Section was usually generated by a visit from a member of Council's national board.

Aided by improving technology in transportation and communication, between 1893 and 1896 board members traveled extensively, sharing enthusiasm, experience, and suggestions. Sometimes they spoke at the invitation of local rabbis. On other occasions they were the guests of relatives or friends who gathered interested women in their living rooms to hear the board member's pitch. For most of its history, Council would rely on members to recruit relatives and friends for the bulk of its expansion efforts. In the first year, such efforts produced thirteen Sections with a total of 1,324 paid members. Despite an economic recession, by Council's first convention in 1896, the organization had grown to over fifty Sections with a membership of just over 4,000.[51] Section membership numbers varied greatly, ranging from seven to several hundred.

Despite Council's successful growth, its first few years were marked by confusion as the organization struggled to find its identity. The national board distributed a provisional constitution in March 1894, but by its own admission, the document was "as simple as possible, defining a broad road within whose borders each Section might choose its own method of traveling."[52] Thirty years later this ambiguous document was still viewed in a positive light by one Council leader, Philadelphia Section president Evelyn Margolis, who explained that "When Council was born . . . the women who attended at the birth had the wisdom to realize that the fewer swaddling cloths, the greater the freedom for growth. Therefore they wrapped the new organization about with as little cumbersome paraphernalia as possible."[53] Yet, to extend Margolis' analogy, every "midwife" harbored differing hopes for the new "child," and opinions on how to translate Council's goals into action varied greatly from Section to Section.

Early projects were usually designed to fill gaps in the institutional structure of local communities. In Chicago, no facilities existed to provide religious training for immigrant Jewish girls, so Council's first project was to open and operate a religious school. In Philadelphia, a city with well-developed philanthropic and religious institutions, Council founders, led by Laura Mordecai, the great-niece of Rebecca Gratz, also devoted their energies to education, attempting to counteract the work of Christian missionaries in immigrant neighborhoods and establishing a sewing school.[54] In contrast, the women of Marion, Indiana began with nothing but their own dedication and were credited with founding Marion's first synagogue.[55]

There was also a divergence of opinion concerning the proper format for Council meetings. Sections led by experienced clubwomen tended to use standard parliamentary procedure, though not always meticulously. Lizzie T. Barbe, a Chicago Board member, recalled that the minutes of her Section's first meeting were recorded in an old cookbook.[56] Other Sections were uncomfortable with the formality of parliamentary procedure, preferring to model their meetings on the social gatherings of literary or sewing societies.

Nor was there agreement about acceptable topics of discussion at Council meetings. State vice president for Colorado, Carrie Benjamin, reported on two Sections that she believed were not engaging in appropriate Council activities. One had listened to music and another had helped an unhappy woman attain a divorce.[57] While these Sections certainly viewed their actions as proper, others criticized the lack of specifically Jewish content. Several Sections that had been founded from preexisting groups like literary or benevolent societies merely continued their original activities under a new name.[58] In some locations meetings were conducted exclusively, or in part, in German, although in most cities English was the only language permitted. In small towns NCJW was often the center of Jewish life, providing the only source of Jewish education, while larger cities provided many religious outlets, causing Sections to concentrate on philanthropic work.

Members, aware of the growing divergence in policy, attempted to conform to uniform standards by addressing questions to the national board. The standing committees on religion and philanthropy, appointed by Solomon immediately following the Congress, issued their reports and recommendations in October 1894. A year later, the newly created Sabbath School Committee issued its recommendations and a study guide for the Prophets section of the Bible. These reports helped direct Section activities down similar paths but often raised more questions about specifics than they answered. Corresponding secretary, Sadie American, experienced the pervasive confusion firsthand, receiving 25 letters a day and writing 7,500 letters in return.[59]

The mammoth task of eliminating this confusion and setting the organization on a clear course fell to NCJW's first convention.[60] The meeting, hosted by the New York City Section 15–19 November 1896, was attended by 250 members, 67 of whom were voting delegates.[61] For the opening meeting, Tuxedo Hall was crowded to overflowing with guests, curious onlookers, skeptics, and the press, which described the atmosphere as "enthusiastic."[62]

The assembly's work was divided into three major areas of concern: legislative process, organizational identity, and work of standing committees. The process debate set rules for the discussions of other business and established the permanent structure of NCJW. Presentation of issues fell to the Committee on the Revision of the Constitution, chaired by Pittsburgh's Pauline Rosenberg. In her opening statement, Rosenberg mapped out the challenges the committee faced, including how to provide an organizational structure that allowed for growth and productivity, how to give everyone in the organization a voice, and how to balance power between the national board and the local Sections. Before arriving at their recommendations, the committee members solicited and considered suggestions from local Sections, distilling out those that did not seem to be generally beneficial to all.

Their first recommendation was that meetings be conducted according to Robert's Rules of Order. Anticipating protest by members unfamiliar with parliamentary procedure, Rosenberg put the process in more familiar domestic language, explaining that, just as there were certain rules of courtesy governing a hostess in her drawing room, "Parliamentary law is the etiquette of assemblies."[63] She continued by noting the problems Robert's Rules could prevent, ending with a litany of situations familiar to anyone who has ever attended an organizational meeting: "There is always a member who will rise to speak on a question and speaks away from it; there are members who would speak on the same subject six times if permitted, and others who would introduce motions whilst another is pending; members who hold private committee and consultation meetings without paying attention to the business in hand. Have you met them? If so, tell me how a Chairman would conduct the business of her session without the rules of order."[64]

Repeating what had become standard ideology in other women's groups, Rosenberg also reminded her audience that participating in ordered meetings provided woman the necessary practice that would "later enable her to meet man on his own basis."[65] The delegates agreed to abide by parliamentary procedure without major objection. In addition, the rules stated that while only delegates could make or vote on a motion, any member could speak from the floor, though she was limited to three minutes on business issues and five minutes for comments on a paper. No one would be given the floor twice until all members who desired to speak had done so.[66] Non-members could address the assembly only with permission of the chair.

Practical concerns and the insistence on equal access to power for all members continued to dominate the discussion of how to form the national board. Added to the normal slate of officers were vice-presidents from every member State and a board of ten directors selected from the membership at large, all of which would be elected by a majority vote of the delegates present. Some voiced concern that this arrangement would make the board too large to be workable, and one pragmatic member questioned how the organization would manage to get such a diverse group to board meetings.[67] The assembly viewed such considerations as subordinate to the ideal of equal representation, and they approved this large national board. Members also agreed that the president would appoint committee chairs and select a corresponding secretary, who, because of the tremendous amount of time required to coordinate all communications between Sections and with other organizations, would be salaried. Acting corresponding secretary, Sadie American, was chosen to be Council's first paid staff member, but she refused the stipend, so Council's first board was not burdened with arguments or jealousies over whose work deserved compensation.

Once the national board was defined, the convention moved on to consider how much power it should wield over local Section policy. Though women had not yet won suffrage, the delegates displayed thorough familiarity with and commitment to American governmental process, both in concept and in terminology. They described local Sections as states and argued about how much autonomy a Section could exert and how the Sections could be represented to balance most efficiently the power of the national board.

Many Council members had lived through the Civil War and were familiar with the potentially divisive ramifications of States' rights arguments.[68] Citing a need for unity, the constitution committee recommended that the convention be modeled after the United States Senate. Each Section, no matter how large or small, would elect two representatives, each entitled to one vote. All major policies would come before an assembly of these delegates and would require majority approval to be adopted. Constitutional amendments required a two-thirds majority for ratification.

Several larger Sections expressed displeasure at this arrangement, claiming that their involvement in a greater number of Council programs than smaller cities entitled them to a greater say in determining policy. These larger Sections favored an arrangement patterned after the House of Representatives with Sections being granted delegates according to membership numbers. The smaller Sections quickly responded that in such an arrangement, they would always be outvoted and might as well not bother to send delegates to the convention at all. Sadie American, always quick in her attempts to minimize potentially destructive schisms, supported the small Sections but added that "When we get large enough we will have both [a House and a Senate]."[69] American's comments, coming from a member of Council's largest Section (Chicago), were effective, and the proposal for a Senate was adopted.

Council rules consistently reflected the desire to share power fairly among all members. Rules guaranteeing that any member could add a candidate to the ballot by nominating her from the floor and that a local Section meeting could be called on the request of any ten members rather than having to wait for the president to act ensured that voices of nonofficers would be heard. Their ideal was to create a prevailing atmosphere of openness and sharing, but later debate would make it clear that a select few national board members exerted more than their share of influence over policymaking.

The constitution for local Sections was, more or less, a replica of the national document with the additional mandate that Sections carry out the policies of the national board through monthly meetings. The most highly contested point of the rules debate was the policy on what percentage of a member's dues was to be turned over to the national board. In this discussion, more than any other, the diversity in Section practice that had become entrenched in the preceding three years was divisive. The highly respected Rebekah Kohut, widow of Rabbi Alexander Kohut and first president of the New York City Section, spoke on behalf of Sections with well-developed local programs. She reminded the convention that the great amount of money needed to run such programs necessitated local fund raising. She argued that such fund raising would be hampered if donors thought the money was going for programs in other States and reported that she had already heard some complaints that too much money was being sent to the national board.

On the other side of the coin were Sections that depended on the national board for basic resources like study guides, speakers, and program materials. They argued that no Section should be autonomous, that the national board should decide which programs most deserved funding, that printing and travel costs engendered in normal board functions should take priority over local needs for funding, and that smaller Sections would not be able to carry out national policies without help from the national treasury.

Kohut's side, which included most of the larger Sections who had earlier failed to convince the majority to adopt their plan for proportional representation, won this debate by suggesting Council follow the pattern of a well-established national women's organization, the Women's Christian Temperance Union. They did not suggest in any way that Council reflect the content of WCTU work. To the contrary, NCJW firmly opposed prohibition.[70] Instead, they viewed the WCTU as a model national organization, large and stable.

Moreover, unlike women's clubs patterned after early New England (often elitist) women's groups, the WCTU was popular in the South as well as the North and respected for its success by the majority of delegates assembled.[71] They proposed to duplicate only WCTU's dues structure, with Council's national board taking one third of all membership monies collected. As a compromise, the convention also adopted several fund-raising procedures that would produce funds directly for the national treasury, including establishment of a patronage system whereby people who were not eligible for actual membership could contribute to the organization.[72] As with other controversial decisions taken at the convention, this debate would only settle the matter temporarily. Within a few years, continuing disagreements over dues policy would bring Council to a major crisis.

Though constitutional debate dominated the business meeting, the more important discussions focused on establishing a clear identity for this patchwork group. Even staunch supporters like the outspoken *American Jewess* editor Rosa Sonneschein were bewildered enough to ask, "What does the NCJW stand for?"[73] Members and observers alike spoke of "renewing Jewish womanhood," but there was little obvious agreement on just what Jewish womanhood was or how one went about renewing it.

Council's constitutional statement of objectives provided more questions than guidance:

Article II

The purposes of this organization are: To serve the best interests of Judaism; to bring about closer relations among Jewish women; to furnish, by an organic union, a medium of communication and a means of prosecuting work of common interest; to further united efforts in behalf of the work of social reform by the application of the best philanthropic methods.[74]

These goals would be summarized in the Triennial's selection of the slogan "Faith and Humanity" as Council's motto, but neither the motto nor the debate over its adoption would clarify just what were "the best interests of Judaism," and what constituted work of "common interest," and who should decide which were the "best philanthropic methods." Because most Jewish women already participated in some form of philanthropy, the last issue seemed the least complicated, and Council dispensed with it first.

Earlier Section and committee reports traced a clear framework of successful philanthropic endeavors. In its first three years, Council founded no less than thirty-three permanent social service institutions,[75] and more than two-thirds of all local Sections actively conducted philanthropic projects. The national board demonstrated its commitment to this work by devoting an entire session to the latest developments in the field presented by such luminaries as Lillian Wald.

The programs described in these papers and in the report of the Committee on Philanthropy would soon become synonymous with NCJW in social reform circles. These programs emphasized services for children and women that provided education, health care, and employment. Specific projects were often modeled after work done by prestigious local women's organizations, as in Chicago, where the Chicago Woman's Club had long been active in running vocational schools for poor girls and in implementing prison reform, especially as it related to juvenile justice. The Chicago Section also took inspiration from the local work of Jane Addams, drawing heavily from her settlement house model.[76] Because Council was founded in Chicago, other Sections often looked to that city's Section for a sense of the organization's true purpose, frequently replicating Chicago's programs in their own cities. Thus, those local projects that influenced the women of the Chicago Section shaped NCJW's programs nationwide. One especially popular program that grew from the idea of settlement house youth clubs was Council's auxiliary of Jewish Juniors. Essentially youth groups for Jewish teens, the Juniors involved both girls and boys in running scaled-down versions of NCJW social welfare programs. Established in 1894 and continuing through the early 1950s, the Council of Jewish Juniors encouraged children to develop a social conscience and acted as a membership feeder for the local Sections to which each Junior group was attached.

In a ground-breaking move for Jewish women, though well within the mainstream of middle-class Progressive social reform strategies,[77] Council urged women to become active in local government, both by seeking elected or appointed office or by agitating for legislation. This directive was carried out by dozens of members at the local Section level. For example, Sante Fe's Flora Spiegelberg developed a sanitary plan for handling the city's waste material and then worked with every Sanitary Commissioner for twenty years until the plan was adopted.[78] Another successful strategy was to start programs in order to demonstrate their viability and usefulness to government officials who would then be persuaded to take over their administration.[79] These policies produced such extraordinary Jewish role models as Belle Moskowitz, who learned how to be a social reformer in NCJW's New York Section. Though Moskowitz was more famous than most of her Council counterparts, her path to involvement and colleagues' perceptions of her exemplified an experience not uncommon for NCJW leaders. In an era when few charitable organizations welcomed women or Jews onto their boards, Council's "all-female, all-Jewish environment gave [Moskowitz] unmatched opportunities to develop leadership skills."[80] With these skills Moskowitz built an exceptionally successful career as a political appointee, culminating in service to the administration of New York's governor, Alfred Smith. Yet those who described her did not emphasize her accomplishments, but rather the fact that she was able to pursue her career without abandoning the outward appearance of True Womanhood. As Rabbi Stephen Wise eulogized in 1933, "Let it not be imagined that . . . hers was the ambition to lead. It was the will to serve and not the desire to lead that ruled her life."[81] Even Alfred Smith felt it necessary to add that "Women in politics sometimes make the mistake of not being themselves and imitating men. In Mrs. Belle Moskowitz the very opposite was true."[82] To Council, as to many moderate turn-of-the-century women's organizations, Moskowitz's model of "ladylike" service over forceful leadership was exemplary. Most important to Council's ideology, however, was Moskowitz's commitment to motherhood. As her biographer noted, Moskowitz reveled "in maternal duties" and never resented being publicly portrayed "first and foremost [as] a devoted mother."[83] Moskowitz was Council's model of traditional Jewish womanhood, committed to motherhood but also successful at forging new inroads to public service.

The ideals of personal service, legislative action, nonsectarian aid, and preventive social work all within the context of traditional womanhood placed NCJW squarely in the vanguard of the social reform movement. Council members expressed no doubt that they were endorsing the newest, most scientific, "best philanthropic methods."

2.

Council Religion

OCIAL reform work would come to dominate Council's activities to the exclusion of other pursuits, but such was not the intention of those who attended the first convention. As Hannah Solomon so bluntly expressed, "It is not the purpose of the organization to establish a Jewish salvation army."[1] Elsewhere she explained, "Philanthropic organizations, no matter how Jewish they may be, are not Judaism. The practice of good deeds should flow from the religious spirit, but it does not answer the moral, ethical need of humanity."[2] Council members valued their philanthropic work as an expression of Judaism, but few were content with philanthropy as their only expression of renewed Jewish womanhood. Most delegates belonged to women's clubs and social reform groups before they joined NCJW (see Appendix A, chart 19). They had no need for Council except as a specifically Jewish organization. Aware that abundant philanthropic opportunities were available elsewhere, Rosa Sonneschein perceptively declared: "The Council is nothing if not a religious organization."[3] Yet, the original draft of Council's constitution did not include the phrase "to serve the best interests of Judaism" in its statement of purpose, and early debate seemed ambivalent about just how Jewishly identified NCJW would be. One delegate asked

that references to Judaism be dropped altogether because a member of her Section was Gentile. President Solomon responded that the Preamble declared Council to be a Jewish organization, even though "Christian women are not excluded."[4]

Concern that such openness might undermine Council's ability to renew and represent Jewish womanhood surfaced during the floor discussion of the statement of purpose (Article II). Noting that the statement contained no reference to Judaism, Julia Richman asked the constitution committee if the omission was intentional. In response, the committee said it had discussed the point at length and had decided to "leave it as is, so that our labors should not be too much restricted."[5] This answer amplified the concern of delegates who had been present at Council's founding. They recalled that the original intent of the organization was to promote a renaissance of Jewish practice by "teaching all Jewish women their obligations to the Jewish religion." Julia Richman had written those words. Never a particularly observant Jew, Richman was an ironic spokesperson for those who insisted on the importance of Council's religious identity, but she persuaded those assembled to send the Article back to committee for reconsideration.[6]

When the issue came up for a second discussion later that day, sentiment ran strongly in favor of declaring Council's *primary* purpose as strengthening Judaism. This time, however, practical considerations required the assembly to pause. Both the national organization and local Sections had been invited to affiliate with a variety of Jewish and secular organizations. Council accepted invitations from charity federations, national women's associations, and governmental advisory boards among others. In Jewish groups, NCJW's representative was often the only woman on the board, and Jewish federations came to regard NCJW as the representative voice of all women.[7]

In much the same way, women's groups viewed Council as representing American Jewry, a role Council took very seriously. By 1908, Sadie American would be able to describe this role with great clarity. "Without the National," she wrote, "the Jewish women as a whole would not be represented where other women of the country as a whole are represented." She based her assessment on the invitations issued Council by "all large movements such as the child labor

Pauline Rosenberg (left), and Julia Richman (right). Drawings are from a newspaper report of NCJW's First Triennial (1896). (Photos courtesy the National Council of Jewish Women)

movement, the Tuberculosis movement, the Consumers' League, etc." American boasted that Council's "hearty and quick response [to Social Legislation] gives Jewish women of the country a standing and a reputation well deserved for being interested in all things that are for the good of humanity. Here is the difference between the Council and a mere benevolent society, no matter how excellent the latter."[8] In 1896, however, American's description was merely a hope.

Just as Hannah Solomon had proved Jews worthy to the Chicago Women's Club, so did the organization she founded want to prove Jews worthy of acceptance into the world of women's clubs, and by association, upper-class social circles. In this effort to earn Jews an equal place alongside their Gentile sisters, NCJW was partially successful. For example, in 1894 Council affiliated with the National Council of Women of the United States (NCW), with Solomon sent to conventions as the organization's representative. Despite her presence, however, the meetings of the NCW were opened with a prayer invoking God's "well-beloved son."[9] Thus, Jewish women were present but not accounted for. Some women's organizations hoped to avoid controversy by keeping religion off their agenda altogether. Such was the position of the General Federation of Women's Clubs (GFWC), but rather than leading to Council's acceptance, the Federation's policy posed an awkward dilemma to those present at NCJW's 1896 Triennial. Though the GFWC had been among Council's first supporters, its constitution forbade the admittance of specifically religious groups. Its understanding of what it meant to be Jewish was not sophisticated enough to identify Jews as an ethnic group, so the Federation requested that NCJW deemphasize its Jewish identity and join as a literary group.

Though Council deeply desired to join the GFWC, such an affiliation would be meaningless unless they could join as Jews. Vocalizing this sentiment, Rebekah Kohut declared that "If the word Jewish or religion is going to prevent our getting into any State Federation, let us put it in. . . . Let us not sail under false colors. This is a Council of Jewish Women. Let us put it into our Constitution, and into our preamble, and everywhere."[10] Kohut's speech evoked empathy and pride. Surrounded by hundreds of supportive sisters, the delegates found new strength in declaring that they would be accepted as is. In the spirit of the moment, the bonds of "Am Yisrael" (Jewish peoplehood) completely overshadowed the social gains that might result from being accepted as a proper women's club. The delegates voted to turn down the Federation's invitation.

In this emotional atmosphere, the convention began its reconsideration of Article II (the Statement of Purpose). Julia Richman suggested that Council's first purpose was "to serve the best interests of Judaism" and proposed that Article II begin with that declaration. With Kohut's passionate words still echoing in the hall, the delegates voted to adopt Richman's amendment.

The great challenge facing Council then would be to describe in practical terms what "serving the best interests of Judaism" meant. Council's approach to religion exemplified its community's attempt to Americanize Judaism, but from a uniquely female perspective.

Grateful for the haven and prosperity America offered Jews, Council women sought a way to demonstrate their gratitude. Forming their organizational identity during the Progressive Era, social reform work offered an obvious way to fulfill civic obligations. Often represented by organizations like the WCTU or Social Gospel leaders, Progressivism was correctly viewed by Council as infused with a Christian spirit. Eager to stand as equals with other women's organizations doing social reform work, yet unwilling to accept such work as inherently Christian, Council sought a Jewish context for its work. It emphasized its efforts as fulfilling the traditional Jewish obligation of "tzedakah" (a term which Council women understood to mean charity) and invoked the language of the Reform movement's ideology of ethical monotheism, which stressed prophetic calls for universal justice. As a result, Council members were among the first American Jews to define social reform work as an expression of Judaism rather than merely a civic obligation.[11]

To NCJW, social reform work was service to God as well as to country. As historian Sue Levi Elwell has perceptively noted, this fusion of patriotism with religion was illustrated in Council's Hymn. Sung as an opening ritual, the hymn set the tone for many Council meetings:

To Thee Thy daughters sing,
Humbly our pray'rs we bring,
    To Thee above!
Into our hearts instil
Reverence for Thy will
Our duty to fulfil
    Through Faith and Love.

When we from Egypt's land
Marched forth a rescued band
    To Liberty,
Then Freedom, noble word,
By mankind first was heard
And human hearts were stirred
    To turn to Thee!

Since then throughout the world
Our flag has been unfurled
    For Thee on High!
Justice, Love, Modesty,
Duty, Fidelity,
"Faith and Humanity!"*
    O, hear our cry!

(* Council's motto)

Composed by Orthodox rabbi Henry Pereira Mendes for the 1896 Triennial, the hymn embodied Council's blending of American and Jewish cultures. Sung to the tune of "My Country 'Tis of Thee," it invoked divine guidance, celebrating the achievement of Council's goals as fulfillment of divine will. Elwell notes that "By transposing the subject of the song from 'sweet land of liberty' to 'Thee above,' Mendes harnessed the patriotic enthusiasm of the singer and directed it heavenward. The overtly religious sentiments in the song reflected Council's self-conscious desire to establish an American Jewish religious identity."[12]

In addition to its religious and patriotic sides, Council's social reform work was born out of a practical need to keep American anti-Semitism in check. As children of recent immigrants, Council members knew well the consequences of anti-Semitism and were always wary that European patterns of discrimination not be repeated in the United States. Events in the years prior to 1893 gave rise to legitimate concern. As German Jews succeeded economically, they expected to succeed socially as well. The Saratoga incident of 1877 publicized the exclusion of Jews from country clubs and other bastions of elite American society. The existence of quotas for Jews admitted to college was commonplace. Even more troubling than social discrimination were challenges to the separation of church and state. Christian interpretation of the Bible was regularly taught in public schools, and Christian missionaries headed many government-subsidized programs to help the poor. In 1888, and again in 1890, bills declaring Sunday a national day of rest were introduced in Congress. In 1892, the Supreme Court held that the United States was a Christian nation (Church of the Holy Trinity v. U.S.). Even at the 1893 World Columbian Exposition, the very event that gave Jewish scholars an equal platform with their Gentile counterparts and where Council was founded, there was a vocal campaign to close the Fair on Sundays. Council members had special reason to be concerned about these attempts to establish Christian hegemony because missionaries often targeted women. Because Americans placed the responsibility for religion on female shoulders, missionaries believed that converting women was a prerequisite to influencing the rest of the population.[13] In her study of Rebecca Gratz, Dianne Ashton noted that "Missionary women did not enter synagogues, they knocked on home doors."[14] Thus, to Council women, the threat posed by Christian proselytizing was not merely political, it was personal.

As an obstacle to assimilation, anti-Semitism strengthened Council's Jewish identity. As a threat to American democracy, which Council women considered basic to the safety of Jews in the United States, anti-Semitism was a common enemy against which all types of Jews could unite. Jewish unity would be important to Council, not only as a show of strength but also as an affirmation of democracy. Sure in its faith that America was strengthened rather than weakened by permitting the expression of diverse points of view, Council insisted that in the Jewish community, anything less than full toleration of varying interpretations of Judaism was hypocritical.

Ever vigilant against injustice, NCJW did more than decry anti-Semitism. It directly responded with several programs. First, it established Jewish Mission Schools in immigrant areas where parallel Christian schools encouraged not only assimilation but conversion.[15] Later, Council created its Committee on Purity of the Press to act as a watchdog and denounce any anti-Semitic statements that appeared in print. Most important, NCJW developed a sophisticated network for legislative action and political lobbying. Like much of the Jewish community, Council members believed that only a secular government could protect the rights of minorities.[16] Motivated by the need for self-protection and by its sense that Judaism demanded just treatment for all people, NCJW consistently supported legislation that it believed protected the fragile equality for minorities under the law (see Appendix D for stands on specific legislation). Yet, aware of anti-Semitic conspiracy theories, Council spokespersons were careful not to paint their opinions as representing all Jews but rather used the language of universal humanism. This approach was more than a practical strategy. To Council women, Judaism demanded justice not only for themselves but for all people.

More than anti-Semitism was a threat from without; assimilation was a threat from within. German Jews did not come to the United States with the intention of abandoning Judaism, although their willingness to leave native lands suggests that most were predisposed to departing from familiar paths, including the path of traditional Jewish religious observance.[17] The demands of life in America made change almost inevitable. The need to work on the Sabbath and the lack of resources like Jewish books and kosher butchers made observance of Jewish ritual difficult at best. Few of the German Jewish immigrants came with more than a rudimentary Jewish education and were thus hampered in creating the necessary institutions on their own.[18] The small Sephardic community that had come a century before had grown lax in its practice of Judaism, providing little leadership or guidance. America's reputation as a "Sodom," where Jews ate "treyf" (non-kosher food) and married non-Jews, kept qualified scholars and leaders from immigrating for fear they would have no support network, no followers and thus, no means of financial support. Moreover, in the last half of the nine-teenth century, the United States had experienced a decline in the numbers, training, and quality of Christian clergy, resulting in a generally low opinion of the profession.[19] This negative attitude compounded the immigrant Jewish community's inability to attract or develop strong religious leadership. .

Believing these problems to be insurmountable or simply not worth the effort, some Jews took advantage of their new freedom to abandon the practice of Judaism altogether. Most, however, simply attempted to adapt their religion to American life. For some immigrants, that adaptation meant identifying exclusively as secular Jews, basing their Jewish lives in social clubs like B'nai B'rith. Most of these German immigrants, however, chose to identify as Reform Jews, an approach which, because of its open encouragement of changes in ritual, they associated with modernity.

Council women grew up in this community of German Jews, and the development of Reform Judaism had a tremendous influence on Council's approach to religion. Without great thinkers to guide it along ideological lines, Reform Judaism in America became pragmatic in its development. Congregations made decisions based on need rather than principle. In the absence of strong leaders to act as religious authorities, synagogue decisions were more often made by congregational boards than by rabbis,[20] and the growth of secular organizations challenged the synagogue as the traditional center of Jewish life.[21] Some rabbis attracted large local followings, but only a few were recognized nationally, and even their decisions were binding on no one in particular. One result of this absence of authority was great variation in local practice, so when Council members from different cities got together and shared what they believed to be appropriate Jewish practices, they found their descriptions diverged greatly. In addition, the absence of intellectual leadership had allowed a great deal of religious change to occur in the Jewish community without serious consideration of the consequence of that change.

Perhaps the most startling of those changes was the shift of religious responsibility from male to female shoulders. Traditionally, public religious observance, especially that which took place inside synagogue walls, was the exclusive province of men. Only men received the training necessary to study the holy texts and perform the complicated rituals associated with public worship. Moreover, according to tradition, God's commandment to perform such rituals was incumbent only upon men. Yet, contrary to traditional Judaism, which reserved the highest rungs of spiritual achievement for men, German Jewish immigrants found that dominant American opinion assigned spirituality, piety, and religious devotion to woman's sphere.

German Jews came to an America where industrialization was taking paid labor, and the men who performed it, out of the home and into a hostile environment of cutthroat competition and physical danger. Believing women to be weak, vulnerable, and incapable of handling the pressures of the work world, men excluded the "fairer sex" from most waged labor, rendering women economically dependent on men. In the idealized version of social relations that grew out of this system (though often not in the reality of poor women's lives), a woman exchanged care of a man's home for his financial support. Men expected that home to provide a safe haven from the burdens of work. They saw woman as creator of that nurturing home environment and attributed the qualities of the object to the creator. As historians Carol Hymowitz and Michaele Weissman aptly describe it, the evils of the world of commerce severed men "from the tender side of their own natures," leading them to try "to regain this aspect of themselves through women. . . . In symbolic terms a wife came to be seen as her husband's better half," the embodiment of "the purity, spirituality, and goodness which his life in business lacked."[22] Dualistic gender roles quickly became the norm in America.

Necessity led Jewish men to center their lives in the business world, which viewed emotion as an obstacle to success. Americans expected men to be rational, depending solely on logic to determine values and influence decisions. When the ideal American man envisioned the future, he did so through the rational prisms of science and technology. In 1895, Rosa Sonneschein observed that over the last thirty years lack of religion had become a fad, a sign of the secular higher education available to Jewish men long before it was socially acceptable among Jewish women.[23]

Sonneschein expected that the creation of NCJW would end this "fad," but her optimism did not take into account the growing

importance of science and technology in American life. The introduction of Darwin's theories in the 1870s, the creation of new
sciences like psychology to reveal the "objective truth" about human
nature, and the dependence on new technologies to provide for
America's future all served to dwarf the importance of religion in
America.[24] The more science and technology advanced, the more
they seemed to suggest that religion was based on emotional rather
than rational commitment. If religion was not rational, then it
could not properly fit into American concepts of manhood.

If, as the Reform movement emphasized, Judaism was more a set
of religious beliefs and practices than an all-encompassing culture,
and if religion had no place in men's rational world, then men
could view observance of Judaism's rituals as essentially extraneous
to their lives. Participation in religious ritual did not help them
advance their careers, gain power, or otherwise fulfill the duties
expected of an American man. Participation in religious institutions, however, could help men do all those things.

Looking to the men whose methods they had emulated to
achieve success in the business world, German Jewish men found
that "respectable" American men were usually Protestants who supported the religious activities of their wives, attended church occasionally (especially on important holidays or life-cycle events),
donated generously to building funds and church charity projects,
and received recognition for such donations. In many cases, membership in the "right" church indicated inclusion in certain social
circles more than it revealed anything about one's faith.

Eager to Americanize and too attached to Jewish identity to attend
church or convert, American Jews began building Reform synagogues. Not surprisingly, those synagogues closely resembled American Protestant churches. The pulpit, from which a robed rabbi would
preach weekly sermons, was placed at the end of the sanctuary like a
stage. Male and female congregants sat together in pews and listened
to English hymns sung by a choir with organ accompaniment. As
with post-disestablishment American churches, the new synagogue
had no way of exercising direct power over congregants. As a result,
men did not always take the synagogue seriously. To most German
Jewish men, the synagogue was a showpiece, important to vouch for
one's character and community standing, but not a place one visited

on a regular basis.[25] Men continued to control American synagogues, serving on congregational boards and reserving for themselves the right to vote on all important congregational policies, but
they rarely attended as worshipers or students.

Women, on the other hand, attended worship services in relatively great numbers. Duplicating the numerical process of feminization which historian Barbara Welter has described for American
churches between 1800 and 1860, wide-ranging segments of the
Jewish community reported that female congregants vastly outnum-
bered male worshipers, despite Judaism's longstanding teaching that
performance of public ritual was an exclusively male obligation. As
synagogue leader Tobias Schanfarber reported in 1908, "The same
complaint [as heard in churches] is heard in the synagog. Some
have gone so far as to declare that there is a danger of an effeminization of the synagog because of the predominance of women over
men in synagog attendance."[26] Though Schanfarber would go on
to argue that the predominance of women had not altered the content of synagogue life, numerically American synagogues had been
"feminized."[27]

This new phenomenon did not go unnoticed in the Jewish press.
Theresa Lesem echoed many earlier writers when, in 1897 she
observed, ". . . year in and year out, for many long years, their [the
rabbis'] efforts in sermon and lecture have been prepared for and
delivered to congregational audiences composed *almost* exclusively
of women."[28] Expanding on Lesem's theme, Rebekah Kohut noted
that women had all but taken over the everyday workings of the
synagogue while their husbands earned a living. "We might say she
is the synagogue," commented Kohut, who felt the situation should
be recognized by changing the popular saying, "The men work and
the women pray," to "the men work, and the women pray and
work."[29] Esther Andrews agreed that "man is no longer the leader
of religious life [but is engrossed in] twentieth century worldly aspirations."[30] Twenty-five years after Lesem's article, the Board of
Governors of Hebrew Union College denied Martha Neumark's
request for ordination to the rabbinate for fear that the synagogue
would "become yet more 'an affair of the women.'"[31] References to
the predominance of women continued for no less than four decades, indicating that it was not merely a minor trend but an ac-

cepted and in some circles even popular feature of American Jewish life. By the time NCJW was founded, the German Jewish community accepted women's attendance at synagogue (and men's absence therefrom) as a natural, if somewhat lamentable, state of affairs.

In allowing their wives to bear the burden of carrying on the religion, men had found a way to preserve their heritage without having to participate in religious ritual themselves. Writing for NCJW's newsletter, HUC faculty wife Irma A. Cohen explained that when women preserved Judaism by keeping a Jewish home and remaining active in synagogues, they were acting as "the guardian of the future . . . providing the men of the morrow and saving *for them* their noblest treasures" (emphasis mine).[32] Elimination of concern for survival of Jewish religious traditions enabled men to live comfortably as secular Jews. That comfort is best illustrated by the success, longevity, and male-only membership of the quintessential secular Jewish organization, B'nai B'rith. In fact, B'nai B'rith would prove to be one of NCJW's greatest allies, not because the organizations were parallel but because they were complementary.[33] Husbands of Council members frequently belonged to B'nai B'rith, and the relationship between the two organizations mirrored the cooperation between the sexes that ideally governed the Jewish home.[34]

Where men found contradictions between their own traditional Jewish roles and new American expectations, they found the opposite for women. Barbara Welter has aptly summarized gender role expectations faced by turn-of-the-century American women naming piety, purity, submissiveness, and domesticity as the "cardinal virtues" by which "a woman judged herself and was judged by her husband, her neighbors and society." Emphasizing the importance society placed on these characteristics, Welter concluded that "Without them, no matter whether there was fame, achievement or wealth, all was ashes. With them she was promised happiness and power."[35] The placement of woman in the home, the expectation that she subjugate her own will to that of the men in her life, and the notion that women were somehow more pure (free of sin) than men, either naturally or through vigilant protection, were all familiar demands to Jewish women. The notion that women were more pious, however, was somewhat problematic.

Some segments of the Jewish community had long believed that women were morally superior to men, but they did not conclude from this position that women were especially fit for public religious pursuit. Rather, they argued that women's moral superiority exempted them from many of the religious duties incumbent upon men.[36] In the American notion of True Womanhood, the opposite was true. Because society believed women to be more pious than men, they concluded that women had a greater capacity for religious activity. Moreover, American association of emotion with both religion and women joined the two in the view that religion was most properly pursued by women. Despite Judaism's history of male dominance in public religious affairs, Jewish leaders, eager to acculturate, were quick to claim this American approach to religion as their own. Rabbi Henry Berkowitz of the Jewish Chautauqua Society echoed common Jewish opinion when he wrote, "Physical inferiority gives [woman] a moral and spiritual superiority over man. This is an established fact. . . . Religion is innate in her heart."[37] The highly respected architect of the Reform movement's Pittsburgh Platform, Rabbi Kaufmann Kohler, agreed that women naturally possessed a special avocation for religion, asserting that women were "more responsive to the tender appeals of religious duty."[38]

The Jewish community would not chastise men for their failure to attend synagogue until it realized that the devaluation of religion in favor of ethnic identity did not produce commitment to Jewish survival in the next generation.[39] Rising rates of intermarriage[40] and the typical conflicts between immigrant parents and their American-born children jarred the Jewish community into reconsidering its attitude toward religious practice. Children, often unfamiliar with even basic Jewish rituals, began drifting away from the community. That meant the older generation could not count on the younger generation to guarantee the future of any Jewish institutions, religious or secular. By 1899, publications like the *Reform Advocate* lamented the lack of young men in Jewish service organizations as well as in synagogues.[41]

Unwilling to let centuries of Jewish survival efforts succumb to assimilation, Jewish leaders began to consider ways to reverse the trend. Many Jewish men, however, were not yet ready to abrogate the acculturation process by challenging gender role definitions and reclaiming religious practice for American manhood. Neither could they depend on the generally weak religious institutions in existence to solve their problem. Even the rabbis had not been successful at countering assimilation.[42] Many Jewish men concluded that because much of traditional Jewish religious observance was based in the home, the home was the key to Jewish survival in America. The next logical conclusion was that because both the home and the religion were women's domain, it would be up to women to save the religion.

The Menorah, B'nai B'rith's journal, explained women's new savior role as a matter of practicality, necessary to combat the "Apathy and indifference [that] characterizes the position of the average Jew of to-day towards his religion." The journal concluded that "The modern Jew is so completely taken up by the struggle for existence that it absorbs all his energies, and if the wife and mother does not resume her ancient function as priestess of the household, our prospects for the future were really discouraging."[43] The esteemed Reform rabbi, David Philipson, cast the savior role in Biblical terms, noting that just as Esther had come to Mordechai's aid to save the Jewish people, so too must women now fulfill their function as "the mainstay of our faith." Philipson even noted that men frequently told him that their wives and daughters had come to represent them in matters of religion.[44]

The declaration of women as Judaism's saviors was both predictable and startling. Given the reversal in Jewish gender roles represented by the declaration, it seems reasonable to expect a great public outcry criticizing the suggestion. Instead, one is struck with the absence of comment, as if no great change had occurred.[45] However, the silence was quite logical. More often than not, Jewish clergy answered to rather than led their congregations. Jewish laymen who had already stopped attending synagogue for regular worship or study had little reason to be concerned that women seemed to be usurping previously male religious responsibilities. No mandate would be forthcoming from them that would encourage rabbis to make a critique of the situation. Nor would the rabbis have been likely to say anything that might alienate the women who predominantly filled synagogue pews.

More importantly, to rabbis and other male Jewish leaders the appeal of declaring women the saviors of Judaism in the United States was enormous because it absolved them of the responsibility for the community's failure to slow assimilation. As Council readily acknowledged, "The fault [for assimilation] lies not at the door of the Rabbis, but with the parents who neither practice their religion in the home, nor help the religious schools that teach real Judaism."[46] Moreover, the casting of woman in the savior role was appealing because it seemed to fit easily into the traditional framework of Jewish womanhood. For centuries the Jewish community had defined woman as man's helpmate, caretaker of his home, and mother of his children. She was expected to exhibit religious commitment by toiling in the material world so that her husband/sons/father might be free to spend time in prayer and study, the ultimate expressions of Jewish spirituality.[47] She was responsible for providing a proper Jewish environment in the home, raising children loyal to the Jewish people, and protecting her home and family from sin. These longstanding views of women's religious nature led many American Jews not only to accept women as Judaism's saviors but also to conclude that the role was a continuation of historical expressions of traditional Jewish womanhood, the Mother in Israel: "She will foster the sacred things of life, the sanctities of home and the sacred ideals of the people. Jochebed saving the child, Miriam enthusing the men, and Deborah leading them. And all for the sake of God and His name."[48]

Such links between Council's expression of womanhood and historical ancestors were a common means of establishing religious legitimacy. In this instance, the depiction of Jewish women as religious leaders allowed men to justify the transfer of religious duties they could not or did not wish to fulfill, but it was a portrayal of Jewish women only peripherally grounded in reality. Historically, for every scholar who praised female piety, another described women's moral weakness, convinced that women were divinely cast as man's inferior, incapable of serious scholarly or spiritual pursuit. In practice, the Jewish community had long excluded women from the most valued religious pursuits, including study, public prayer, and the rabbinate. And Rebekah Kohut recognized the contradictory attitudes, summarizing, "The exemption of the woman from the performance of all legal and ceremonial obligations imposed by Jewish law on the male has placed her in an anomalous position where she appears virtually ignored, whereas, morally, she is an object of exaltation."[49]

No Jewish community had ever viewed public religious activity as properly belonging to women, yet, despite women's obvious lack of preparation, American Jews were proposing that women take responsiblity for their religion's future. Women would be expected to staff religious schools,[50] fill synagogue pews, and ensure the religious devotion of the family by rejuvenating Jewish practice in the home.

This new role for Jewish women was especially important as a parallel to notions of American womanhood that extolled woman's religious nature and emphasized the home as the source of morality and religious devotion. This notion had been popularized by organizations like the WCTU, which portrayed its members as both saviors and patriots. Thus, in addition to providing a practical solution to the problem of men's decreasing religious practice, the assigning of the savior role to Jewish women was a welcome synthesis of modern American culture with Jewish tradition.

Where men found no compelling reason to make religious observance central to their lives, women found abundant reason. In addition to the opportunity religion offered to fulfill gender and social roles and the sense of power obtained from participating in a previously forbidden activity, the propriety of Jewish women's new religious nature was affirmed in the reality of their day-to-day lives. If men found religious activity out of place in the work world around which they centered their lives, women found themselves surrounded by religious debate. The Gentile women with whom they cooperated in social reform work pushed Jewish women to study Judaism. More than one woman lamented the fact that Christian women seemed to be well versed in the Bible and its interpretation while many Jewish women could not recite even the most famous Biblical stories.[51] As they became more active in secular women's organizations, Jewish women could not help but be immersed in the "hot topic" of the day, suffrage. Because that debate was religiously charged and because some misguided Christian feminists attributed their religion's oppression of women to Judaism, Jewish women found it necessary to become Jewishly literate.

Because it was dedicated to renewing Jewish womanhood and it claimed to be a national voice for Jewish women, NCJW was entrusted with the task of saving Judaism. Writing in *The Menorah*, Rabbi Joseph Silverman posed this challenge directly to Council's first convention: "To this Council we submit the problem of a revival of religion in the Jewish home, and of the re-institution of those ceremonies that gave the Jewish home and synagogue a religious sanctity."[52] In another article, *The Menorah* actually portrayed NCJW in messianic terms, comparing the organization to Elijah.[53] The expectation that Council women would preserve Judaism while the right to define the tenets of that Judaism was reserved for men would be one of the greatest ironies of Council's early years.

Nevertheless, Council welcomed the challenge. No one believed more strongly in woman's ability to save Judaism than did Council women themselves. As one woman declared, "I cannot detach Jewish motherhood from Messiahship."[54] Just as society's valuation of women as morally superior served to increase women's self-esteem, the declaration of Jewish women as saviors confirmed Council women's belief that they deserved more status and power in the Jewish community than they had been accorded.[55] Although Council women welcomed the new respect that they presumed would accompany their new responsibilities, not all members shared enthusiasm for the prospect that men were relinquishing control to women. Some lamented the change, remembering a time when "Judaism was not . . . so decrepit, so maimed . . . that it needed the leaning crutch of women to bolster it up."[56] This was a minority opinion, however, and most members, like most of the Jewish community, saw the change as inevitable, and they sat back to watch Council's development "with more than ordinary interest."[57]

The immediate obstacle was that most Jewish women knew even less about proper religious observance than their unobservant husbands. Council's founders claimed that NCJW's proposal to organize women in a national campaign to renew Jewish womanhood by training women how to be Jewish mothers was the only viable solution to the problem.

The cornerstone of all Council's policies would be the elevation of motherhood to a holy pursuit. In Council language, as it had been in domesticity expert Catharine Beecher's language half a century earlier,[58] the home was a sanctuary and the woman its high priestess.[59] Sadie American set the tone at Council's founding insisting that organizational work would not take women away from their homes. She rooted her certainty in religious doctrine, asserting that no matter how much the societal position of women advanced, the home would remain primary and sacred to women because "When, in the economy of the globe, an allwise Creator made male and female, and assigned them varied functions and duties, this variety of function and duty became a law of being, and no advance of civilization can change these functions nor abrogate these duties."[60]

American's speech highlighted the first internal conflict posed by Council's emphasis on renewing Jewish motherhood, namely, how to devote time to learning how to be a Jew without neglecting the home duties of Jewish motherhood. If the patterns of later Council members reflected those of their foremothers, the concern was well placed. Interviews with NCJW leaders of the 1950s, for example, indicated that most of them devoted anywhere from forty to eighty hours a week to Council activities, leaving them little time for homemaking.[61] These leaders also reported, however, that such levels of activity were generally reserved for years when they had no or grown children. They also indicated that their ability to devote time to Council was due, in large part, to supportive husbands, a sentiment also widely expressed by Council's founders.[62]

Although concern that Council women would neglect home responsibilities haunted the organization for many years,[63] no one ever voiced concern that Council might actually undermine the institution of marriage. Rebecca Gratz notwithstanding, the Jewish community had never accepted what historian Lee Chambers-Schiller termed "the cult of single blessedness," which touted singlehood for women as positive if devoted to good and glorious deeds.[64] In this attitude, Council did not differ from other Jews. In fact, NCJW's emphasis on home made it almost impossible for the organization to support singlehood. In Council ideology, the home was the ultimate source of power because it was there that the character of children was best shaped. If home was woman's source of power, then marriage and motherhood were necessities.

Recognizing that occasionally special circumstances caused women to remain single, Council tolerated members who never married, though in its first thirty years, only two such women became prominent national leaders within the organization. One was Sadie American, who often found herself in conflict with other members and who eventually was forced out of NCJW amid controversy. The second was Rose Brenner, who, after her mother's death raised her younger siblings, thus fulfilling the traditional responsibilities of motherhood, though without a husband. Both women had primary lifelong relations with other women, though the possibility that they were lesbians does not seem to have colored Council's relationship with them. NCJW never hesitated to work with and even praise women who were paired in "Boston Marriages" (the turn-of-the-century term for lifelong lesbian relationships), including settlement house experts Lillian Wald, Jane Addams, and WTUL leader Pauline Newman.[65] In 1929, Council's newsletter published a positive review of Radclyffe Hall's lesbian classic, *The Well of Loneliness*, observing that the novel provided insight into lesbian life.[66] One can only wonder if the author was merely following homophobic convention in labeling the sad conclusions of the story as insightful or whether she was writing from experience, but the fact that a review was written and that it called for understanding suggests that Council members acknowledged the presence of lesbians in their midst. More often than not, however, Council publicly ignored the question of lesbianism, partly out of discretion and partly as the result of their belief that a society that could not tolerate diversity was not likely to be safe for Jews. Still, toleration was not support, and Council never came to view singlehood, for any reason, as an acceptable option for women. This attitude was reflected in the composition of Council's general membership, where single women never constituted more than 10 percent of the entire organization (see Appendix A, chart 7). NCJW was never a haven for single women, lesbian or otherwise.

To those who accused NCJW of taking women away from the

home rather than encouraging a return to it, Council answered sarcastically. Knowing that most prospective members were financially well-off, many with servants or recently invented labor-saving appliances and thus able to fulfill household duties with time to spare, member Nellie L. Miller responded, "we might mildly insinuate to those mistaken women that to spend an hour or two [at Council activities] may not be more derogatory to their love and devotion for home than a two hours' gossip, or shopping, or dressmaking."[67] Council frequently portrayed itself as a superior alternative to the stereotypical shallowness of women who confined their leisure activities to the drawing room.[68] It insisted that skills acquired in Council activities could only improve domestic life. Recognizing that in many homes money was a source of conflict and that husbands admired economic efficiency in their spouses, Milwaukee member Rae C. Ruscha concluded that the Council member was superior to her socialite counterpart because she "has a more intelligent understanding of the domestic situation. She budgets her expenses carefully as does her husband when he inventories his stock." Like many members, Ruscha believed that a Council member was more attractive as a wife than other women because Council activities made her a more interesting person and gave her enough of a taste of her husband's world to understand him truly. Ruscha extended this reasoning to motherhood, concluding that because the Council woman's life was filled with interesting and informative experiences, "She [the Council woman] becomes a delightful companion to her family. . . . As a mother she is a friend and a joy."[69] Through analyses like Ruscha's Council defined its activities as an essential component of Jewish womanhood.

Council's position was backed up by a history of Jewish women's economic activity outside the home. For generations of Jewish women, motherhood included helping to provide for the material needs of the family. As a result, it was not unusual to find Jewish women working outside the confines of the private dwelling. Most Council women did not need to contribute to family income, but this history did foster their perception that activities outside the home were well within the bounds of traditional Jewish motherhood. Added to their increasing ability to care for home with time to spare, Council members simply did not see participation in Council and complete fulfillment of the responsibilities of Jewish mother-hood as mutually exclusive. In addition, most Council women were themselves mothers (see Appendix A, chart 8). They certainly did not see themselves as deficient, and they would have found insult-ing the notion that their concern for their children was in any way diminished by Council membership.

Why, then, would the members so frequently repeat American's assurance that the home came first? One possibility is that Council's constant invocation of Jewish motherhood was a smokescreen in-tended to shield them from attacks by Jewish men.[70] Some male leaders insisted that Council's activities were counter to Jewish law, opposing such projects as Study Circles by citing Talmudic passages declaring the teaching of women as blasphemy.[71] Some Council leaders experienced such opposition in person, as Rebekah Kohut reported: "When the Council of Jewish Women was organized I was sent on a series of speaking tours, and I frequently had to face hostile crowds." She explained the hostility as an outgrowth of the percep-tion of Council as "revolutionary, because, no matter what Gentiles did, Jewish women were expected to stay at home and occupy themselves with housekeeping, sewing bees, card playing and tea parties." Her attempts to counter this view were met with resistance because for women "to have opinions and to voice them was not regarded as good form, even in the home."[72] To quell this opposi-tion, Council women may have used domestic feminist arguments because they were expedient and not necessarily because they actu-ally believed in them. It would be correct to conclude that had NCJW's radical policies not been cloaked in a language that seemed to reinforce tradition, the organization would likely have faced in-surmountable opposition. However, much evidence suggests that it would be wrong to conclude that Council members did not in-ternalize the centrality of motherhood in their renewal of Judaism. To claim that Council women used domestic feminist arguments to ensure that seemingly radical programs would gain acceptance is to assume that such programs faced a good deal of opposition. Such was not the case.

The great variety of members and the frequency with which they repeated statements similar to Sadie American's, which insisted that the responsibilities of home and children were woman's primary raison d'être and that no Council activity or position would ever lead a woman to abrogate those responsibilities, suggest that Council members truly believed what they said rather than viewing it as an expedient political tactic. An essay embracing the primacy of home and the extension of motherhood into the synagogue was among the most requested materials distributed by NCJW's national essay bank.[73]

Moreover, the argument was addressed to audiences of Council women, themselves, as often as it was spoken in settings open to the rest of the Jewish community. Addressing the New York Section, Hannah Solomon indicated what she believed was the commonly accepted attitude of her audience, describing the ideal Council woman as one who expresses and acts on her convictions and who dares go out into the world, but who also is "the woman who stays at home in the smallest, narrowest circle, forgoing all the world may have to offer her, if there her duty lies" and that as a result, "never should any secondary duty take away from us the sacredness of the first, the near duty, for I am satisfied that there is not a woman here who needs that advice."[74] The mothers in Council (most members) saw themselves as living proof of Solomon's declaration that being a woman involved in pursuits outside the home and being a devoted Jewish mother were not mutually exclusive. To think otherwise would have been to deny the reality of their own lives.

Council's pervasive acceptance of Jewish motherhood is further illustrated by continued reiteration of its responsibilities. Even the official prayer used to close Council meetings praised the Divine power who "consecrated our lives by self-sacrifice to serve Thee as priestesses at the fireside and to be builders and guardians of the home, to make it a sanctuary of piety, of love and peace for the upbringing and uplifting of man."[75] Though penned by a rabbi (Kaufmann Kohler), the prayer was adopted with the expectation that it would be recited with earnest devotion at every Council gathering.[76]

Even after NCJW had established itself as a respected Jewish organization with little reason to fear that outsiders would threaten its survival, Council leaders continued to push Jewish motherhood as a prominent Council theme. In 1929, Portland, Oregon's Blanche Blumauer, who had served as a national Council vice-president, repeated the call that home came first, and that only proper fulfillment of responsibilities there would allow woman to expand her sphere of influence,

> We say lightly that the youth of today will not be led; but have we sufficiently tested the influence that goes out from the best type of family life, or the example of religious loyalty and religious devotion in the home? . . .
>
> Until Jewish women and Jewish mothers are willing to give themselves sincerely and devotedly to the re-establishment of the Jewish home, we are failing in our influence in the religious life of today.
>
> Ours is the opportunity, and only as we take it as a solemn duty in the daily affairs of life, shall we be a living force in solving this problem of the age. Then, and then only, shall the Jewish womanhood of our country express itself nobly and self-consecratedly, not only in preserving the religious spirit in the home, but in doing our part in the great national movements of our day, through our organizations, and in our devotion to Temple and Synagogue.[77]

Blumauer's lengthy affirmation of the primacy of motherhood appeared in Council's own journal, a publication intended for Council members, not the general public. It is unlikely that this publication would include rhetoric intended to pacify a resistant Jewish community. Rather, it contained the materials most important to members themselves. Even if Council's founders viewed their remarks on motherhood as a political strategy, the membership they recruited based on those remarks both endorsed and internalized the notion that motherhood was their primary responsibility, both as Jews and as citizens.

The best evidence of the pervasiveness in the belief that woman's first allegiance was properly to home and family is the influence of this ideology of motherhood on Council's subsequent programs and policies. In particular, motherhood affected Council's policies in four areas: Study Circles, philanthropic projects, woman's role within Judaism, and woman suffrage.

Study Circles

Jewish tradition had always insisted that women receive at least enough religious instruction to perform adequately the duties of a good wife and mother, but Council leaders found that for most of the women they hoped to attract, this system had broken down.[78] Even where formal religious training was provided for girls, as in the case of America's Sunday Schools, the education stopped when childhood ended. In the adult world, when questions about practice arose, the community expected men to provide the answers, or as Sadie American phrased it, "the Jew was supposed to have enough [knowledge] for all the female members of his family."[79] Many Council members found, however, that the men in their lives were no better equipped to answer questions than were they. Recognizing that members were not likely to create exemplary Jewish homes without significant knowledge of Jewish religion and history, Council developed Study Circles as the organization's "backbone . . . the nerve-force upon which it must depend for its true usefulness."[80] In doing so, Council set up a pattern of adult religious education that seemed innovative, especially in requiring Jewish women to continue formal regular study of religious texts as adults, but was in reality neither especially innovative nor radical.

Historian Anne Firor Scott has noted that nineteenth-century obstacles to women's education often produced pedagogical innovation in women's educational institutions.[81] Study Circles, the core of American women's clubs' activities since 1860,[82] were not a Council invention, though NCJW was the first organization to apply their methods to the study of Judaism. The adoption of secular women's study club techniques came to NCJW quite naturally as several Sections traced their roots directly to such clubs.[83] Optimal Council Study Circles comprised approximately ten members who would gather on a regular basis to study Judaism. Influenced by Reform interpretation, Protestant America, and the limited number of Jewish texts available in English translation, study was frequently Bible centered. As Buffalo member Elizabeth Hirschfield pointed out, Bible study was fully accepted by the upper class, validated by its inclusion in the course offerings of the most prestigious Ivy League schools.[84] Once basic familiarity with Bible stories was achieved, most Circles attempted to gain a wider sense of the development of the Jewish people by studying Graetz's *History of the Jews*. However, each Circle's autonomy produced a great deal of variation, and Triennial reports mention more than seventeen different books on Jewish subjects in use. Those same reports listed discussions on more than forty topics, ranging from the Prophets to works by contemporary Jewish authors Josephine Lazarus and Grace Aguilar. Discussions attempting to define women's responsibilities to the Jewish community were also popular.[85]

NCJW encouraged its own members to lead the Study Circles, either by covering texts in an area of personal expertise or by rotating leaders with each assigned to present research on a specific topic at designated meetings. This process was so demanding of participants that it earned secular women's study clubs a reputation for being surrogate colleges.[86] By the time American universities admitted female students on a regular basis, many clubwomen were too old to attend or they shunned the maverick reputation earned by the first women to receive degrees.[87] Some women desired to take college courses but felt that family obligations kept them from traveling to the nearest school. Clubs provided these women an opportunity to select their own coursework, and by bringing in occasional speakers, to select their own teachers. The Chicago Woman's Club, on which much early Council activity was modeled, boasted a study program that rivaled college core curricula.[88] Participants in these programs gained research skills as well as an introductory-level knowledge of their subjects.[89]

Many participants in NCJW Study Circles had never formally studied Judaism and certainly had no other opportunity to study it as an adult. As Study Circle participant Elizabeth Hirschfield reported, "Many a young woman is forced from her books just as her mind begins to crave for them. . . . To these, study in circles is a remedy, almost a salvation."[90] By the first Triennial, over half of NCJW's membership participated regularly in Circles, indicating that American Jewish women both needed and wanted to study.[91] For Council members, Study Circles functioned as a kind of middle-class women's yeshiva for the study of Jewish culture. They certainly helped prepare participants to work as educators in the Jewish community, a role soon to be common for NCJW members (see Appendix A, Chart 10). For Jewish women already well versed in Judaism, Council Study Circles provided the only forum in which to share knowledge with other adults and be recognized as scholars. Undoubtedly, some of these learned women viewed Council as a substitute for entering the rabbinate.

On the surface, Study Circles appeared to open new doors for

Jewish women, but what they offered behind those doors was a path back to traditional Jewish womanhood. The potential for change in concepts of Jewish womanhood that might have been fostered by Council's study program was circumscribed by the justification NCJW gave for such study. Borrowing again from the secular women's clubs of the nineteenth century, Council invoked the standard arguments of Republican Motherhood: that a woman could not be expected to make good citizens out of her children if she did not possess an adequate education. Applying this argument to Council's battle against assimilation, Chicago member Florence Herst reminded her colleagues: "It is up to the mothers to know their religion, not merely for the wonderful inspiration it gives them, alone, but also for the example and assistance it will give their children in preserving a faith which brings to us joys, and shows us the paths of righteous living."[92]

This was not the first time such ideas had been introduced in the Jewish community. A century before Council was founded, Isaac Leeser, a traditional Jew and supporter of Rebecca Gratz's establishment of America's first Jewish Sunday School, reminded his readers that "when the child first begins to think, it is his mother who infuses into his mind the first ideas . . . who instructs him concerning the great Being who is the Creator of all." Leeser concluded that Jewish women "ought to be deeply and early impressed . . . with a profound respect for the divine ordinances, and be carefully instructed in the duties which are demanded of us as Israelites."[93]

Nor was this idea original to Leeser. Because this type of argument for women's education reinforced the prevailing social order in the United States and in the Jewish community, it was echoed by a wide variety of Americans.[94] This approach put women's education in the service of a society that placed women in the home rather than in the service of women who wished to break out of Victorian notions of womanhood. Ann Douglas' summary of the resulting nineteenth-century women's education aptly describes Council education as well: "Feminine instruction, as they presented it, was simply a guarantee of masculine rights; the well-educated girl was advertised largely as a better and more understanding wife and mother."[95] Put in this domestic framework, Council Study Circles were neither original nor a threat to traditional Jewish roles for women. Because Council justified its methods with domestic feminist arguments, it reaffirmed the status quo for women rather than providing a vehicle for change.

Some scholars have argued that despite its reiteration of traditional values, women's higher education was an important conduit for the diffusion of feminism because it expanded women's horizons while presenting such expansion in nonthreatening terms.[96] This argument would also apply to Council Study Circles if the traditional language used to justify the Circles cloaked nontraditional goals. However, the ideology of motherhood provided not only the central justification for Study Circles, it served as the primary content as well. Ultimately, Study Circles' potential to challenge traditional Jewish notions of womanhood was limited by the topics and texts studied. Nothing illustrates this point better than Nahida Remy's book, *The Jewish Woman*, so popular that it was reprinted by Council in 1916. Remy suggested that assimilation would become extinct if every Jewish woman returned to her home as a loving servant and ensured that her husband and children properly observed the Sabbath and holidays. Louise Mannheimer, then president of the Cincinnati Section, connected Remy's exhortations to the Council in her introduction to the book: "The same spirit of enthusiasm which animated the organizers of the NCJW is manifested in the writings of Nahida Remy. It is a spirit of renaissance which strives to reestablish the lofty, pure, and beautiful ideals of humanity as found in the oldest document of Monotheism—the Mosaic Law."[97] For Council, a return to Judaism meant a return to traditional notions of Jewish womanhood, even if that return meant women were required to participate in untraditional pursuits like study.

This traditional view, that Jewish womanhood could not and should not be defined outside of Jewish motherhood, was reaffirmed in Council members' own limited Biblical scholarship. In her address to the Jewish Women's Congress, Mannheimer described the most pronounced characteristic of the Matriarchs not as devotion to God or the Jewish people but rather as "devotion to the duties of home and the deep and tender love for their children."[98] At the same convention, Sadie American reinterpreted Eve to be the ultimate civilizer of men, a model she expected Council members to accept unquestioningly.[99]

Other Council members took inspiration from Grace Aguilar's

book, *Women of Israel*, which frequently appeared on the recommended reading lists prepared by Council's national Committee on Religion. Aguilar claimed that "the woman of Israel . . . was debarred in not a single instance of the spiritual privileges and solemn responsibilities which had been bestowed upon her by the law of God."[100] Aguilar's optimistic portrayal of women in Judaism was frequently repeated by Council members. One Charleston Section member claimed that Jewish women were not interested in women's rights because "From the earliest Biblical times the Israelite recognized with joy whatever ability his sister might possess, and the Jewish woman so gifted might freely make a study of the laws, and enter the councils of the wise men, prophets, and judges." Moreover, she claimed that such status was granted to Jewish women not as a reward for independence but "because of their innate womanliness, for we read that though there were those among them who in times of need rose even to the rank of prophets, judges, and leaders in battle, yet they were essentially *womanly women*, who, after the hour of peril passed, claimed as their greatest glory the title of 'Mother in Israel.'"[101]

Nahida Remy expanded on these inflated claims, incorrectly alleging that in pre-Enlightenment generations, Jewish women were fluent in Hebrew.[102] Mrs. Carl Wolf of Terre Haute summarized: "because his [the Jew's] religion centered in the home, of which the wife and mother was the priestess, she had no small share in the [religious] training of the child, as well as in the formation of public opinion."[103] Council members clearly romanticized woman's position in the Jewish community and awarded her more rights than she ever actually possessed. In so doing, they depicted a tradition so enticing there was no reason to challenge it.

Historian Theodora Penny Martin has drawn the analogy between Women's Study Clubs' discovery of women and the rejuvenation of black history that accompanied the civil rights movement in the 1960s, noting that such study reinforced students' identities as it provided role models.[104] Council's studies succeeded in reminding American Jews that Jewish history had not been exclusively shaped by male hands, but rather than challenge the status quo, NCJW chose as role models the foremothers who conveniently reinforced mainstream American visions of womanhood.

The best example was Council's choice to observe Council Sabbath (a yearly occasion when synagogues would recognize Council members) on the Sabbath preceding Purim in honor of Esther. Esther was an appropriate role model because her success in coming to her people's aid and saving them after men's efforts to do so had failed paralleled Council's ambition to save American Jews from assimilation.[105] Yet, as Chicago Section president Nannie Reis observed, Esther did not challenge traditional gender roles (as had Vashti), but had obeyed "the commandment of Mordechai like as when she was brought up by him."[106] In other words, Esther succeeded in saving the Jews because she had deferred to a man. In fact, several voices in the Jewish community had come to identify Esther with the moderate domestic feminism supported by NCJW while associating Vashti with militant feminists. A poem entitled "A Purim Fantasia," which appeared in the *American Hebrew*, offered one such depiction:

Vashti, The New Woman

She was the first of "New Women," Queen of the olden
    time,
Founded the rights that are Woman's and lost crown and
    thrown for the "crime;"
Lost she the crown and the Kingdom, monarch and glorious
    name,
But now do we hail thee: "The Woman's Right Martyr, heiress of
    Fame!"[107]

In a reaffirmation of their rejection of militant feminism, NCJW chose to observe Council Sabbath on the Sabbath preceding Purim to honor Esther's courageous actions *within* the system, not Vashti's rejection of it.[108]

Despite participation in Study Circles, Council members never believed themselves to be sufficiently competent to make their own decisions in religious matters.[109] When a debate about Biblical history arose at Council's first Triennial, the women called upon the few rabbis present to discuss the issue and eventually decided that the question was best left to the male "authorities."[110] In many smaller towns, members complained that they simply could not find any qualified women to lead their Circles, and they depended upon rabbis to guide them. Such practice reinforced the traditional hierarchy wherein Jewish men possessed knowledge and chose what and when to share with Jewish women. It failed to provide potentially revolutionary models of female leadership or the possibility of advancement beyond the level of student. Council board member Emma S. Rosenstock lamented the "tendency on the part of some Sections to give up individual effort and let the thinking be done by professionals," questioning whether dependence on others would "help our own minds? Does it help to bring out the best that within us lies, as doing our own thinking and writing our own papers?" She answered her own query with an unequivocal *"decidedly not."*[111]

Hannah Solomon illustrated her attitude toward the value of women's scholarship in a presidential report to the national board, then considering whether to take a stand on the Sunday Sabbath controversy: "Now we may go on splitting hairs about the 'Sabbath in its pristine purity' until we fill volumes, and our generation can have a woman's Talmud as well as a woman's Bible. Let us rather avoid it, since we cannot settle it."[112] Here Solomon recognized the revolutionary potential for women's scholarship, no doubt referring to Elizabeth Cady Stanton's *Woman's Bible*, yet she chose not to pursue the task for want of a permanent, definitive outcome.

Study Circles might have encouraged Council women to mirror feminist activity in the Christian community by pursuing further study, reinterpreting texts from a woman's perspective, entering the rabbinate, or beginning to question the awe in which they held Jewish male scholars. As in most Women's Clubs, however, such was not the intent, and such was not the outcome.[113] Blaming the shortcomings of American Judaism on men's rational approach, even educator Julia Richman insisted that what women most needed to bring to Judaism was emotion, not intellect, and that while Study Circles nourished the head, "God needs hearts more than heads in His service."[114]

Sadie American made the point clear in her address to the 1896 convention, stating bluntly that it was not Council's intent to produce scholars.[115] Instead she predicted that Study Circle participation would produce "high thinking [which] shall lead to noble living, to a finer, truer, fuller womanhood; that knowledge may bring wisdom, and our women be an influence and an instrument for the very best in every relation of life, whether crowned as wife and mother, in the family, as friend, or as a light and guide in the dim realm of the unfortunate."[116] According to American, woman's efforts to achieve wisdom were directed at making her a better wife and a more effective social reformer, both of which she could place squarely within the parameters of traditional Jewish womanhood. In other words, while Study Circles challenged traditional Jewish notions of womanhood in form, they posed no such challenge in content. They were an accommodation to modern life in America that did not require a compromise in traditional Jewish values—a model of acculturation.

This reinforcement of, rather than challenge to, societal norms was not unique to NCJW. Study Clubs in general were populated by women who counted themselves among those who had succeeded in America. They had no intention of challenging the order that produced their success. One key to that order was the acceptance of gender roles that were complementary and distinct. Delineating that distinction, one clubwoman noted that while man was "the inventor, the explorer, the discoverer," woman was "the *conserver, preserver*, and helpmeet" [emphasis mine].[117] According to this definition, it was contrary to American womanhood to do anything but continue the status quo. Theodora Penny Martin summarized the resulting function of study clubs saying, "They were a way for women to identify with others like themselves and a way to prevent that identity from changing."[118] NCJW followed the study club model precisely because it did not have a reputation for upsetting the social order.

Several members claimed that participation in Study Circles had increased commitment to philanthropic work and "quickened the religious feeling of the community."[119] Yet, even the author of these words, New York City Section's second president Rachel H. Sulzberger, was quick to add that her reference to religious feeling was not merely among women, "For, so closely do men and women act and react upon each other that whatever deeply affects one must of necessity leave a lasting impression upon both, and in rousing woman, the Council has carried its message to every home where her influence is felt."[120] Later in the same speech Sulzberger would, like Sadie American, caution her listeners not to pursue their studies to any great depth, claiming that most members were simply not yet prepared to do "textual criticism."[121] Instead, the goal was merely to bring devotion and spirituality to the home.

In this ambitious goal, Study Circles were only partially successful. The Circles' design assumed that devotion at home would be sparked by the increased knowledge gained through study, but several Sections reported inconsistent attendance and a failure to address topics seriously. Reports at every Triennial convention in Council's early years indicated that almost half of all Section members never attended Study Circles, and as the years passed, fewer members continued to attend the Circles. The decline led Hannah Solomon to observe, "While its fundamental interest has always been the study of Judaism and Jewish affairs, it is significant that each successive convention finds greater stress laid upon social legislation, social welfare, international relations and all problems of aliens."[122] This decline occurred despite the crucial role Circles played in Council's plan to renew Jewish womanhood.

One source of the decline was competition with newly offered synagogue adult education courses, to which Council responded, "Congregational classes, composed of women of largely similar viewpoint, cannot adequately supplant the Council classes, with their varied memberships."[123] This attempt to portray Council's religious diversity as a source of strength, however, did not address the main problem, which was that most Council women did not pursue any formal religious study, in or outside the synagogue. The president of the Syracuse Section explained that the difficulty in attracting women to Circles was not due to ideological objections either from within or without, but reflected the reality of members' lives. She reported that in her experience, members were "either too advanced in age to study, or those who, never having had educational advantages, are unable to apply themselves to books at this late day. Such women can only do philanthropic work, and, except at our monthly meetings, derive no advantage from the study of religion pursued by the other members of our section."[124] As Sue Levi Elwell in her study of NCJW so aptly phrased it, "For many women, the lack of interest in study circles did not represent a weakened commitment to Council aims, but simply served as a clear expression of their preference for action over contemplation."[125] Sadie American had recognized this preference in her earliest recruiting efforts. In 1895 she remarked, "Strange as it may seem it is much easier to get people to *do* some definite thing for others than to get them to think for themselves; it is easier to interest people in philanthropy than in purely religious work."[126]

It is also likely that the decline in Study Circles reflected the trend of secular Study Clubs. NCJW was founded just as these Study Clubs were beginning to shift their emphasis from cultural studies to social reform work.[127] The Chicago Woman's Club was actually founded by younger members of the prestigious Fortnightly Club who were unsatisfied by the older group's reluctance to add social reform work to its agenda. In a statement of purpose that contained many elements later to be found in NCJW declarations, the new group explained, "The Chicago Woman's Club is essentially a practical organization, made up of earnest intelligent women, banded together not in the mere pursuit of intellectual culture, but to promote the higher ends of a purer social state and the true enlightenment of mankind."[128]

As with the Chicago Woman's Club, the decline of NCJW Study Circles was precipitated by the increasing demands of urbanization and poverty-stricken immigrants. The decline also reflected the limits of Women's Clubs' study. Few groups possessed the resources to go beyond a basic examination of any given subject. Introductory courses were exciting to those who had never studied at an advanced level, but they could not hold a student's interest forever. Can we imagine a college senior who would not be bored and frustrated by being restricted to first-year courses? Moreover, for the vast majority of participants, the education received in Council Study Circles was a dead end. It did not lead to careers, open up leadership roles in synagogues, earn participants respect from male Jewish scholars; nor, as Council members would soon discover, did it guarantee that their children would not assimilate. Given these trends, the decline in Study Circle attendance was inevitable. That decline marked a shift in Council programming from efforts geared to serve the needs of members as well as those less fortunate, to an exclusive focus on serving clients. Not until the 1980s would Council programs again blur the lines between members (who provided aid to the needy) and clients (who received the help offered by members).

Though regular participation in Study Circles would come to be replaced by attendance at occasional Council-sponsored lectures, members' enthusiasm for less demanding educational projects did not diminish. For example, Council members played a key role in the development of the Jewish Publication Society (JPS). Many members made individual contributions, like Mary M. Cohen, who was the only woman on the JPS first executive committee, or Nina Morais Cohen, who completed her father Sabato's translation of Jeremiah for the press, or the otherwise anonymous Mrs. Lewis, who is credited with inspiring the collection of stories compiled in *Under the Sabbath Lamp*.[129] In addition to these individual efforts, Council cooperated with JPS in the issuing of the *Papers of the 1893 Jewish Women's Congress* and the proceedings of NCJW's first convention in 1896. Council members who purchased these volumes helped JPS grow and stabilize. In return, several early JPS titles were geared toward women, and JPS's call to issue an English translation of the Bible was, in part, due to the fact that NCJW had placed Bible study at the core of its adult education program.[130] As consumers, Council members would continue to influence the development of cultural institutions like JPS long after Council's own adult education programs had faded.

As Council women worried less about their own religious training, they became increasingly concerned with their motherly duty of religiously educating the youth of the Jewish community. Leaders like Rebecca Gratz and Isaac Leeser had established religious schools early in the nineteenth century, but attendance at those schools dramatically declined with the secularization and growth of America's public school system.[131] By the time NCJW was founded, Jewish education in the United States was, at best, erratic, and religious schools that admitted girls were often underfunded and too few in number to meet basic needs.[132] Because many immigrant mothers did not have the time, the resources, or the understanding of a new generation growing up in America to teach their daughters the skills necessary to keep a Jewish home, many American Jewish girls went without religious instruction. Council was quick to recognize the potential loss to the community inherent in this situation and established religious schools for girls as one of their early projects.[133] As the Chicago Section discovered, the demand for such schools was tremendous. When its school opened at the end of the nineteenth

century, three hundred girls enrolled immediately, and many more
were placed on a waiting list. By 1905, the school had over four
hundred students.[134]

Like Study Circles, curriculum content in these schools was
quite traditional. Rather than posing a new challenge to Judaism,
Council religious schools acted as a substitute for the mother who
could no longer provide her daughters with lessons traditionally
learned at home. Council's curriculum emphasized subjects like
holiday observance and familiarity with basic Bible stories, long
considered topics appropriate for women. Because Council hoped
their graduates would easily find employment if necessary, even
their vocational education remained within the boundaries of accepted women's tasks, concentrating on sewing and domestic science, and for the most advanced students, perhaps teaching or
writing.[135] In Rosa Sonneschein's words, "Compelled to become a
breadwinner, she has successfully entered industrial and intellectual
fields, but her foremost mission will forever be the propagation of
the race. . . . Men will never replace women in the home realm,
and her physical and mental structure will exclude her from avocations befitting a man."[136]

Sonneschein included in her list of "male avocations" handling
freight, building railroads, and being a soldier, a mathematician, or
a logician. She insisted that training women for such fields (in
which they could never compete) was a complete waste of time,
claiming that "Marriage is the foremost aim of the American Jewess, as it was of her grandmother."[137] Coming from Sonneschein,
who left a disastrous marriage and who, as publisher of the *American Jewess*, worked in a "male" profession, these comments were
particularly ironic, a further underscoring of how central the ideology of True Womanhood was to Council thought. Council schools
provided hundreds of Jewish girls with their only opportunity to be
educated, a vital contribution to both women and the Jewish community, but rather than opening doors to the world at large, Council education led girls back into the home.

Council would continue to reflect the primacy of motherhood in
the types of social reform projects it chose to sponsor (see chapter 5).
Its greatest fame came from its battles to protect the virtue of immigrant girls and from providing programs like parenting classes and

penny school lunches. Thus, while it may have seemed revolutionary to have Council women participating in American politics or running large social welfare projects, it was easy for the women to see such work as an extension of their role as mother. As Philadelphia member Mary M. Cohen put it, "she is a worthy daughter of Israel in the home first, and then everywhere."[138]

Women in the Synagogue

Not only did Council use motherhood to justify woman's foray into secular projects, it also based its arguments for increased religious activity on women's responsibilities for rearing children. Because a mother's daily tasks grounded her in the material world, traditional Judaism defined the daily routines of motherhood as essentially secular. Council women, however, accepted motherhood as woman's primary *religious* obligation, just as study and prayer were men's responsibility. They insisted that mothers, as important religious functionaries, were entitled to some power in the religious community.

Initial Council efforts to transform conviction into action concentrated on seeking a greater say in synagogue policy. Such a demand was not new. As early as the 1860s, Isaac Mayer Wise called on synagogues to "require that woman be made a member of the congregation, of equal rights with every man" and that "All laws contrary to this principle, on any statute book of a congregation, should be wiped out as reminiscences of barbarism and degrading to the cause of religion."[139] Significantly, such calls for religious equality were made at a time when men were beginning to devalue the synagogue and religious practice. Not surprisingly, Central Conference of American Rabbis resolutions[140] and Wise's pleas for equality were largely ignored, and when NCJW was founded, most synagogues listed as members only the male head of household. Council demanded that women, too, be recognized as synagogue members. In response to that demand, most synagogues began listing membership as "Mr. and Mrs." Of course, women's first names remained hidden behind their husbands' names, but Council women believed they had taken a first step toward getting synagogue men to take women's contribution seriously.[141] Two years later, Temple Isaiah, a Chicago congregation with many Council members, became the first American synagogue to admit women to full membership.[142]

Like the members of the first Women's Club who campaigned for seats on Boston's school board in the 1870s, Council pressed for, and often won, an end to the exclusion of women from synagogue and religious school boards.[143] The results of a survey done by NCJW's first national Committee on Religious School Work (1893–1896) indicated that Council efforts had placed seventeen women on religious school boards in ten different cities.[144] By the 1905 Triennial that number had grown to seventy-two women in twenty-nine synagogues.[145] Continuing in the secular Women's Club pattern, Council developed the justifications for their demands directly from the text of domestic feminism. They argued that because woman was "in charge of almost all religious duties [in the home]," from ritual observance to the education of children, that "in the administration of synagogal affairs she can be and should be a potent factor . . . to her should be assigned the inner life, the housewifery of the synagogue."[146] One Council committee report took this role of congregational housewife quite literally, arguing that women should be included on religious school boards because "In addition to paying close attention to the matter and manner of teaching, women are more apt to look after the physical requirements, such as keeping the rooms well ventilated, properly heated, sanitary and attractive."[147] To phrase it another way, Council women argued that they could not possibly educate their children properly without a say in the process and preparation of that education.

The limits of such an approach became clear when the community began to debate the ordination of women into the rabbinate. Following the common pattern of leading Protestant suffragists, several of whom were themselves ordained, a strong minority in Council believed women could and should be rabbis.[148] They believed that just as women had made advances in other professions and proved themselves capable, so, too, should they be given the opportunity to become rabbis, arguing that "The woman who is fitted by nature and experience to occupy the pulpit, should do so. There is no sex in spirituality."[149] Others connected their position to the phenomenon of synagogues' feminization, arguing that the large percentage of women congregants would be better served by women rabbis.[150]

Council had already laid the groundwork for the ordination of women by demanding a greater formal role for women in synagogues, by structuring their own meetings to provide a forum in which women could preach, and by accepting invitations to have its leaders address the Jewish community from the pulpit. With the establishment of Council Sabbath in 1920, during which Council members often led or took active roles in the worship services of their individual congregations, women's occasional presence on the pulpit would become commonplace. In Council's early years, however, a female on the pulpit was so rare it was newsworthy. One typical headline described Hannah Solomon's first appearance on a Chicago pulpit:

WOMAN ACTS AS RABBI

IN THE SINAI TEMPLE PULPIT

Mrs. Hannah G. Solomon the First of
Her Sex in the History of Judaism
to Fill the Position—Will
Create a Sensation.[151]

In her memoirs, Solomon claims that Council's influence was responsible for the invitation to speak at Sinai.[152]

Despite the opportunity Council seemed to hold forth, the great majority of Council women opposed the ordination of women. In her address to Council's founding convention, Ray Frank would summarize Council's prevailing attitude, "Innovation is not progress, and to be identical with man is not the ideal of womanhood. Some things and privileges belong to him by nature; to these true woman does not aspire; but every woman should aspire to make of her home a temple, of herself a high priestess, of her children disciples, then she will best occupy the pulpit, and her work will run parallel with man's. She may be ordained rabbi or be the president of a congregation—she is entirely able to fill both offices—but her noblest work will be at home, her highest ideal a home."[153] This statement is all the more ironic because Frank's own life contradicted the notion that the rabbinate was male "by nature" and contrary to being a "true woman." Her invitation to address the convention came directly from the notoriety she had earned preaching from Jewish pulpits on the West Coast. Though she was not ordained, many people mistook her for a rabbi, and the congregation in Portland, Oregon, that she helped found invited her to be its spiritual leader, an offer she turned down.

That Frank's success did not lead her to question the ideology of True Womanhood was certainly ironic, but it was not surprising. Frank's position presented women with the best of all worlds. While affirming what Council women believed to be divinely ordained differences between men and women, she did not rank those differences to favor men. Instead, she asserted that women were certainly capable of being rabbis, but there was no compelling reason that would lead them to desire such a career. Here, again, Frank was not expressing a new ideology, but rather, was echoing a common argument from the domestic feminism of the mid-nineteenth century. Catharine Beecher, for example, used a pattern of thought similar to Frank's to oppose women's entrance into politics. Beecher claimed that the ultimate human goal was happiness and that such happiness could not be found in public pursuits, but could be found readily in a moral home. She concluded therefore that women should concentrate on the fight to remain supreme within the home.[154]

Just as Beecher's argument appealed to women who were either restricted to the home or who enjoyed great success there, Frank's position was popular with women who wanted greater recognition within the Jewish community but who did not wish to upset the status quo that guaranteed the good life they enjoyed. That the Jewish community seemed to be waging a losing battle against assimilation seemed ample evidence to Council women that rabbis did, indeed, lack the power to influence Jewish life. As Frank knew from her own experience, the effect of pulpit persuasion was temporary at best, and even the finest orators addressed audiences of adults who generally were already set in their ways. She looked instead to those who had the best opportunity to shape young minds: mothers.

Perhaps because she had not borne children herself, she romanticized the mother-child relationship, propounding the exceedingly optimistic belief that properly raised children would undoubtedly carry into adulthood the religious values of their mothers.

Yet, Frank was correct to conclude that mothers had a better chance of ensuring the Jewish identity of Jewish youth than turn-of-the-century American rabbis. Council women generally agreed that instilling commitment to Judaism in the next generation was the most important task facing the Jewish community. Compared to motherhood and its presumed opportunity to influence husbands and children, then being touted by the majority of the Jewish community as the only possible savior of Jewish life in America, the rabbinate seemed like a second-rate opportunity, that which men did because they could not be mothers.

Other Council arguments would flow from this position, including the claim that both motherhood and the rabbinate required full-time devotion, so a woman could not possibly do both, and given the choice, she should choose the superior option: motherhood. To condone women in the rabbinate would have meant admitting that, in fact, motherhood was not always the best way for women to serve in the Jewish community. To an organization that had based itself on the notion of divinely ordained separate spheres and renewal of tradition, this position was unacceptable. Not least it would have contradicted Council's assumption that mothers wielded greater influence over the Jewish community than rabbis ever could. To Council members, this notion of influence was no trivial matter. As Ann Douglas has demonstrated in her work on Christian women and the clergy, women were excluded from the direct exercise of power in American society, so they focused their energies on maximizing their ability to influence others.[155] With no other access to power, women depended on their talents of persuasion to guarantee themselves a valued place in society.

Rabbis, as rabbis, also depended on their ability to influence others, but as men they had access to power in a variety of other arenas, so admitting that mothers might better influence children was not a total denial of power. For Council women, however, acknowledging that rabbis could influence the next generation more effectively, or even as effectively, as mothers was to admit that in the

Jewish community women never had the final say, that is, women were powerless. Unwilling to condemn a religion to which they were devoted, Council women (like Ray Frank) devalued the rabbinate, and without devaluing women's capabilities, developed a model of women's power through influence that effectively excluded women from the rabbinate.

Given the ramifications of supporting the ordination of women, it is not surprising that those Council members who favored it did not manage to bring the subject up for debate or vote on a convention floor prior to the late 1960s. Even when the issue was hotly debated elsewhere in the Jewish community, as in 1923 when HUC denied ordination to Martha Neumark, Council did not comment. Members would carry on a dialogue in the Jewish press and Council publications,[156] but either for fear of defeat or fear that the issue would be divisive enough to damage the organization, NCJW did not take an official stand on the ordination of women.

Rather than challenge tradition, Council demanded that American Jews live up to their religion's concept of separate but complementary (and equal) gender roles by according mothers the respect and status given to male scholars. Historically, the Jewish community had paid women tribute more by lip service than by offering any substantial reward. Council recognized this situation as ultimately devaluing women, leading it to seek reassurance of women's importance, not only in statements of praise for good Jewish mothers, but by demanding concrete changes like full synagogue membership. Yet, Council never sought direct power in the Jewish community. Though it fought for synagogue membership, it did not demand ordination or the right to become officers in either synagogues or other communal institutions.

Instead, Council glorified and expanded motherhood, extending women's scope of influence in the process. As Ann Douglas has noted for other American women, this pursuit of greater influence rather than direct power led Council to exert a "conservative influence on their society."[157] Though some Council members would support radical changes in Judaism proposed by male leaders (like Sunday Sabbath), Council never proposed such challenges itself. In the Victorian ideology of separate spheres, the home represented permanence, stability, and unwavering morality in the face of societal corruption and constant change. In this context, the centrality of motherhood in the development of Council policy guaranteed that the organization would preserve rather than challenge traditional Jewish roles for women. Though the members demanded some expansion of women's role, Council's vision was circumscribed by its resolve to renew rather than recreate Jewish womanhood.

Suffrage

Council's limited demand for equal rights within the synagogue paralleled its attempt to extend this demand to the American political system. Council's most influential leaders, including Hannah Solomon, Sadie American, and Rebekah Kohut, openly declared their support for the suffrage movement.[158] They considered leaders of the suffrage movement like Susan B. Anthony and Carrie Chapman Catt friends.[159] They sympathized with suffrage ideals and, as Kohut wrote, they identified those ideals as Jewish: "I associated the work of [suffragists] with the history of the women of my own people, and found much similarity in their ideals and aspirations. Deborah became to me not a prophetess but a great political emancipator."[160] Kohut concluded that because she was a Jew, she was obligated to work for suffrage.

Though not fully supportive of all suffragist tactics, Council leaders were quite comfortable with those suffragists who used domestic feminist arguments to justify their demands. Already skilled at using these arguments to their own advantage, they found domestic feminist arguments for suffrage compelling. Most agreed with Toledo Section president Pauline Steinem, who believed in woman suffrage because "the perfect equality of man and woman is founded on Divine Wisdom." Steinem combined Kohut's sense of religious obligation with domestic feminism to conclude that "Women need today the larger vision and the wider experience which the world's work would give them . . . in order that they may become better wives, better mothers and better homemakers."[161]

Council received positive reinforcement for their pro-suffrage stand on many fronts. Several of the organizations with which

NCJW affiliated or worked, such as the Chicago Woman's Club, the National and International Councils of Women, the WCTU, and the settlement house movement, promoted the suffrage cause. Even women's clubs that shunned militant suffragists voiced public support for the vote in the first years of the twentieth century.[162] In addition, much of the Jewish community, particularly in Reform circles, supported suffrage.[163] Thus, when an official resolution was finally brought before the 1917 Triennial convention, Council leaders had every reason to expect the organization to endorse wholeheartedly their position. Rebekah Kohut had already assured suffrage leaders of Council's support.[164]

Convention planners had invited several speakers to address the issue prior to the motion. From the widely respected Hannah Solomon to the somewhat obscure delegate from Terre Haute, the speakers called for support for woman suffrage. The official motion was proposed by Mrs. Henry Weiller, a member of the St. Paul Section:

> Whereas, The question of Equal Suffrage is now one of great moment; and
>
> Whereas, Every body of women organized for progressive work along lines of special and civic betterment is forced to recognize the imperative need for woman's enfranchisement; and
>
> Whereas, This organization is co-operating with all groups organized for bettering conditions for women and children; be it
>
> Resolved, That the National Council of Jewish Women, in Convention assembled, endorse the bill now pending in Congress providing an Amendment to our Federal Constitution granting to all the women of the United States the same political rights now enjoyed by the men, and that a telegram to this effect be sent to our President at Washington, D.C.[165]

The resolution highlighted several important Council goals, including being counted among America's preeminent women's organizations and protecting the welfare of women and children. It also reflected Council's trust that legislation would help solve social problems. Despite the strongly grounded expectations of the motion's supporters, however, the resolution was defeated by a vote of the convention.

Observers at the time attributed the defeat to strong opposition by a few influential women, including Annie Nathan Meyer, who wrote, "There are some women—I won't say a few, but I am convinced they are not the majority—that think they cannot influence sufficiently this world of ours unless their opinion is backed by the ballot. But I should like to say to such women: How have we met the obligations of the past? Let us consider this before we yearn to take on new obligations. . . . The woman that brings up her son to be the right kind of voter is not ballotless."[166] Using the familiar political technique of discrediting the movement by limiting her description to its most extreme elements, Meyer further characterized suffragists as "man haters" who would oppose Council's efforts to strengthen the family.[167] She also insisted that the vote would not bring the rewards suffragists promised. Meyer's arguments were familiar to Council members on both sides of the issue. Council based its activities on the assumption that one could influence adult decisions to live Jewishly by providing the proper upbringing during childhood, so when Meyer said "The woman that brings up her son to be the right kind of voter is not ballotless," most Council women nodded in agreement. Those who opposed suffrage were further bolstered by claims that militant suffragists intended to disrupt the American political system. While Council members saw room for change, they fundamentally believed that American democracy afforded Jews the best life possible. As a result, they were unwilling to support any movement which might seriously threaten that system.

Of course, Meyer did not address the situation of those women who had no sons or husbands, and not all Council women found her position satisfying. Yet, most Council members enjoyed the cooperation of their husbands in their Council activities. They were well educated, active in public cultural and political life, successful in obtaining community support for their issues, and they had received recognition for their efforts in both the Jewish and the Gentile communities. That is to say, Council members believed they had already achieved what moderate suffragists claimed would be won only with the vote.[168] Thus, even to Council suffragists, there was no compelling reason to risk splitting their infant organization for the sake of something that would bring little real change.

In addition, Council women had good reason to see other issues as more pressing than suffrage. Discussions at the 1917 Triennial were dominated by the Great War, not votes for women. Moreover, for three decades, the vast amount of Council energies and monies were spent helping the millions of newly arrived immigrants. Compared to starving Russian Jews living in the squalor of America's urban slums, suffrage must have seemed a minor issue rather than an immediate need. Ironically, 75 percent of the immigrants Council was serving supported suffrage. [169]

The presence of increasing numbers of immigrant Jews presented a challenge to Council women, not only in terms of resources, but also to their self-concept of what it meant to be Jewish in America. One of Council's functions had been to aid in the process of Jewish acculturation to the United States, and before the arrival of these new immigrants, many Council women, though proud of their Jewish heritage, had come to identify predominantly with Gentiles of their own class. They viewed themselves as American club-women, belonging to NCJW as only one among many organizations, most of which were secular (see Appendix A, Chart 20). However, anti-Semitism inherent in American anti-immigrant sentiments and the American tendency to rely on stereotypes that obscured differences between groups of Jews made such identification increasingly difficult. Historian Nancy Cott has argued convincingly that those who traditionally led the fight for women's rights were those who had the luxury of identifying as women first because their class and ethnic identities were of the dominant culture and therefore invisible. [170] That is, what most distinguished the leading fighters for women's rights from mainstream American culture was their womanhood. Had Eastern European Jewish immigrants never arrived on American shores, such would also have been true for many Council women. The presence of these highly visible Jewish immigrants and Council members' inevitable multi-layered identification with them made it increasingly difficult for Council women to view womanhood as their primary identity. As Council's focus on womanhood faded, so did its active support for issues exclusively focused on that identity, especially suffrage.

Moreover, Council women had good reason to be suspicious of much of the women's rights movement. Council members were familiar with Elizabeth Cady Stanton's *Woman's Bible*, debated hotly in feminist and Jewish circles in the mid-1890s.[171] In all likelihood they were also familiar with Matilda Joslyn Gage's *Women, Church and State*, the monumental exposé of the Church's mistreatment of women throughout history. Gage's study was published in 1893, the same year Council was founded, and received much press because it was so widely criticized by the religious establishment. Both books argued that Judaism and Christianity inherently and irreversibly oppress women and therefore should be abandoned.

Even feminists who believed Christianity could be used to justify women's equality, like the Reverend Anna Howard Shaw (leader of the nation's largest suffrage organization and a Council supporter), echoed Gage's claim that the "doctrine of woman's secondary creation and subordination was a part of Judaism engrafted upon Christianity," or more bluntly, that the oppressive facets of Christianity lay in its Jewish roots.[172] Like other suffrage leaders, Shaw accompanied this attitude with anti-immigrant sentiment, as in her assessment of South Dakota where she blamed counties inhabited by Russian Jewish immigrants for failure to win suffrage. To Shaw, "The fact that our Cause could be defeated by immigrant laborers newly come to our country was a humiliating one to accept."[173] Just a year before NCJW's first Triennial, Shaw had innocently queried her friend Rebekah Kohut about why the Jewish woman "had not emerged from the home and taken up her position with the others of her sex in fighting for women's rights."[174] If such naiveté and subtle anti-Semitism were all Jewish women could expect from suffrage leaders, then Jewish women could hardly be expected to feel an obligation to serve the movement. Given this attitude, even Council members who supported suffrage were hesitant to join suffrage organizations, and they certainly were not willing to risk serious division within Council to support a movement toward which they could only feel ambivalent.[175]

Following the passage of the nineteenth amendment, Council's approach to women's rights continued to be dominated by moderate domestic feminist arguments. Responsive to its emphasis on education, NCJW quickly affiliated with the League of Women Voters. Jennie Franklin Purvin, longtime officer of the Chicago Section, articulated the rationale for supporting the League using the classic domestic feminist extension of home into the public world saying, "We should be especially interested in our new citizenship since we are ambitious to see our homes and our city, the big home of us all, well taken care of."[176] Purvin concluded by urging women to vote for whatever candidates best supported NCJW's legislative plan, irrespective of party, a policy that Council quickly adopted as its own.[177] Despite this position, many Council members harbored conflicting attitudes about female politicians. Even in 1959, a Council survey of 240 members showed that 91 would not vote for a woman for the presidency of the United States.[178]

Council also actively opposed the passage of the Equal Rights Amendment, not only because it was proposed by the militant wing of the suffrage movement, but because it seemed antithetical to Council's support of motherhood.[179] ERA supporters argued that the legislation was necessary to open up higher paying and more satisfying professions to women, but only women who were well educated would actually have access to such a career, and the requisite education was generally beyond the reach of the lower classes. Council believed that middle- and upper-class women had already won equality by gaining the right to vote, so this pro-ERA argument seemed superfluous. Viewing legislation primarily as a tool to help the downtrodden, Council concluded that ERA served the interests of the wrong people and therefore sought a solution to the problems faced by working women in protective legislation rather than the ERA.[180]

Council's anti-ERA resolution underscored its belief that only protective legislation best bolstered the family by keeping children out of the workplace and improving the health of mothers:

> Whereas, The Blanket Equality Amendment proposed by the National Woman's Party is an attempt to give equal rights to men and women by a Federal Amendment; and
> Whereas, We believe that its enactment would imperil the rights and privileges secured by women in industry and would render insecure the legal and economic basis of marriage and the family;
> Be it resolved, That the National Council of Jewish Women opposes blanket legislation on these subjects and endorses the

method of securing separate, specific legislation to remedy the existing inequalities involving injustices to woman in the laws of most states of the nation.[181]

Council would remain steadfastly opposed to the ERA until the 1960s.

Council's approach to equal political rights for women reflects its interpretation of equality between the sexes. Even Council's most traditional members agreed with Rabbi Emil Hirsch. Commenting on the growing number of women in the workforce, Hirsch supported equal pay for equal work and claimed that, at least in the abstract, women were capable of pursuing previously male-only occupations. However, he also reminded his readers that women and men were naturally different, claiming that psychological studies proved beyond a shadow of a doubt that "Woman is stronger in the affections and emotions, man in reason and action." Therefore, Hirsch reasoned, "Man is destined to be the provider, woman the preserver. This inequality is fundamental equality. Both are equal in function."[182] He concluded that instead of struggling for the emancipation of women, it would be more productive to struggle for the emancipation of society. In Hirsch's view, an emancipated society was one in which woman did not have to work—one in which she was free to devote herself to the natural calling of motherhood and in which motherhood was valued as highly as men's paid labor.

Nearly forty years after Hirsch penned those words, Council member Elizabeth Stern writing in support of career women concluded that woman "chooses her career, but God chose her first— the woman of the race—to be the mother of the race. She can never forget that solemn duty encharged to her despite whatever paths or plans she may elect to take. She may challenge the conscience of society and question its judgement, but she cannot challenge her own. So long as her children need her they come first, and the job must follow."[183]

To Council women, motherhood was the divinely ordained function of womanhood. It was beyond challenge. In Council eyes, women could seek higher education, could work before marriage or out of economic necessity, but to pursue a career to the exclusion of motherhood was to try to be a man, and above all, Council prided itself as representing, not abandoning womanhood. Even career woman Rosa Sonneschein cautioned intelligent women not to lose their femininity, saying, "to be a genuine woman is far more preferable than to evolve into an imitation man."[184] Pittsburgh Section president Bertha Rauh phrased it, "No sincere, modest woman unsexes herself by educating her mind for the battles of this life." In Rauh's view, "woman only improves herself as sister, as daughter, as wife, as mother: she dignifies her home and she benefits mankind thereby."[185]

Given this view that preserving the differences between the sexes was preserving Divine natural order, and that difference did not imply inequality, Council's opposition to the ERA was quite logical. The members could not support legislation that might blur the line separating gender roles or threaten the elevation of motherhood to heroic status.

3.

Jewish Leaders Respond

CONCOMITANT with Council's belief that inequality between the sexes was "fundamental equality" was the desire to cooperate rather than compete with men.[1] As historian Janet Wilson James observed, compared to women in other faiths, Jewish women worked more closely with men in charitable undertakings.[2] Hannah Solomon even insisted that Council's "sisterhood does not exclude brotherhood" and that "Jewish women cannot conceive of a Convention in which we should not have some honored gentlemen with us."[3] According to Solomon, Council expected "to admit them [men] whenever they clamor for admission." But, as she observed, despite her presidential invitation, "Up to the present time they have not clamored."[4] The idea of actually joining a woman's organization was ludicrous to most men, an act beneath their dignity. Council's size and the extent of its programs, however, would not permit men to ignore it.

In the premier issue of the *American Jewess*, Rosa Sonneschein astutely recognized that history depends on who does the telling and that "Not what has happened, but what is recorded makes history. . . . It is therefore difficult," she said, "to predict with certainty the effect which the National Council of Jewish Women may have upon the mental and religious development of American Jewesses."[5] Like Sonneschein, male Jewish leaders also reacted to Council with uncertainty, some viewing it as a mixed blessing, others as an insult, and still others as an enigma.

Many early male observers expected the organization to reflect their stereotyped notions of women as flighty, superficial, and incapable of serious discourse. The *American Hebrew*, voice of the Historical School, reported on NCJW's first convention with surprise: "All traditions have gone to naught! Here have we had a roomful of women for over three days, and the ubiquitous reporter has not been able to catch a word passing between them concerning servants or fashions."[6] Though emphasizing that the women present "looked charming,"[7] most publications also admitted that the caliber of discussions was of high quality. *The Menorah* described Council members as "some of the best gifted and noblest women of America."[8] The *Jewish Messenger* went further, invoking the power of ancient heritage by placing the women alongside their Biblical foremothers, writing that "just as in olden times woman could prophesy in Israel and attain queenly dignity, so at Chicago she was seen in the role of teacher and preacher. Most of the papers read by Jewesses were marked by much breadth and insight."[9] Council members' reputation for being intellectually sharp was so pervasive and accurate that it persists even today.[10]

The *American Hebrew*, which devoted a full issue to coverage of NCJW's first convention, was also quick to point out that Council women did not fit their negative and mistaken stereotype of women's rightsers as "specimens of humanity notable mainly for scragginess of physique, with a predominance of old maids. The Women's Council was a notable exception in this regard. The women were either matrons or young girls, all of whom seemed to enjoy the good things in life."[11] This description was important to Council's image, placing members in the mainstream of upper-class Jewish society rather than painting them as political activists disdained by the establishment Jewish community.

Perhaps because NCJW was accepted by the core of the Jewish community and because its members were recognized as intellectually capable, some Jewish men viewed Council as a threat. Tobias Schanfarber, writing in the *Chicago Israelite*, described a familiar fear "that with women taking the major interest in synagog matters the feminine element of religion will supersede the masculine and we will get a religion of vapid emotionalism and sentimentality."[12]

Women's presence in the synagogue presented a paradox to the rabbis. On the one hand, women were essential to the support of the rabbi, often raising funds for his salary and, through their volunteer labor, implementing the programs he directed.[13] At the 1896 Triennial, the Committee on Religion reported that many rabbis had acknowledged this work and had expressed appreciation of Council's efforts "to promote the ends they [the rabbis] have constantly striven for."[14] Moreover, as in Christian America, the rabbis saw women as responsible for the religious commitment of their families.[15] Without devoted women, the rabbis could be sure that synagogue pews would be largely empty. At the same time, the rabbis had reason to fear the rise in women's participation in synagogue life unaccompanied by a similar rise in male participation, or as Schanfarber put it, the "effeminization" of the synagogue. As a result, the rabbis' position toward Council's efforts to renew women's commitment to the synagogue was riddled with all kinds of contradictions.

American historians are familiar with the pattern of occupational status being downgraded as women entered an occupation in large numbers. German Jewish men, who based much of their assessment of life in America on their experience in the work world, had witnessed such a feminization in occupations like typing and teaching. Rabbis, long accustomed to officiating in sanctuaries filled predominantly with women, had the most to lose if the synagogue should suffer a loss in status, and they expressed the most concern about synagogues becoming "effeminized." While they applauded the return of Jewish women to religious practice and to the synagogue, they were wary that those women not change the character of the religion from underneath them. They wanted Jewish women to be followers, not leaders, a position to which the rabbis claimed exclusive rights.

The American rabbinate, especially in the Reform movement, also placed heavy emphasis on intellectualism over spirituality.[16] Council supporters like Emil Hirsch seemed to welcome women's new religious enthusiasm as an opportunity to balance "the thought autocracy of our religious philosophy by the heart's influence upon our code of practice."[17] Even supporters, however, cautioned women not to go too far in their pursuit of spirituality or scholarship because, while rabbis feared that women might make Judaism overly emotional, neither did they want them to master the intellectual skill that might enable women to participate in the high level of rabbinic discourse. Rabbi Leo M. Franklin warned those assembled at NCJW's 1898 Omaha convention that Council women cannot solve theological problems or become great scholars. Rather, he argued, Council's role was to plant love for Judaism in the heart, not the mind.[18] Henrietta Szold was among those who pointed out the irony of this position, stating that "If the fear of feminization ever becomes a reality, it will be because Jewish women are ignorant, not because they are too learned."[19]

The possibility that women might compete with rabbis for the ability to wield the greatest amount of influence over the Jewish community in shaping the future of American Judaism made the relationship between Council women and their rabbis a complicated one. In *The Feminization of American Culture*, Ann Douglas paints women and American clergy as allies with much in common. She notes that both women and clergy were the primary functionaries in life-cycle events and both had substantial reasons to promote increased religious devotion. More important, both had been disempowered, women by removal of paid labor from the home and clergy by disestablishment. As a result, Douglas argues, both groups were forced to exercise power indirectly by becoming emotional necessities and by exerting influence over others. Though Douglas was analyzing Christian experience, her description is also accurate for American Jews.

In the Jewish community, however, these commonalities not only produced an alliance between women and rabbis but also spawned serious competition. With various movements struggling to develop cohesive ideologies, each hoping that American Jewry would come to be unified under the banner of their specific interpretations, and with all movements battling to strengthen Judaism against future disintegration through assimilation, turn-of-the-century American Judaism was in a state of flux. Rabbis engaged in this effort to shape American Judaism found themselves in an awkward position. While they spoke of preserving Judaism for the future, many had received their training in the Old World, and as representatives of an ancient religion, they appeared to symbolize a world to which American Jews had no intention of returning. Faced with the need to be seen as thoroughly American, rabbis adopted the basic values of American culture, including the notion of True Womanhood that emphasized women's natural vocation for religion. Confronted by their own failure to stem the tide of assimilation, rabbis recognized the interests they shared with American Jewish women and, like Jewish laymen, declared that clergy alone could not save Judaism. The rabbis argued that true love of Judaism could only be produced in the home, not the synagogue, and that because the mother governed the home, it was her responsibility to instill that commitment in her family.

This responsibility for the religious devotion of her family was a familiar role to Christian women, and Jewish women eager to acculturate welcomed their new status as saviors in the Jewish community. The rabbis, however, by declaring women the true preservers of Judaism, were admitting that their own influence was limited. Because their own power in the Jewish community depended upon how well they influenced others, the rabbis were, in effect, relinquishing much of their control over the Jewish community to women. This situation was acceptable while women remained unorganized. They were easily influenced by individual rabbis and appeared as allies rather than as a threat. When NCJW was founded to organize Jewish mothers, however, that situation began to change.

As a national organization, NCJW was both visible and beyond the control of any single rabbi. As a new and purely American organization Council often seemed more attuned to the needs of American Jews than were many rabbis. Moreover, as bearers of the next generation, Council women concretely represented the future in a way rabbis never could. Most important, Council demands for greater participation by women in the policymaking of synagogues reminded the rabbis that their depiction of mothers as saviors was not without consequences.

Prior to Council, rabbis assumed that mothers would limit their influence to the home while clergy would continue to control synagogues. Council's definition of the responsibilities of Jewish motherhood dissolved that boundary, declaring that the synagogue was also properly women's domain. Immersed in a tradition based on separate gender roles, most rabbis were not interested in sharing their leadership with women. They resented Council's renewal of Jewish motherhood and the infringement on rabbinic territory it represented. Rabbis who vocalized their resentment chastised Council for overstepping the bounds of acceptable gender roles and warned that participation in Council would lead women to neglect the home. Even NCJW supporters like Emil Hirsch cautioned women to "keep to their proper sphere and not presume in school or synagogue to dictate what shall be taught and what shall be believed [because] to be a theologian in Judaism more is needed than an easy pen and a nodding aquaintance with the Bible. . . . Would it not be wiser to leave the expert in Jewish theology to his legitimate functions?"[20]

While many rabbis feared that women's increased synagogue participation (sparked by Council membership) might challenge their leadership or transform their institutions, they were not prepared to discourage women from such participation. Just as women had become essential as consumers in the American economy, women had become essential as congregants in the American synagogue.[21] Many voices cautioned NCJW not to compete with the synagogue or pull women away from their duties there. Guarding the institution that made them central to the American Jewish community, rabbis like Joseph K. Arnold insisted that Council would prove its worth by how well it functioned as an "auxiliary society to the synagogue, a society which the synagogue cannot well spare, but nevertheless a society which depends upon the synagogue for its sustenance. . . . [NCJW] should be the helpmate of the minister in the temple and of the teachers in the temple's school, for woman is the best, the truest helpmate, and especially in matters spiritual is her service appreciated."[22]

That so many rabbinic voices sounded the caution indicates the importance they attached to Council, especially because Council women had given no sign that they intended to end their longstanding synagogue memberships.[23] In fact, quite the contrary. Not only did most Council women retain their synagogue affiliations, they were frequently among the most active members, volunteering for various committees and teaching in synagogue religious schools.

Even when Council's own religious programming waned, it encouraged synagogue membership, cooperated with national rabbinic and congregational organizations, and in 1927 joined the rabbis in a strong endorsement of the "Back to Synagogue Movement."[24]

NCJW never intended to pose a threat to established Jewish institutions but rather hoped to strengthen them. It developed strong cooperative relationships with organizations such as the Jewish Chautauqua Society and the Jewish Publication Society and fully intended to duplicate that relationship with synagogues.[25] In her capacity as national president, Hannah Solomon described the relationship: "The council is not antagonistic to the synagogue. On the contrary, we urge the women to use their influence toward strengthening and increasing their [synagogue's] power. Some of the rabbis are yet opposing us and are preventing organization in their cities lest they detract from their individual greatness by allowing a rival synagogue to have credit for a 'woman's society.' A little feminization would do them a world of good. However, these are exceptions. Wherever we are organized we have the warm support and assistance of the rabbis, and in the name of the organization I thank them heartily."[26] The organization welcomed rabbinic guidance much more often than it placed itself in competition with rabbis. Thus, though many rabbis were quick to caution NCJW not to carry its campaign to renew Jewish motherhood outside acceptable bounds, they more often perceived Council as an ally than as a serious threat.

Some rabbis found it difficult to take NCJW seriously altogether. Several observers correctly pointed out that while a few Council women occasionally presented worthy papers, most Council women were hardly scholars of Judaism. Hebrew Union College faculty member Rabbi Gotthard Deutsch, who led a Council Study Circle, commented, "If one should think that I use dark colors in painting the Women's Council, let him go to any of their meetings and ask the ladies present to find a passage in Malachi, and I should not be surprised if one of them should ask, whether Malachi was the title of an Italian opera."[27] His colleague, Rabbi David Philipson, concurred: "I cannot expect ladies who are busy with one hundred things every week to be able to bring their minds to such a [serious] state on Tuesday afternoon that they will be interested in abstruse questions of higher Biblical criticism."[28] Council members who had devalued their own capacity for scholarship were strained to respond to such criticism. Chicago member Jennie Franklin Purvin claimed that women's scholarship suffered because Council did not have access to the best teachers, noting that the great Jewish scholars would not speak to "lowly" women's clubs.[29] Although Purvin's accusation might have been true, such apologetics were unconvincing and did not alter opinion even in Council.

Others took Council lightly because they misunderstood its issues. For example, despite its support, the *American Hebrew* criticized Council for the amount of time devoted to debating whether or not women should be addressed by their own first names or by their husbands' first names.[30] The reporters viewed this issue as inconsequential in the general scheme of renewing Jewish womanhood, but to NCJW delegates it was symptomatic of the invisibility of women in the Jewish community. To them, the issue betokened not merely how delegates would be addressed, but rather in what ways Council would begin to demand from the Jewish community the recognition due women, a point that the *American Hebrew*'s reporter clearly missed.

Confusion also clouded attempts by observers to place NCJW on the continuum of turn-of-the-century feminist organizations. To some, Council's suggestion that women should begin to have an impact on the world outside the home and the description of that process as a renewal of Jewish "womanhood" seemed to be an endorsement of the feminist movement's "New Woman." Several scholars associated the "New Woman" with the most radical elements of the women's movement. Isaac P. Mendes, for example, held the "New Woman" responsible for Elizabeth Cady Stanton's *Woman's Bible*. Mendes believed that the benefits of equal rights and opportunities promised by the "New Woman" were a myth and that traditional Judaism's exaltation of motherhood actually secured women a much higher place in society. He concluded that advocates of the "New Woman" were "trying to indulge in every known kind of folly, and are trying their utmost to stand neck and neck with the stronger, sterner sex, in order to be so recognised for their facilities in doing everything to the discredit of those who have been for so many years, ay, for so many centuries, her true champions and her staunch defenders."[31]

Council wished to be seen as thoroughly modern but at the same time generally agreed with Mendes' position. As clubwomen Council members counted themselves among the pioneers in expanding women's rights and improving their status, but they found militant feminism distasteful (if not offensive) and in no way wished to be associated with its aims or tactics. Rather than relinquishing the term "New Woman" and its implications of modernity, Council assured observers that they had misunderstood what the term "New Woman" represented. Writing in the *Jewish Comment*, member Emma Rosenstock explained,

> Despite the comic papers, and the assertion that the new woman is merely a product of the imagination, into the existence of the average Jewish woman during the past few years, a new order of intelligence and of enlightenment has entered, awakening her to a more active interest in the life about her. The new woman is not here to be regarded as the exponent of "woman's rights," with a multitude of views on the suffrage question, nor as the seeker after notoriety in the everlasting denunciation of woman's garb and the desire for dress reform, but as the sweet womanly woman, who is being aroused to the great responsibilities of life and the duties awaiting her outside her own narrow circle. The title "New Woman" is in a measure ambiguous, as she is merely the old woman with modern ideas.[32]

Despite Council's justification, most American writers would continue to use the term "New Woman" to refer to the more militant wing of the women's movement, ultimately forcing Council to abandon its use of the term so as not to alienate the majority of the Jewish community.

In general, male Jewish leaders were pleased that NCJW existed, but only if they could define its parameters. This qualified acceptance was particularly true because they had annointed Council as the savior of the Jewish community. As B'nai B'rith's journal put it, "There has been no time in our history when such a movement was more needed than at present. Apathy and indifference characterize the position of the average Jew today towards his religion. . . . We greet the meeting of the Council of Jewish Women as a harbinger of resurrection as the Elijah that might in course of time make the American Jewish family and American family life the example for the world to copy."[33] Because Jewish leaders believed that Council was the key to Judaism's survival they were understandably concerned about what form of Judaism Council would promote. Ten years before Council's founding, Hebrew Union College held a banquet intended to underline the unity of the American rabbinate. In a much publicized scandal, non-kosher food was served, offending the more traditional rabbis present. The offended clergy stormed out of the hall, formally drawing lines that eventually divided the Jewish community into Reform, Conservative, and Orthodox segments. By 1890, a power struggle was under way, each movement attempting to become the dominant representative of Jews in America.[34]

Despite their divisions, the various interpretations shared basic notions of Jewish womanhood, so when NCJW was founded to renew that womanhood, each movement expected Council to promote its interpretation of Judaism. The *Jewish Messenger* put the challenge succinctly: "There is not a loyal Jewish heart throbbing in this land that will not hail with delight the efforts of woman to regenerate a backsliding generation. The question to be answered is: Are they who stand at the head of that organization women of reverential sentiments, mothers of religiously trained families, souls of Jewish loyalty?"[35]

Reaction to subsequent Council policy depended on how well Council seemed to be fulfilling each movement's expectations. To the Reform movement, NCJW seemed to be a tremendous success. Through Emil Hirsch's Reform eyes, the organization founded by his congregants represented Judaism's entrance into the modern world. He applauded NCJW's refusal to back any single interpretation of Judaism as a challenge to the rigid demands of Orthodoxy and believed Council's role was to insist that Judaism treat women according to modern American standards, a role he considered to be "without exaggeration . . . an epoch in the history of modern Judaism."[36]

Those Jewish leaders who favored a more traditional interpretation of Judaism did not share Hirsch's enthusiasm. Convinced that

the concept of renewing Jewish motherhood was the key to Judaism's survival, the Reverend Henry Iliowitz wondered whether
NCJW was the proper organization to undertake such an endeavor:

> If thy gatherings mean to restore Jewish womanhood to faith and
> reverence, the Jewish home to its beauty of holiness, and Jewish life
> to its consecrating influences; if it means that there shall hereafter be
> no poker-playing by Jewesses, no shopping on Sabbath, and no ham
> on the Jewish table; if it means worship at and sanctification of the
> Jewish home, an ideal Friday eve, and a spiritual Sabbath, then will
> God and man bless thy doings. But if it means to put thyself on
> exhibition, educate thyself to turn beautiful phrases instead of turn-
> ing out beautiful souls . . . then the sooner thy Council dies the
> better for the cause of Israel and the Jewish family. [37]

Traditional Jewish hopes for NCJW were dashed at the first Triennial, when Council refused to endorse traditional Sabbath observance and elected Hannah Solomon president despite her adoption
of the radical Reformers' Sunday Sabbath. The Reverend Meldola
de Sola recounted the events through the eyes of the opposition that
had been led by his wife Katherine, who had declared before the
assembly in no uncertain terms that according to God's holy law,
only "the seventh day is the Sabbath."[38] De Sola termed his wife's
utterance "brave" and angrily questioned whether her plea even
touched "a sympathetic chord in that assemblage of so-called 'Jewish' women?" Solomon's election to the presidency provided a negative answer to de Sola's query.

From his Orthodox viewpoint, a Jew was bound to follow
halakhah (Jewish law) and Council arguments that Jews were
entitled to freedom of opinion exemplified "the utter ignorance
of Judaism which distinguishes certain officers of the Council."
De Sola's sarcastic citation of examples to bolster this point made
clear that his criticism of NCJW was not based on its stated ideals,
but on its leaders' association with the Reform movement:

> The present president of the New York Section of the Council
> [Sadie American] occupied the pulpit in Dr. Hirsch's [Emil G.
> Hirsch of Sinai Congregation] Ark-less and Sepher-less [Torah-less]
> temple in Chicago a few years ago. With the intensely amusing

assurance which once fortified her (an unmarried young lady) to hold forth upon the duties of the Jewish mother, she distinguished herself in the Chicago pulpit by advocating the Sunday Sabbath. And she proved crass ignorance can vie with monumental impertinence by endeavoring to strengthen her ludicrous attempt at argument with the bewildering announcement that Sunday is recognized in all parts of the world as the Lord's Day!

At a recent meeting of the Philadelphia Section of this Council of "jewish" Women it was moved that, for a certain entertainment, no rehearsal be held on the Sabbath. The motion was lost.

These are merely specimens of the absolute contempt for all that Judaism holds sacred which characterizes the rising generation of Reformers.[39]

The great bulk of subsequent criticism of NCJW and its leaders centered on the perception by observant Jews that Council was a Reform organization.[40] The most scathing criticism was voiced by Israel H. Peres in an address before a Tennessee YMHA. He claimed that Council was founded only to imitate non-Jews, that it had no real purpose, and that Judaism was not dying and therefore was not in need of a "nurse and preserver in the shape of a council of Jewish women."[41] He found no redeeming value in any Council programs and denied that Council brought anything but ridicule to the Jewish community. Resorting to sexist slurs, he commented, "The Council of Jewish Women meeting once a year for a social chat on a large scale—a gigantic Kafee Klatch so to speak—can accomplish no practical results for faith or humanity." Peres revealed the source of his great animosity at the end of his speech when he concluded that it was simply ridiculous for an organization that intended to preserve Judaism to be allied with the Reform movement.

Peres' accusations were ably answered in several forums, beginning a debate over Council that would crop up from time to time in the Jewish press well into the first decades of the twentieth century.[42] Traditional Jews would continue to level attacks, often on individual leaders as well as Council itself. Such attacks were not based on perceptions of feminist challenges or on objections to women's participation in public life, be it religious or secular. In fact, much of the Jewish community recognized Council's emphasis on the home, even in its efforts to expand woman's sphere. The *Jewish Exponent* voiced a common sentiment when it concluded that "In this [NCJW] we have no marked departure from the most anciently accepted principles."[43] Instead, primary opposition focused on Council's failure to endorse and promote traditional Judaism, in particular, the traditional Sabbath.[44]

Defenders of Council recognized that the source of objections was not Council policy or programs, but its leaders' acceptance of the Sunday Sabbath and Reform Judaism. Emil Hirsch, prime advocate of the Sunday Sabbath, responded to attacks on his followers, Hannah Solomon and Sadie American, in an angry editorial:

> The Council rendered all Judaism a service by ignoring the shrieks of these doughty champions [spokespersons of conservatism]. . . . The ladies against whom this campaign of calumny was waged . . . knew very well that the assault was directed only against their persons. . . . Even the delegates from more conservative Sections could not help feeling that the attack had been inspired by motives of the most contemptible order. . . . Viewed from a higher altitude, the outcome means this: the blustering champions of conservatism must know that it is not for them to trace the lines beyond which none may dare proceed. In all Judaism, the Sunday worshiper has as clear a title to his Judaism as has the Saturday observer.[45]

Council was caught in a power struggle between Reform and traditional Judaism. The emotionalism of the arguments reflects the importance of NCJW to the plans of both sides. German Jewish men could conceivably have tried to recruit Eastern European immigrants to their respective sides rather than seeking women's help, but for class reasons, they did not consider this an option, nor did they see the addition of Eastern European Jews to their ranks as a benefit. Instead, each movement, unsuccessful at achieving dominance by itself, declared that it needed the help of Jewish mothers to preserve Judaism in America. NCJW, as the only organization that could justifiably claim to represent those mothers, was therefore an essential prize. If, as the rabbis believed, Jewish motherhood would be the greatest influence on the Judaism practiced by American Jews, and if Council was the organization to mold that motherhood, then the interpretation of Judaism adopted by Council would become dominant in America. Such was the hope of many male Jewish leaders, and such was the source of their vehemence in claiming Council as their own or denouncing Council as heretical.

Despite the hopes of Jewish men and despite Council's early Reform leanings, both sides of the struggle for hegemony over Jewish interpretation would ultimately be disappointed. Like most of American Jewry, Council leaders hoped that America's Jewish community would heed calls for unity.[46] For many male leaders, the last hope for that unity was destroyed at the 1883 HUC banquet. Council leaders, however, were not prepared to let the dream of unity die. Though many of them were married to the leaders involved in the banquet scandal, they did not accept that the differences among Jews were irreconcilable. Hannah Solomon suggested that "Women may not analyze as carefully as men do [but they have the advantage of] extending to each other the hand of fellowship, recognizing one God above all, all mankind as His children."[47] Perhaps because they agreed with Solomon's assessment, believing women were natural nurturers capable of healing when men insisted on arguing, or perhaps because their lack of advanced Jewish education caused them to underestimate the deep ideological divisions in religious interpretations, Council leaders committed their organization to "enable all groups of Jewry to meet on a common platform."[48] They intended to show Jewish men that people with varying interpretations of Judaism could still work together in a religious endeavor.

Its commitment to unity would lead Council to avoid making decisions on controversial religious questions. New York Section member Lillian Hirschfield explained, "I have a great deal of reverence and respect for those people who feel one way, but I have the same feeling for those who feel the other way, and it seems to me it is beyond the aims of this Council to interefere in any way whatsoever with the individual convictions or observance of any member. I feel as though we were standing upon the very rock that we are afraid is going to split under us."[49] Hirschfield's words underscored the potential threat to the organizations posed by religious debate. Council leaders believed that as long as they remained committed to a pluralist model, the organization could incorporate all views.

They failed to recognize that some issues might be viewed by members as non-negotiable. Such was the issue of Sabbath observance.

Finding it impossible to appease all religious views, Council refused to deal with religious issues. By way of justification, one member concluded that it was probably impossible to teach spiritual devotion anyway.[50] By its twentieth anniversary, NCJW would divest itself of most of its religious character and goals. Referring to this abandonment of religion, even Reform leaders would conclude that while NCJW had provided the Jewish community with new visions and expectations, it had not provided the renewed spirit hoped for.[51]

Defending Council, Rosa Sonneschein noted that while rabbis admonished Jewish women for not being as religious as their grandmothers, they did not similarly admonish Jewish men to mimic their grandfathers.[52] Yet, such an argument could never win acceptance, even within Council circles. Council women heartily endorsed the designation of Jewish mothers as the saviors of Judaism in America. The flip side of that argument, as *The Menorah* pointed out, was that if the next generation's ties to Judaism wavered, women were to blame. The journal declared that wives were responsible for neglect of Sabbath observance because men often had to go out and work while women had no such excuse. It further claimed that Jewish children leave the faith "for *no other reason* than the disappearance of religious warmth from the Jewish family home" [emphasis mine].[53] Early hopes that Council would save Judaism easily turned to criticism for failing to achieve that goal.[54]

The most common call was a demand for Council to take a stand, either for Reform or for tradition. Solomon recognized the community's frustration at NCJW's apparent ambivalence, responding that the organization simply did not yet have sufficient experience to risk permanent damage by alienating any segment of its membership. She attempted to paint Council as a positive example of pluralism in action, acknowledging that "This seeming lack of definiteness has been one of our main obstacles," but suggesting that "It has been called our weakness, whereas it is our strength. Do any expect an infant to outline its career?"[55]

Solomon's words, however, would not satisfy Council's detractors. Male Jewish leaders criticized NCJW not because they viewed it as a threat, but rather because it was a disappointment—it had failed to fulfill their goals. That Council's objectives might go beyond those goals never occurred to these men, leading one rabbi to write, "The National Council of Jewish Women should never have organized. . . . These one-sex organizations have a tendency to widen the breach that already exists between the sexes. It is contrary to social instinct, it is unnatural. . . . The Jewess has no mission apart from the Jew."[56] Of course, the author leveled no such criticism at exclusively male Jewish organizations.

Council women shared men's hope that NCJW would rejuvenate Judaism in the United States, but their goals did not stop there. Had Council's vision been so limited, it would not have survived the Sunday Sabbath controversy. The story of that controversy and of the success of the resulting organization demonstrates that Jewish women did not limit their goals to those expressed by male Jewish leaders.

4.

The Sunday Sabbath Controversy and the End of Council Religion

OUNCIL'S religious idealism precluded inclusion of specific religious questions on the agenda of its first Triennial. Council policy assumed that theological discourse could only be conducted by properly trained male scholars. In addition, Council leaders expected that their commitment to uniting all Jewish women would override any attempt to institute policy favoring one interpretation over another.

The first hint that NCJW could not remain neutral on religious questions came during Julia Felsenthal's report as chair of the Committee on Religion at the 1896 Triennial. The report recommended for study Claude Montefiore's *Bible for Home Reading*. Several traditional scholars had condemned Montefiore's book as irreligious because it used modern methods and non-Jewish literature to explain the Biblical narrative.[1] Two members of the Committee on Religion had refused to sign the report recommending the book's inclusion. After brief discussion noting that scholars disagreed about the book and that Council did not wish to censor any valid opinion, the report was accepted by the convention. Those who opposed the inclusion of Montefiore's book did not feel strongly enough to force a showdown over the issue, and though unhappy, compromised by having their protests officially entered as part of the convention record.[2] The ease with which this issue was settled may have lulled Council leaders into thinking that religious controversy had run its course. They were unprepared for the frequency and ferocity with which religious issues would continue to surface, especially in debates over Sabbath observance.

In its theological aspects, the Sabbath is important as the ultimate symbol of the Covenant between God and the People of Israel. Theology, however, was not Council's primary concern. Through its home celebrations, the Sabbath had also come to symbolize family strength and well-being. In Esther Ruskay's words, "In how many families, but for the regular weekly Sabbath reunion, would members drift apart, each becoming unconsciously alienated from the other, or, at least, losing the strong interest in and regard for one another's well being which are the whole charm of family life."[3] Given Council's focus on motherhood, home, and family, it was natural for Sabbath observance to overshadow other religious concerns.

Rebekah Kohut expressed a common Council sentiment when, in her opening address to the convention as president of the host Section, she said,

> Sabbath! That is the word which we, as Mothers in Israel, must brave again. Ours is to be the saviors of our people. Ours is to arouse courage and hope in the leaders of the nation's destiny. They need our sympathies, our active aid. Even into the Promised Land of the old the command went forth, "take the women and children with you," and when down Sinai's mighty heights the Lord's voice rang out in thunder tones, "Remember the Sabbath day to keep it holy," even the women joined in the answer, "We will do and we will hearken." This be the spirit of this convention. Let us not only hearken, but let us do.[4]

Although the sentiment was popular, the question of just how Council could help restore Sabbath observance plagued the convention. The problem was exacerbated by the knowledge that NCJW's top leaders, Hannah Solomon and Sadie American, endorsed the observance of Sabbath on Sunday. To the traditional women of Council and to many Reform women, such observance was sacrilege of the highest order, paramount to eating on Yom Kippur or converting to Christianity.[5] Led by Katherine de Sola, these traditionally minded women vowed not to leave the convention without explicit Council endorsement of the historical Sabbath.

De Sola first attempted to force the issue by proposing to include the phrase "All of whom must keep the Jewish Sabbath" in the statement of who may serve on the Committee on Religion. Chairing the meeting, Solomon responded, "I don't think this is the place for [discussion of the Sabbath question]. . . . Let us leave all religious questions to the quarrels of the Rabbis for the present; we will fight later." Not willing to back down easily, de Sola retorted, "No, if we are an organization of Jewish Women, then we must do what Jewish Women do, and therefore must keep our Sabbath on Saturday and not on Sunday." Solomon temporarily settled the question by declaring de Sola out of order. No reference to the Sabbath was included in the constitution, angering de Sola and her sympathizers and setting the stage for the next clash.[6]

The de Sola forces would not have to wait long for their next opportunity. That evening, Henrietta Frank, Solomon's sister, delivered a paper entitled "Our Opportunities" in which she detailed the classic Reform defense for the Sunday Sabbath:

> The Sabbath is one of the best gifts of Israel to humanity. The Sabbath-idea is essential to Judaism. The choice of the day of rest conforms in practice, if not in theory, to the general custom of the people among whom we live. . . . What we need is to consecrate that day of rest in accordance with the spirit of Judaism and its message. . . . Jewish men cannot give up one day of the six devoted to work, without separating themselves from the community in secular interest, which would be most undesirable. . . . Not the choice of the calendar day, but the manner of its observance makes of it a Sabbath. . . . We keep our religious ideals more alive by devoting a part of the day of rest to the study of Judaism, its history and evolution, its message to us and to the world, than by wasting it and celebrating the traditional Sabbath-day more in the breach than in the observance.[7]

Katherine de Sola and those who shared her opposition to the Sunday Sabbath must have been quietly fuming as Solomon opened up the floor for comment and then called on two speakers who agreed with Frank's general premise. She then quickly closed the discussion saying,

> I am sorry that I cannot allow the floor to anyone further. We might talk from now until the next Convention, and we would not settle this question. I want to say for myself that in this Convention I have endeavored to keep every theological question out. This has been my ruling. I feel that there are such great things that we can all do together that we can well afford to let the Rabbis light for three more years [until the next Triennial].
>
> The essayist had the same right to the floor that we have granted to everybody. She has expressed her individual opinions. They are just as honest and just as strong for Judaism as any the most orthodox have expressed.[8]

Solomon's "out of sight-out of mind" policy and the perception that she was using her position as convention chair to silence the opposition angered de Sola's supporters. The events of the following morning made it clear that discussion had continued well into the night.

The opposition began the day prepared to make it clear that they would not be silenced by Solomon's politicking or even by her sincere wish to avoid religious controversy. No sooner had Solomon called for the day's first committee report than she was interrupted by an inquiry from the floor about whether the convention had officially accepted Frank's paper. Solomon answered that papers were only the expressions of individual presenters and then reminded those assembled that they had but one day left in which to discuss the great number of pending resolutions. She attempted to appease the opposition by suggesting they could voice their concerns when it came time to discuss new business.[9] Of course, according to parliamentary procedure, new business appears last on the agenda. Having already implied that the convention barely had time to consider its current business, Solomon had good reason to think that new business would have to be postponed until the next Triennial. Already suspicious of Solomon, those who backed the historical Sabbath took her suggestion as further insult. They had not, however, played their last card.

Knowing Sabbath observance was the subject of an upcoming resolution, members opposed to the Sunday Sabbath patiently waited until the resolution was read: "Whereas we believe the observance of the Sabbath to be of paramount importance to the proper exercise and influence of religion, be it resolved that the members of the Council shall use all possible influence against the desecration of the Jewish Sabbath, and resolve to reinstate it in their homes in its pristine purity."[10] In the ensuing discussion several speakers, including the influential Rebekah Kohut, spoke in favor of the historical Sabbath. One member voiced concern that the reality of the work world would prohibit Council members from following through on the resolution, no matter how devoted some members might be. Only Henrietta Frank defended the Sunday Sabbath, and that in response to a specific comment on her paper. Solomon's opposition felt the tide of discussion going their way, and before a speaker could rise who might change the atmosphere, they called the question. The resolution passed unanimously.

The traditionalists believed the resolution supported their position, but its unanimous passage indicated that others felt the wording was open to a broader interpretation. Surely the Sunday Sabbath observers would not have voted in favor of a resolution which implied that their observance was less than Jewish. The opposition had won a small victory, but unless they could ensure that the resolution would be backed up with specific action, they could not be satisfied. The Sabbath resolution vote had already passed, however, leaving the opposition no clear opportunity to air the issue before the convention's quickly approaching close. Katherine de Sola found her chance in the last order of business that day, the election of officers.

After Nominating Committee chair, Cleveland Section President Flora Schwab, presented a slate of officers (headed by Solomon for president), parliamentary procedure required that the floor be opened for other nominations. First to rise was Katherine de Sola, who had been a member of the nominating committee. Thinly disguising her animosity toward Solomon she said:

I feel deeply the unpleasantness of having to differ in a matter of this kind where unanimity and harmony should prevail, but "peace at any price" cannot hold good where the price is sacrifice of principle. . . . Hence I must make another nomination. Mrs. President, most solemnly do I proclaim my reluctance to do this, for the ladies named here, without exception, have worthily gained our deepest obligation by their sacrifice of time, strength, and thought. But if this Council stands for anything, it stands for Judaism, and if Judaism stands for anything, it stands for God and God's Holy Law. In that Holy Law it is written, Remember the Sabbath day to consecrate it, and it adds that the seventh day is the Sabbath.

De Sola was briefly interrupted with a reminder that a motion was before the convention. Solomon acknowledged that de Sola was out of order, but perhaps aware of the anger generated by her earlier conduct as chair and eager to make amends before the Triennial ended, she asked the convention to grant her the courtesy to speak. De Sola continued, "The President of the Council stands for the Council, and therefore for Judaism and its Holy Law. Much as we may regret it, much as I personally regret it, I cannot but feel our loyalty to that Law makes it impossible for us to vote for any lady to be President of this Jewish Council who does not consecrate the seventh day as the Sabbath. The question is loyalty to God or loyalty to the lady named for President. For myself, I cannot, I dare not hesitate. I declare for God and His law."[11] De Sola then nominated Minnie D. Louis for president.

Solomon's response, widely quoted in the Jewish press, became one of her trademarks: "I forbid the Council or any member of it to be a censor over me as to what day I shall keep. I do consecrate the Sabbath. I consecrate every day in the week."[12] The specific question of Solomon's presidency was quickly solved when Minnie Louis declined the nomination. Solomon, as the only remaining candidate, was elected by acclamation.

Perhaps to emphasize that Council's president was not elected merely by default, Sadie American rose to extol Solomon's virtues. Solomon, in all likelihood anxious to drop the issue, tersely interrupted American and insisted that the convention was not the place to discuss personal affairs. Despite Solomon's wishes, the matter was not yet closed.

Just before the end of the meeting, Minnie Louis, who as a member of New York's prestigious Reform congregation, Temple Emanu-El, but backer of the historical Sabbath, had the respect of those on both sides of the Sabbath issue, requested the floor. Hoping that she could heal some wounds and concerned that members not depart from this first convention feeling negatively about the organization, she stressed the value of pluralism. She begged the participants to respect each individual's integrity, exhorting them not to leave the convention "without feeling that every one is a Jewess at heart, no matter what her convictions about a ceremonial may be." Perhaps feeling betrayed, de Sola quipped, "I beg to say that the keeping of the Jewish Sabbath is not a ceremonial." Julia Richman brought the debate to an uneasy close by reminding the delegates of the late hour and the need to finish selecting the Board of Directors. [13]

Failing to heed the warnings of the discontent at the Triennial, Solomon and her Executive Board continued to insist on acceptance of all religious views and forbade debate of religious questions at national Council gatherings. Following patterns established in the years before the first Triennial, Sadie American and Hannah Solomon took on the bulk of Council's recruiting efforts, traveling the nation speaking as representatives of Council. On several occasions American and Solomon were invited to address congregations from the pulpit, which some Jews found objectionable, but both women had a reputation for eloquence, so if their appearance generated negative feeling toward NCJW, those feelings were buried beneath the surface. [14] That situation would change dramatically in 1898.

Council's attention frequently focused on Chicago as the site of the organization's founding, the home of its leaders, and the location of the very first Council Section. In January 1898, the *American Jewess* reported that Chicago's Jewish "Society" had begun to hold charity balls on Friday nights, a violation of the historical Sabbath. [15] Though these were not officially controlled by NCJW, many of the women involved were Council leaders who, the *American Jewess* claimed, were responsible to uphold Council principles by opposing such activities rather than attending them.

Despite the *American Jewess* article, the Chicago Section not only did not speak out against the balls but instituted questionable programming of their own. Many of Chicago's members belonged to Sinai Congregation, which observed the Sunday Sabbath. Unwilling to exclude the entire weekend from programming, they held a bazaar on Saturday.[16] Many Council voices were quick to call foul, arguing that official Council policy dictated respect for, if not observance of, the historical Sabbath. The bazaar blatantly violated traditional Sabbath laws, and observant Council members took it as a slap in the face. To them it appeared that no matter what the general membership mandated at convention, Council's leaders would do whatever they pleased.

Later that year, Sadie American was invited to deliver a sermon at her temple, Sinai Congregation. In that sermon she reiterated her support for Sunday Sabbath observance. The widely circulated *American Hebrew* and subsequently other smaller Jewish papers reported American's remarks as proof that NCJW had abandoned Jewish tradition. Editorials abounded challenging Council's central claim that it was restoring Jewish womanhood.

The *Reform Advocate*, edited by Hirsch, came to American's defense claiming it was unfair "to hail with loud acclaim every orthodox sentiment expressed by a member of the council" while condemning all "their liberal utterances."[17] Though Hirsch's intentions were good, his remarks further publicized the event and implied that American had, indeed, been speaking as a Council representative.

Those Council members who had pinned their hopes on the passage of the Sabbath resolution at the 1896 Triennial were disillusioned. Even the previously supportive Rosa Sonneschein editorialized, "Fourteen months have passed since the C. of J.W. have made the sacred declaration to try and restore the Jewish Sabbath to its 'pristine purity' but as yet not even the first official step has been taken to redeem the divine promise. . . . The inconsistency with which the Council pursues its religious mission is almost tragic. To consecrate everyday is no substitute for the Sabbath."[18]

The growing criticism made it difficult to recruit backers of the historical Sabbath, both Reform and traditional, into the organization, ensuring the issue a hearing at the Second Triennial. The 1900 convention afforded American an opportunity to respond to the critics, which she did at length. American claimed that she had been maligned by the conservative press, which she accused of misreporting her statements. She insisted that she had been speak-

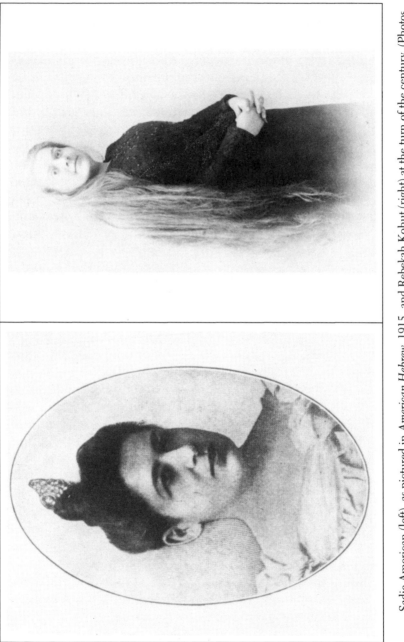

Sadie American (left), as pictured in *American Hebrew*, 1915, and Rebekah Kohut (right) at the turn of the century. (Photos courtesy the American Jewish Archives)

ing as an individual rather than as a representative of NCJW. She further explained that while she preferred the Sunday Sabbath, she also supported those who observed on Saturday, though the press had claimed she called for abolition of the traditional observance.[19] American also personalized the issue by chiding her audience for believing the press without bothering to confirm the story's accuracy. In particular, American painted herself as antagonist to Rebekah Kohut, who had been a vocal supporter of the historical Sabbath. Kohut had attempted unsuccessfully to silence American by calling the question before American could speak. American responded sharply, "I claim to have the right to reply, with these ladies before me, not one of whom in the hotel or otherwise has come to me, but who all around me have been talking about this thing, some taking clippings from place to place and showing them to each other, and then they get up and call for the question."[20] American's comments sharply drew the lines of the debate to include not only the substance of the issue but also personalities.

The Second Triennial ended with general endorsements of Council's efforts to revive religion but without an explicit decision on the Sunday Sabbath issue. The events of the convention further clouded the issue by focusing on the dominant personalities on each side and thus resulted in continuation of the debate through personal attacks, especially on the outspoken Sadie American.

In a letter to the *American Hebrew*, Maud Nathan, founding member of the National Consumers' League and NCJW's New York City Section, described American's private support for the Sunday Sabbath as akin to a politician running as a Republican but privately proclaiming to be a Democrat.[21] To underscore its support for Nathan's position, the *American Hebrew* editorialized, "If the Council of Jewish Women stands for the Seventh-day Sabbath but nevertheless its president and secretary may privately favor Sunday-Sabbath, what is the difference between the council and a temperance society whose president and secretary have private whiskey flasks in their pockets?"[22] Though the *American Hebrew* agreed that Council should not split itself over the issue, it insisted that the Sunday Sabbath was untenable.[23]

Though NCJW would continue to disagree about Sunday Sabbath observance, it became increasingly clear that what was untenable was Council's refusal to take a clear stand on the issue. Those committed to religious pluralism had not accounted for the possibility that some religious beliefs would be mutually exclusive.

For the next thirty years, calls for increased devotion to Judaism and greater toleration of religious diversity as well as demands that Council set minimum standards of religious practice would continue to surface in the Jewish press and at NCJW Triennials. These repeated attempts to grapple with religious policy were intended by all sides to strengthen Council's ties with Judaism. In reality, however, the debates weakened Council's commitment to religious identity. By 1913, other circumstances had contributed to the decline of Council religion, and Council's identity focused on its role as a social welfare organization rather than on its claim of renewed Jewish motherhood.

One factor contributing to that shift was the difficulty in documenting religious commitment. In most areas, Council relied on statistics to assess its success or failure. Reports of social reform work overflowed with charts enumerating how many clients had been helped, how many settlement houses were in operation, how much money had been raised, etc. An increase in religious devotion, however, was not so easy to quantify. What is somewhat surprising is that no Council committee even tried. They did not seek statistics on intermarriage, observance of Jewish holidays, or affiliation with Jewish institutions. Without such statistics Council could never prove its claims that its approach to renewing Jewish womanhood was increasing the Jewish commitment of Council members or their children. Two decades after NCJW began its efforts even Council members still lamented the low level of religious enthusiasm in the Jewish community and the absence of men from synagogues.[24]

Worse, in the one area for which Council did have statistics, attendance at Study Circles, the numbers indicated a decline.[25] By 1908, Study Circles were such an insignificant part of Council's programming that their numbers were not even included in regular Triennial reports. Three years later, Council abandoned distribution of Study Circle syllabi, referring interested people to Jewish Chautauqua publications.[26] By 1923, advanced secular education took priority, with many Sections arranging for members to take courses at local colleges for reduced tuition rates.[27]

Council's identity as savior of Judaism was weakened further by the advent of synagogue sisterhoods. Though the National Federation of Temple Sisterhoods (NFTS) was not founded until 1913, increasing numbers of synagogues had established their own women's auxiliaries in the previous decade. For women to whom a religious identification with Judaism was particularly important, the sisterhood was an easier and more rewarding organization than Council. In general, a sisterhood's position on religious issues was defined by the policy of the synagogue with which it affiliated. Because Jews generally supported the religious approach adopted by the congregation they chose to join, sisterhoods were free from the kinds of difficult and emotional religious debates that plagued Council. Many women, tired of constantly having to defend their religious interests in Council circles, retreated to the supportive religious environment of the sisterhood.[28] Even those women who retained dual affiliation had less time to devote to Council. The energy they did reserve for Council was not likely to be in the area of religion.

Once NFTS and its counterparts in the Conservative and Orthodox movements were established, NCJW could no longer claim to be the only American organization representing the religious interests of Jewish women. This situation, combined with Council's failure to prove success in saving Judaism, posed a tremendous threat to all of NCJW's accomplishments. Council had based its claims for women's greater participation in the governing of the Jewish community on its claim of renewing Jewish motherhood. If, indeed, NCJW was not renewing traditional Jewish motherhood, then the community had no reason to back its programs or accept its demand for innovation in the role of Jewish women.

Council itself relied on its ideology of motherhood to justify its programs, providing its membership no other ideology on which to base their activities. The consequences of Council's definition of religion through motherhood and the subsequent weakening of that religion ended Council's chances to change woman's place significantly within Judaism. Always targeted toward renewing rather than recasting Judaism, Council never seriously challenged traditional Jewish views of womanhood.

Council had nonetheless made progress in expanding woman's role beyond the home. For example, no other organization did so much to foster Jewish women's entrance into the ranks of professional social workers, even subsidizing the college training of many members and employees.[29] Yet, without its traditional justification that such expansion was essential for Council's attempt to save Judaism, even these achievements began to be reversed. Where once NCJW members had been included routinely on boards of directors overseeing projects that Council had founded or worked on, with the decline of Council religion many of the new boards excluded not only Council members, but all women.[30]

Even Council's conquest of the synagogue proved temporary. Where, in 1896, the *Reform Advocate* celebrated the fact that with the advent of NCJW it was no longer a novelty for women to speak from the pulpit,[31] by 1912 the *American Hebrew*'s "Of Interest to Women" column noted that "It is now some years ago that we were threatened with a woman rabbi. . . . During the time Miss [Ray] Frank was in the public eye other Jewish women believed they had a message to give from the pulpit and they got the opportunity to be heard; but in recent years Jewish women have been content to leave the pulpit, as they are ready to leave their religion—to the rabbis."[32] Just as in the Christian community, as the Jewish population grew it experienced a growth of institutions and bureaucratization resulting in the tightening of authority and fewer positions available to women.[33]

Council members unquestionably laid the groundwork for future feminist efforts. Their organizational skills provided a model for later Jewish women's organizations in both the United States and Europe. Their reputation for superior intelligence and wit would continue to challenge portraits of women as intellectually incapable. Their conquest of pulpit and politics proved to Jewish women that they could cross forbidden thresholds successfully. However, when NCJW could not live up to the standards on which those accomplishments were based, the Jewish community became disillusioned and retreated. Ultimately, Council's religious policy failed to make significant long-term gains for women in the Jewish community.

With the advent of sisterhoods, a Council declaration favoring any particular movement would have been self-defeating, a poor duplication of existing efforts. Unable to unite Orthodox, Reform, and Conservative women in religious work, Council opted to avoid religion as much h as possible. In 1905, Council's "bat mitzvah" year, its emerging "adult" identity was underscored by a changing of the guard. At the 1905 Triennial Hannah Solomon declined the nomination for another term as president, citing concern for her health and a need to rest. She was replaced by forty-year-old Pauline Rosenberg, a Council founder who had delivered a paper at the Jewish Women's Congress and been instrumental in organizing Pittsburgh's Section. Like Solomon, Rosenberg acknowleged the importance of home and family to women's lives. She also believed, however, that woman had an equal responsibility to care for the needy beyond her doors. Rosenberg's administration extended Council's social welfare work, instituting many of the immigrant aid programs that would come to be the core of NCJW's reputation. [34]

Ultimately Council would not be able to sustain its original religious vision. Rather, it would come to emphasize philanthropic efforts in a secularized expression of religion common among Jewish institutions. [35] Having thus removed religion from the center of Council's identity, leaders expected to move on peacefully with the business of the organization, only to be met in 1908 with another crisis of major proportion. The transition from religion to philanthropy would not go smoothly.

In addition to the election of a new president, a 1905 convention vote to double Council dues from $1 to $2 also signaled a greater emphasis on philanthropy. The Cleveland Section objected to the increase vociferously, claiming its members would simply not accept the change, no matter what the leaders did. [36] Despite promises by Cleveland's delegates to abide by the majority decision, much of the Cleveland Section had not paid the increase when credentials were being checked for the 1908 Triennial. The Executive Board notified Cleveland members that if they did not pay, they would be expelled from the organization. Correspondence on the matter was conducted by Council's Executive Secretary Sadie American. Viewing American as a troublemaker, the Cleveland Section did not address correspondence to her but rather contacted other Board members. Ultimately, despite a presidential visit to Cleveland, the national board and the Section could not come to an agreement. Rosenberg, unwilling to take the full burden of expelling one of Council's larger Sections on her own, said that the Triennial assembly was the final arbiter and instructed Cleveland to present its grievances at the convention.

In the meantime, the discord had been leaked to the Jewish press. By the time the Triennial actually convened, accusations of maliciousness, dishonesty, and official misconduct abounded on both sides. Cleveland claimed it had been expelled illegally, that the national board had informed the Jewish press of the expulsion before informing the Section, that the board had ignored sincere attempts by the Section to cooperate, and that the board had overstepped its jurisdiction by dictating policy to the local Section.[37] They presented to the convention copies of their correspondence with the board as supporting evidence. The remainder of the Triennial was dominated by discussion of the Cleveland Section, in both formal and informal sessions. The national board denied the accusations, presenting correspondence of its own to counteract those presented by Cleveland and pointing out that Cleveland was the only Section in the country not in compliance with the constitution and that, therefore, the board was within its rights to act.

Accusations continued to mount. Pauline Rosenberg was accused of abandoning Robert's Rules of Order when it served her purpose. The delegates finally agreed to convene a special arbitration committee headed by Hannah Solomon. The conclusion of that committee was to rescind expulsion provided Cleveland abide by the constitution to the best of its ability. The night following the announcement of Solomon's committee, a special meeting was called by the Executive Board to discuss the situation. While the meeting was declared open to everybody, many people, including Hannah Solomon, were never informed of its purpose and did not attend. That meeting, led by Rosenberg and Sadie American, overturned the decision of the Arbitration Committee. They further concluded that Cleveland owed the Council money for the time of its affiliation and could not withdraw from the organization until its bill was paid.

Solomon justifiably thought the board had betrayed her by over-turning the committee's decision. In her anger she "refused to be Honorary President of an organization where the will of one is set against the will of a democratic house as expressed in the vote," reminding the Board of Council's principles of unity and pluralism, and accusing them of breaking faith with her.[38] Rosenberg subse-quently rebuked Solomon in the Jewish press, perhaps because she felt somewhat insecure in her leadership after taking the job from the overwhelmingly popular and highly respected Solomon.

Bitterness and division overshadowed everything else at the Fifth Triennial. Some delegates hoped the issues would be settled ul-timately with election of new officers. Rosenberg had offered to step down, and many predicted that Lizzie T. Barbe, first cousin to Solomon and officer of Chicago's original Section, would be in-stalled. However, a sizable number of delegates believed that the Cleveland Section was setting up a double standard for themselves. They were insulted that Cleveland might retain its membership without having to pay the same dues as did other Sections. The convention eventually chose a more neutral president, Marion Misch, a forty-three-year-old businesswoman from Providence, Rhode Island, who was a Reform Jew but not associated with Chi-cago's radical Reformers. Lizzie Barbe chose to run against the Board member seen by many as the real source of trouble, Sadie American. In the closest recorded vote in NCJW history, American retained her position as executive secretary, 37 to 36.[39] Following elections, the convention ended, but the controversy raged on in the Jewish press. Supporters and critics alike chided Council leaders for allowing a relatively minor issue to debase the proceedings.[40] The Jewish press failed to recognize, however, that the dispute between Cleveland and the Executive Board went far deeper than a disagreement over payment of dues.

Cleveland claimed the right to secede from Council, disavowing any obligations to the organization, but it did not close the door to future affiliation. Rather, it demanded that the current leadership, in particular American, resign.[41] In so doing, it successfully recast the issue. Now, instead of causing a constitutional problem, the Cleveland Section said that Council could have the peace and unity it so deeply desired if only the current board was replaced. Cleveland's demand planted the seed of doubt in the minds of many members, who began to scrutinize the activities of the Executive Board. Attention centered on the outspoken and sometimes arrogant Sadie American, the only woman who had retained her board position since Council's founding.

American had moved to New York City in 1901, and by the 1908 Triennial was president of the New York Section as well as a national board member. No records exist to tell us why American moved to New York City, but with her move, much of Council's focus shifted away from Chicago. This shift resulted from Council's increased emphasis on American's pet project, immigrant aid work. Because so many Jewish immigrants came through Ellis Island, the burden of immigrant aid work fell to the New York Section. As Council shifted its emphasis away from religious work to social welfare work, immigrant aid became Council's primary focus. That change enhanced the power of the New York Section and its president, power that other Sections resented.

On more than one occasion, American was accused of making important decisions on her own rather than consulting the board. In other instances American was portrayed as being out of control, ignoring presidential orders and board mandates.[42] Some Council leaders accused her of spending Council funds on petty extravagances, in particular traveling first-class to do Council business and taking cabs rather than less expensive streetcars.[43] The Baltimore Section had invited American to speak, hoping that a visit from an enthusiastic national board member would inspire local members to greater commitment, but they reported she was not well received. Resentment continued to build as the board narrowly interpreted a constitutional mandate that national funds could not be used for local projects. Though several Sections' requests for funds were denied, Ellis Island was defined as a national project, in essence placing the control of a large percentage of national funds in the domain of the leaders of the New York Section, especially American.

Prompted by her desperate desire to save her organization from crumbling under the weight of this controversy, Hannah Solomon began talking to other Council leaders about calling for American's resignation. Once American's friend, Solomon had broken with her after the events of the 1908 Triennial. She believed that American's self-righteous defense of her positions, once a boon to an infant organization trying to attract adherents, was now an obstacle to Council's continued success. Solomon found several willing listeners, particularly in Chicago, Boston, and Baltimore. In May 1911, coinciding with the national board's planning meeting for the upcoming Triennial, the Baltimore Section circulated a letter to Council members and the Jewish press. The letter enumerated American's supposed faults, called for her resignation, and threatened secession should she refuse.[44] The Baltimore letter set the stage for a repeat of the disastrous Cincinnati Triennial, highlighting Council's discord rather than its accomplishments.

Marion Misch attempted to avoid a public confrontation by visiting Baltimore and appointing a committee to investigate American's conduct. She also arranged for an experienced and neutral (male) parliamentarian to be present at all business meetings. The parliamentarian was empowered to decide all procedural questions, effectively protecting the Executive Board from accusations of favoritism. It is to Misch's credit that the convention was able to conduct its immigrant aid business, but once again, as the *American Hebrew* headline described it, "Opposition to Administration Overshadows All Other Issues."[45]

Despite the headlines, dissatisfaction with the Executive Board and American was not universal. The New York Section distributed its own letter defending American, recounting her contributions and devotion to NCJW, and reaffirming support for her. Several individuals had written letters in the *Reform Advocate* and the *American Hebrew* supporting American's leadership in guiding NCJW toward increased immigrant aid work and chiding American's detractors for publicizing libelous accusations.[46] The convention continued the ongoing exchange in the Jewish press, both in formal sessions and behind the scenes. Misch's investigating committee reported that it found no wrongdoing and that, in fact, compared to other organizations NCJW was more efficient.[47] That report reinforced the feeling that the board was covering for American and that the general membership had lost all power to the national officers.

Because Baltimore's demand had been the installation of a new national board, elections were the focus of the conflict. The *American Hebrew* provided a detailed description of the scene:

> The elections were conducted in a manner that did not reflect credit on the delegates. The disorder at times was tumultuous. There were charges and counter-charges, and so insistent were some delegates upon having the floor, that the business of the convention was blocked and the president refused to go on until order was restored.
>
> Mrs. Henry G. [Hannah] Solomon, of Chicago, who was considered the leader of the opposition, was nominated by the administration as honorary president in order, it was alleged, to get her out of the way as a candidate for the presidency. Mrs. Solomon was elected, however, by the secretary casting one ballot for her.
>
> Mrs. Caesar [Marion] Misch was the only candidate for the presidency, and a motion was in order to have the secretary cast one ballot for her. Miss American, recognizing the objection to the action of the administration in electing Mrs. Solomon as honorary president, moved that the other two nominations be re-opened, but the motion was declared out of order. The Washington delegates then refused their consent to the casting of one ballot for Mrs. Misch, and when the vote was taken, it was found that Mrs. Misch was elected with 88½ votes against 13.[48]

Accusations that Solomon's nomination for honorary president was a diversionary tactic reflected the total absence of trust in the proceedings. That Solomon was elected by acclamation when Misch was not indicates that the accusation was false. Misch's win with only 88½ votes despite running unopposed demonstrated serious opposition. The ½ vote meant that at least one Section split its vote, indicating that the divisions cut deep within cities, not just between them.

As at the last Triennial, the opposition tried to oust American by running a popular candidate against her, in this case, Chicago member Julia Felsenthal. American convincingly retained her position by a two to one margin. To the National Board, the margin of victory signaled the end of the controversy. For the opposition it merely dictated a change in strategy. Within two weeks the Washington, D.C. Section seceded, intending to continue its work by reconstituting under a different name. It was promptly joined by Baltimore, Boston, and Chicago. Once again, the debate spilled over into the Jewish press, with both sides exchanging letters. Administration supporters accused the opposition of withdrawing simply because it had lost the elections. Several authors continued to attribute the split to personal differences, but a few particularly thoughtful members began to put the situation in perspective, recognizing that it went beyond personalities.

Past national vice-president Alma D. Cowen of Chicago opposed the Executive Board because she believed it had departed "from the original purposes of the Council, and from the democratic principles erstwhile underlying the same." Her language indicated support for Solomon's original vision of a pluralistic religious organization. Sarah Bernkopf, president of the Providence, Rhode Island Section, defended the Board, writing: "I am convinced that the Administration is doing its utmost to carry out the religious as well as the philanthropic ideals of the Council."[49]

The letters of these two leaders suggest that the petty personal grievances disguised a power struggle between those who wanted Council to stay true to its religious roots and those who favored the centrality of social welfare work instituted by the Rosenberg administration. Sadie American, the primary leader in immigrant aid work and a Sunday Sabbath observer, was associated closely with the decline in Council religion and continued to be a focus of the debate. She also remained central because she continued to travel in behalf of the organization. Those concerned with Council's religious identity were wary of the more secular picture of Council they feared American presented to the public and were naturally eager to see her replaced.

Though real personality conflicts and serious questions about how much power the national board should wield over local Sections stoked the fire of the ongoing controversy, the central issue was whether the core of Council's identity would be revival of Judaism or social reform work. The more social reform work seemed to dominate, the louder the voice of the minority opposition became.

By the 1914 Triennial, things had gone from bad to worse. Several months prior to the Triennial, American had opened up a bank account with Council funds, but the account was in American's name. For some reason, unknown to American, her secretary changed it to a Council account and, according to American, proceeded to mismanage it. American consulted several attorneys on the matter to ensure that neither she nor Council would be held responsible for the error, and she fired the secretary. Once American had discussed the matter outside Council meetings, rumors quickly spread in the community that NCJW was mishandling its funds. Considering that Council's philanthropic projects depended heavily on fund-raising, the national board could not afford to ignore this rumor. Leaders planned an Executive Board meeting to discuss the situation, intending to exclude American from attending so they could speak openly. They scheduled that meeting for the day following the close of the 1914 Triennial. A supporter informed American of the pending meeting, and American then stunned the Triennial by opening the second day of proceedings with her resignation. Having come under increasing attack over the course of the last nine years, American now felt betrayed by the national board as well. Her announcement sent the assembly into an uproar. The Jewish press uniformly described the scene as hysterical, bitter, and heated.[50] The *Reform Advocate* even reported that one woman was "brought out limp" from an executive session, having fainted from the excitement.[51]

Earlier in the convention, Marion Misch had pointed out that despite Council's internal strife, its programs had grown, its membership had increased, and less than a sixth of Council's members were involved in secession efforts. The implication was that the overwhelming majority of Council members supported the board. That support was quickly marshaled to attempt blockage of American's resignation. Led by the delegates from New York City, the convention did not convince American to reconsider, but they did manage to propose three separate resolutions in support of her. The first resolution expressed Council's esteem and appreciation for American's years of devoted service. The second highlighted her special contributions to the Department of Immigrant Aid. The third urged the Board to offer American a paid position in that department. All three resolutions passed unanimously, leaving the national board the task of how to employ American without offending the opposition.[52]

The minutes of the Executive Board meeting held the day after the Triennial and conducted by a new president (Janet Harris of Pennsylvania) were recorded verbatim to avoid accusations of insider manipulation. Those minutes totaled 650 pages. Their details of personal slurs, confusion, miscommunication, and fatigue cannot be recounted here. Several strong voices kept the meeting from disintegrating by the earnestness with which they approached the survival of the organization and a genuine desire to treat American fairly. Their final decision, passed by a narrow 8 to 7 vote, was to offer American a low-level secretarial position in the Department of Immigrant Aid but at an inflated salary of $4,000.

American, recognizing the offer was an effort to buy her off, refused the position. Disillusioned by her experience, American would never again return to national prominence in Council. Though many Council members acknowledged her unparalleled contributions to NCJW, they accepted her departure with relief, believing, like Sara Schottenfels, former secretary of the New York Section, that it was essential to the continued success of the organization: "Wherever I went, or whatever mission I was sent, I was sure to find it necessary to defend her [American] against some attack. Finally, like all the other women who had preceded me, I had to resign because working with her became an impossibility. Personally, Miss American does not interest me, but as a member of the Jewish community she does. She has clogged the wheels of the working machinery of a large National Organization, and made a sorry spectacle indeed of the N.Y. Section. Members want to resign on account of the constant strife, and they say as soon as there is peace they will join again."[53] The New York Section, however, did not agree with their former secretary. It promptly followed the pattern in vogue among dissatisfied Sections—it seceded.

The secession gave rise to great concern for Council's future. New York was the nation's largest Council Section, and the membership dues it paid constituted a seventh of NCJW's entire budget. Moreover, New York was instrumental in conducting Council's immigrant aid work, and it was on this issue that the Executive

Board forced the Section to back down. New York claimed that because its members conducted all of Council's Ellis Island and New York City programming, it had a right to continue to do so, despite its secession. That is, the New York Section had no intention of disbanding, but rather, under the experienced leadership of Sadie American and under a new name, it would usurp all Council's New York programming. Because most immigrants lived either permanently or temporarily in New York City, NCJW could hardly afford to surrender its New York operations and still continue its leadership in social welfare activities.

Rather than submit the conflict to a public court, both sides agreed to binding arbitration. They chose three leading male Jewish philanthropists to settle the dispute: Jacob Schiff, Felix Levy, and Louis Posner. The hearings took more than a month and deliberations by the arbitrators several weeks more. The final decision favored the national board. The arbitrators concluded that according to Council's constitution, to which New York had pledged loyalty, the national board (or majority vote at Triennials) had sole right to set Council's national policy. They further concluded that programs at Ellis Island were national, not local projects, and therefore should remain under the jurisdiction of the national board.

The arbitrators also invalidated New York's secession because only 4 percent of the Section's membership had been present at the meeting during which the secession vote took place. In the wake of the controversy, the Section's leaders who had pushed for secession, including American, were forced to resign. Almost a year after it had seceded, the New York Section returned to Council. American left Council for good, though her reputation for immigrant aid work and for troublemaking persisted.[54]

Shortly after the conclusion of the New York dispute, Janet Harris took ill. Marion Misch, who had been elected chair of the Committee on Religion, was asked to fill in as the only board member with presidential experience. The combination of the chair on religion with the presidency, as well as Misch's own talent, did much to foster the healing process.[55] She met with disaffected Sections, helping them translate their resentments into workable demands. The Boston Section asked that Section reports, often tedious now that Sections numbered in the seventies, be replaced by

Rose Brenner (left), Marion Misch (right). (Photos courtesy the National Council of Jewish Women)

a conference of presidents to take place at every Triennial. That request was adopted. The Chicago Section wanted one fourth of their dues to remain under the control of local Sections. On further questioning, it became clear that Chicago's real concern was that too much national money was given to the New York Section to do immigrant aid work. Misch made sure that all disaffected Sections understood that though Sadie American could still serve as a Section president if the Section reelected her, she would not have any say in national policy, even in matters concerning immigrant aid. Misch promised a clear statement of immigrant aid funding and the basis for such funding decisions. In addition, the national board declared the office of Executive Secretary, American's former position, to be ex officio.[56] Before the next Triennial, the disaffected Sections had returned to the fold.

Misch's most important efforts, however, were devoted to guiding Council back to religious work. Misch knew that the tide toward increased social reform work was irreversible, so she developed a series of proposals aimed at combining social welfare and religious work. Her board's suggestions, most of which were adopted by at least some individual Sections, included arranging for local rabbis to conduct services in jails. Rather than handpick the rabbis and be accused of favoritism, Council simply left it to the rabbis to decide who was willing to go. In an attempt to foster respect for Jewish observance and facilitate sensitivity to Jewish needs, Misch's committee also suggested that Jewish calendars be distributed to all schools and civic organizations. They further added that notice of all available Jewish worship services should be placed in hotel rooms, allowing guests to choose which (if any) service they might wish to attend. These creative proposals were easy to accomplish and promoted Judaism without favoring one movement over another. On many occasions over the next several years, both in speech and writing, Misch emphasized the positive side of Council's unique unification of all Jewish women using a familiar analogy. "Judaism is," Misch wrote, "mother, and her daughters are the Orthodox, Conservative, Progressive, Reform, Radical branches— any and all the various phases of Jewish thought. They all love their mother, though they often neglect her and disobey her teachings. They have an unsuspected love for each other, for although they may quarrel bitterly among themselves, if one is attacked the others rush to her protection."[57] Like a mother telling a story to comfort an upset child, Misch then situated her analysis in the context of Council itself:

> Twenty-nine years ago there came to them a Good Fairy, the Council of Jewish Women, who said: "Come children, my home is neutral ground. Meet there and learn to know and to love each other. We will organize Study Classes, where we can discuss our individual thoughts and beliefs and where each can learn how beautiful and worth-while is the religious life of the other. If the Orthodox sister clings to old traditions, let the Reform sister learn here the beauty of those traditions and how they have held Judaism intact amidst persecution and torture. If the Reform sister seems to be breaking away from these traditions, let the Orthodox sister learn here the reasons for the widespread acceptance of Liberal Jewish thought and of that Higher Biblical Criticism which cuts away only the clogging underbrush and which lets the strong trees grow the straighter for this pruning."[58]

Having recognized positive aspects in both sides of the religious split and referred to Council's original goals, Misch's statement was that of a skilled negotiator.

Yet, even Misch's best intentions could not gloss over the deep religious schisms within Council. The 1917 Triennial would pass a resolution calling for greater holiday observance on the part of its membership, but it would not comment on how those holidays should be observed. Throughout the next two decades, every Triennial and Executive Board gave lip service to increased Jewish activities, but little changed. So tenuous was Council's ability to keep any vestige of Jewish religion in its programming that in 1927 the national board found it necessary to remind the membership that "the policy of the National Council of Jewish Women be that no woman may hold office nationally or officially represent the National Council of Jewish Women who has any Non-Jewish church affiliation."[59] On several occasions, Council actually seemed to be anti-religious, as at the 1935 Triennial in New Orleans where the entrées for Sabbath dinner were "Baked ham aux legumes or Swiss and Bacon," neither of which was kosher.[60] This menu was despite calls throughout the 1920s that all cookbooks issued by Council Sections "delete any recipes that may offend those members who strictly observe the dietary laws."[61] As the steady stream of immigrants increased the need for social welfare programs, it was easy for NCJW to justify emphasizing immigrant aid work over the promotion of religious practice. By 1920, Council had come to see itself primarily as a social welfare agency. The Jewish community at large also questioned Council's attachment to religion, ultimately concluding that Council was only peripherally committed to Judaism, a perception that even today remains dominant.[62]

This perception, however, mislabels Council's intentions. Rather than a shift away from religion, Council's increasing emphasis on immigrant aid work was part of its continuing attempts to redefine Judaism in ways that would incorporate members' understanding of what it meant to be American Jewish women. From the organization's inception, social reform and social welfare efforts had been forms of religious expression. NCJW President Gladys F. Cahn summarized what had become for Council a common homily when, in 1958, she urged members to "rededicate [them]selves to the worship of God through service to mankind."[63]

The most detailed description of this approach to religion has been provided by Jonathan Woocher, who used sociologist Robert Bellah's terminology to describe the phenomenon as a Jewish "civil religion." Woocher correctly understood that for organizations like NCJW, secular meant nondenominational, not anti-religious.[64] As if analyzing Cahn's statement, Woocher explained that "Though it may invoke the concept of divinity, civil religion is not primarily concerned with God (or the Transcendent)."[65] Rather, civil religion is focused on Jewish peoplehood. It does not ignore religious practice, but it expands its understanding of religion to incorporate everything that sustains the Jewish people, including cultural expressions, efforts to foster Jewish unity, and political and philanthropic efforts aimed at preserving or enhancing Jewish life. Thus, as Woocher points out, "the prime bearers of civil religion are not . . . clergy or religious institutions," but community institutions and their leaders.[66] NCJW was among the first of such institutions, which have now come to dominate the skyline of American Jewry.

Council leaders were not visionaries who consciously encouraged their organization to forge a Jewish civil religion. However, neither was the adoption of civil religion an accident. The next chapter details how Council members' unique experiences *as women* led to the centrality of philanthropy in the organization's attempts to find a viable means of religious expression. [67]

5.

Immigrant Aid Work

T IS IRONIC that al-
though Sadie American was central to the controversy that nearly
provoked Council's demise, the immigrant aid work she so carefully
nurtured was Council's key to survival. Even as Council struggled
internally, it developed social welfare programs that would earn
NCJW international acclaim. Three factors dominated this development of Council's distinctive approach to philanthropy. First, the
organization consciously avoided duplicating programs already in
place. Second, it functioned as a main conduit through which
Progressive ideology entered the Jewish community, in particular
blending old forms of charity with the newer settlement house philosophy. Finally, it developed a gender-based understanding of its
philanthropic mission and designed its programs to reflect its understanding of proper notions of American womanhood.

These factors are visible in Council's earliest philanthropic
efforts, even though initially such work was loosely organized and
defined largely by local needs, the creativity of Section members,
and scattered requests for cooperation from established women's
organizations. Rather than adopt specific projects of national concern, Council's national board adopted a series of principles to
govern the work of local Sections.

For example, eager to be efficient and aware that the novelty of their organization might elicit objections from a community unaccustomed to the vocal participation of Jewish women in public life, Council leaders warned Sections not to intrude on the territory covered by other agencies. The Sections tailored their efforts to fill gaps in existing programming rather than duplicate work done by others, thus earning NCJW a reputation for innovation and producing great variation in Section activities.

Council also insisted that Sections operate according to the highest professional standards of philanthropy, a reflection of many Board members' attachment to the settlement house movement. This insistence was a marked departure from the typical model of Jewish philanthropy, which raised money locally to meet situations as they arose. A few agencies, such as United Hebrew Charities (founded to serve New York City in 1874), had made scattered attempts to implement new "scientific" methods of giving, but case-by-case giving was common until NCJW came on the scene.[1] Often the results of such philanthropy were temporary, with recipients returning for additional handouts as needed. Council associated this method with the benevolent societies founded by their mothers, an old-fashioned model that had outlived its usefulness.[2] In its place NCJW championed the watchword of the new science of charity: preventive philanthropy. Accordingly, Council stressed efficiency of services, set up programs to help a broad range of clients become self-sufficient[3] and consciously designed its projects to solve problems rather than treat symptoms.[4] As founding member Henrietta Frank had described for the Chicago Woman's Club, "in undertaking such practical work it is not the purpose of the club to become a charity organization, but rather a discoverer of the best methods of advancing humanitarian principles, and of helping individuals and organizations to become self-sustaining."[5]

Applying scientific technique to philanthropy was particularly important for women. At the turn of the century, American society believed that science and the technological advances it produced were the key to humanity's future. At the same time, women generally were excluded from its practice and study, and science was used frequently to justify discrimination against women based on supposed proof of inherent female weakness. As a way of claiming science for themselves and guaranteeing at least a piece of the future, women applied science to the spheres that they controlled. Council adopted both the domestic science first developed by Catharine Beecher, and the science of philanthropy practiced by women's clubs and settlement houses. NCJW was certainly not the only women's organization to adopt scientific philanthropy, but it was the first to apply it nationally in America's Jewish community.

In addition to establishing a new style of Jewish philanthropy, Council's national board laid an ideological foundation for their social welfare work that explained it as an expression of NCJW's threefold identity as an organization of Jews, of Americans, and of women. Echoing Reform Judaism's emphasis on universal ethics and rejuvenating Jewish women's traditional responsibility for giving charity, NCJW defined its new style of philanthropy as inherently Jewish: "In no other religion is *charity* linked up with the idea of *social justice* as in ours. The Jewish philosophy which is expressed in the adage, 'The whole world rests upon the Torah, the practice of religion, and the practice of social justice,' is so inextricably interwoven with the idea that it is our religious duty to give to the poor with a view of helping them to rehabilitate themselves, that it completely dominates our conception of philanthropy. The abandonment of this controlling idea might indeed be tantamount to weakening our Jewish social structure."[6]

Defining Council's philanthropic work as religious expression also fit nicely into American notions of womanhood, which contended that religion was woman's natural vocation. Philanthropic work was fashionable as well, having been endorsed by America's clubwomen. Because most of those clubwomen were Christian, working at a time when the Social Gospel movement was gaining popularity, their charity often was defined as Christian. Council, seeking to place itself on an equal footing with other women's organizations, wanted to make sure Jewish contributions were also recognized. Aware that the growing number of immigrants were the most visible Jews, Council's fifth president Rose Brenner asserted, "Through the medium of our civic contribution shall the Council re-interpret the Jew and Judaism to America."[7] This role of interpreter was common to liberal Progressives and thus served as a way of solidifying Council's Jewish identity as well as its American identity.[8]

Council members took their civic duty quite seriously, not only because they wished to prove Jewish patriotism but also because they viewed citizenship as a privilege that imposed obligations.[9] Council women sought a means to serve the country as their way of showing appreciation for the unparalleled opportunities America afforded Jews. Because its notions of womanhood precluded serving as soldiers or professional politicians, NCJW, as well as other women's organizations, met its obligation through philanthropy.

Like most philanthropic organizations, Council's attention was immediately drawn to America's immigrant slums. Sections in large cities developed a variety of local programs, and a cohesive national program was in place by 1903. That year, word of anti-Jewish persecution in Russia, particularly the Kishineff pogrom, reached America. NCJW members expected that other philanthropic organizations, sharing their sense of social justice, would also express their outrage in concrete action, but as Sadie American observed, "No cry of indignation nor any word whatever have I heard from Christian womanhood over the murder of a hundred thousand Jews . . . and no offer of material aid."[10] Actually, there was some response, but it was anti-Semitic. The National Council of Women of the United States agreed that the pogroms were an "outrage," but only because it was worried that such persecution would force to U.S. shores hordes of untrained immigrants who could not be accommodated by industry or the already overburdened immigrant aid services.[11] NCJW remained committed to the concept of nonsectarian philanthropy but discovered a serious gap to fill that would consume the lion's share of Council energy for the next twenty years.

Of course, Council's motives were not entirely altruistic. Many Council members shared the common German Jewish attitude that "Because the Jew is criticized and attacked as a tribe, he is obliged to defend himself as a tribe, whether he likes it or not."[12] Many Jews did not like it, resenting the challenge the new immigrants seemed to pose to their hard-won acceptance in America. Some Council members, like many Americans, attributed U.S. socioeconomic problems to cultural differences and conflicts with the new immigrants.[13] Implying superiority, one Council member gave voice to her concern at the 1902 Triennial, announcing that "We, who are the cultured and refined, constitute the minority, but we shall be judged by the majority, the Russian Jews, by the children of the ghetto."[14] Annie Nathan Meyer shared this elitist attitude of supporting immigrant aid out of a sense of "noblesse oblige."[15] The most common sentiment, however, was expressed by Chicago's Jennie Franklin Purvin: "we should enter civic fields as a matter of self-defense."[16] In this spirit, German Jews mobilized efforts to Americanize the newcomers so that the foreign ways of those newcomers would not jeopardize the gains Jews believed they had made in becoming an accepted segment of American society.

Despite the pervasiveness of this attitude in the German Jewish community and despite the many Council members who had internalized it, it did not dominate Council's approach to the immigrant community. As in the rest of its philanthropic work, NCJW explained its immigrant aid efforts as an expression of Jewish womanhood. To Council, womanhood implied motherhood. Building from this central foundation, Council based its programs on a family model in which Council women were mothers and immigrants were members of their extended family.

It is important to note that Council women viewed motherhood as distinctly different from fatherhood, seeing the latter as financial provider, the former as nurturer. Council leaders routinely condemned the paternalistic attitudes common in social welfare circles and viewed their own emphasis on motherhood as a more sensitive alternative. They spent a great deal of energy trying to counteract the attitude that the immigrant was a "poor relation for whom one had to apologize."[17] The result was a policy that revised the old-style charity practice of "friendly visiting" to include individual pieces of Jane Addams' settlement house ideology.

Like Addams, NCJW insisted that donation of funds could not substitute for giving time. Because it was an organization of middle-class women who, unlike men or poor immigrants, were not constrained by the expectation or necessity of devoting the majority of their time to earning a living, Council was able to design its programs to provide immigrants face-to-face contact with their benefactors. Rather than receiving help from an impersonal, large organization, NCJW clients got to know Council members through repeated contact with the same person(s). Such personal contact made it difficult for either party to generalize about the other and reduced "mutual suspicion and ignorance."[18] Also like Addams, Council demanded that interaction between immigrants and volunteers should be conducted on a foundation of mutual respect. NCJW counseled members of its Committee on Immigrant Aid to "visit the girl in the same way they would visit someone recommended by a personal friend, without patronage and merely in the friendly spirit," noting that visitors using this approach would "always be welcome."[19]

Continuing in the Addams mold, NCJW demanded that even volunteer workers receive proper training for their tasks, a policy producing programs and standards that contributed to the professionalization of social work. Ironically, that professionalization would drive many volunteers out of social service, only to be replaced by their daughters who took advantage of new opportunities to obtain college degrees in social work as their way of continuing the work of their mothers, just as their mothers had continued the work of the benevolent societies by reshaping philanthropic practices. Once social workers began to earn significant wages, however, even those daughters would be replaced, this time by men who now saw social work as a career and therefore appropriate for males but not for females.[20]

In NCJW's formative years, nevertheless, women still dominated the settlement house movement,[21] and Council women adopted as heroes the luminaries of the burgeoning social welfare movement. Leaders such as Jane Addams and Lillian Wald provided inspiration as Council opened settlement houses in more than a dozen cities.[22] Settlement houses were attractive to Council because they espoused an ideology calling for immigrants' "gradual assimilation and recognition of the need to create a sense of continuity between the old and the new, in an atmosphere of mutual respect, toleration, and understanding."[23] That is, settlement houses encouraged immigrants to find ways to preserve their ethnicity by means of expression appropriate to American culture. This encouragement, of course, was precisely Council's function. Settlement houses were also a popular first step for Council women because the volunteer work they required often duplicated familiar domestic tasks. Through settlement houses, Council women became surrogate mothers to the immigrant community while gaining the experience and confidence that allowed them to create one of America's most intricate and influential immigrant aid programs.

In fact, NCJW placed its entire immigrant aid policy in the framework of family and motherhood. Members believed that strong families were the key to their own success, a conviction from which flowed Council's conclusion that if immigrant life was to have any sense of stability, immigrant women, like Council women, would have to become strong mothers. It did not take more than a cursory glance to see that the needs of immigrant Jewish girls (future mothers) and women differed from those of other immigrants, and that no organization, Jewish or secular, addressed those needs. NCJW tailored its programs to fill that gap. Thus guided by its mission of motherhood, Council set out to protect its immigrant Jewish daughters. Informed by the 1894 report of New York State legislature's Lexow Committee[24] and reports from England's Union of Jewish Women Workers[25] and despite hesitancy in the Jewish community to expose publicly its vices,[26] NCJW concluded that the greatest single threat to female immigrants was the white slave trade. Often traveling alone, unfamiliar with the language or American customs, full of grand myths about the availability of American wealth, and in desperate need of employment, immigrant girls were easy targets for white slavers. Promising easy money or marriage, or simply posing as understanding friends, pimps coaxed girls into dependency and then forced them into prostitution. Apparently, these pimps enjoyed a good measure of success. One source estimated that half the prostitutes on Chicago's West Side were Jewish.[27] The involvement of Jews in the white slave trade was no secret. Many Jews simply accepted prostitutes as part of the local scene.[28] Male-run organizations were slow to act, their first formal efforts coming six years after NCJW began their attack.[29]

Like other organizations that eventually entered the fight against the white slavers, Council was concerned because Jewish prostitutes and pimps provided fodder for anti-Semites. Attorneys defending pimps claimed that Jewish girls were not forced into prostitution, but rather chose it freely because Jews instinctively wanted to line their pockets with easy money.[30] Anti-Semites repeated this claim outside the courtroom, blaming Jews for society's ills and insisting that Jews be deported before they corrupted America's morals.[31] Desiring to remove the excuse for this anti-Semitism but primarily concerned with the tragic effects of the slave trade on girls' lives, Council's initial efforts concentrated on juvenile court work (where as volunteer probation officers Council women acted as surrogate mothers to their charges) and on developing methods that would keep girls from meeting the white slavers in the first place. Early aid included providing safe housing for single women and guiding un-accompanied women from the docks to their families.

These efforts were distinctly different from early Reformers' attempts to redeem "fallen women" by introducing them to Christian salvation. Though such Council members as Alice Davis Menken, founder of the Jewish Big Sister movement and noted New York social worker, invited Jewish defendants to Sunday morning meetings at local synagogues,[32] Council did not bombard the girls they served with religious ideology. In part, this was a natural outcome of its emphasis on prevention over cure, and in part a product of its need to de-emphasize Judaism to avoid fracturing the organization, but mostly it was because Council did not see the girls as "fallen." Not only was such a concept foreign to Judaism, but it contradicted Council's settlement house-inspired belief that its clients were essentially good people who had been forced off life's proper path by outside circumstance, not internal deficiencies of the soul. As long-time national board member, Hattie Kahn, summarized, "the Jewish immigrant does not belong in the class in which we find her but has been forced there by untoward circumstances."[33] NCJW's focus, therefore, was on providing material, not spiritual help.

Council's efforts to protect its immigrant "daughters" quickly won acclaim. Members like Maude E. Miner and Alice Davis Menken earned national fame for their prison and judicial reform work. In 1925, Menken attributed New York City's 40 percent decrease in Jewish women arraigned for sexual offenses to Council's preventive programs.[34] Sadie American, representing NCJW at an international conference on the white slave trade in Spain, was granted an audience by Spain's king and queen, who praised Council's work. By 1903, NCJW had so clearly established itself as the undisputed leader in this unique work that the U.S. government sought its help in preventing immigrant girls from falling into the hands of white slavers. In response to that request, Council's Department of Immigrant Aid (later renamed Service to the Foreign Born) was established. By 1905, just two years after the government first sought its help, Council created a permanent aid station to receive Jewish women at Ellis Island.[35] The Ellis Island station was staffed both by paid agents and by volunteers. Council recruited employees who could speak Yiddish and attempted to team them with volunteers who could speak other European languages, hoping to address a diversity of immigrant needs. Securing names from ship manifests and detention lists, Council agents interviewed every female Jewish immigrant between the ages of twelve and thirty.[36]

These interviews revealed that immigrant conceptions of life in America were often based on the glowing descriptions of German Jewish success in mid-nineteenth-century America. Council women, often vocally appreciative of the social and financial benefits they reaped from American liberty and capitalism, now had to temper their patriotic praise. Though few Council women publicly attempted to explain the change, most recognized that freedom would not be as sweet for these new immigrants as it had been for their own families, at least not at first. Knowing that disillusionment stemming from false expectations would likely lead young girls into trouble, NCJW tried to provide a more accurate picture by printing a leaflet which it distributed in Russia and in European ports of embarkation. The leaflet provided information on how to seek help from Council and warned young women to "Beware of those who give addresses, offer you easy, well paid work or even marriage" because "there are evil men and women who have in this way led girls to destruction."[37]

Believing that informed people would act intelligently, Council hoped their warnings would prepare girls to fend off the advances of white slavers. The leaflets also tried to counter false notions about America, stating that U.S. law prohibited the employment of anyone under the age of fourteen and required youths to attend school, concluding with a final warning that failure to abide by these laws

In 1906 immigrant women report to an NCJW agent at Ellis Island. At the top of the stairs, friendly visitor Ray Perlman waits to help the women reach their final destinations safely. (Photo by Underwood Park Place, courtesy NCJW)

could result in deportation. The leaflet tempered its harsh tones by adding assurances that Council would help the immigrant make necessary adjustments.

By 1907, Ellis Island was the hub of Council programming, providing the model used by Council representatives at every major American port of entry. Acting as advocates for the immigrants, Council translators often helped smooth difficulties with customs officials, easing entry for many who would otherwise have been detained.[38] The key to Council work, however, was the personal interview. In addition to informing the immigrant of Council programs the interviewer would ascertain the intended destination of the woman. For cases in which only a name and city were available, port workers would cable the Section (or in cities without a Section, a designated correspondent) who would then attempt to locate the family. Once Council agents were sure that the name was not phony (indicating the work of white slave traders), they would instruct the client on how to travel to her destination, frequently escorting her to the door of the train and occasionally paying her fare.

Volunteers at the final destination would be cabled to expect the immigrant's arrival and with her relatives (if possible) would meet the train. That volunteer would accompany the immigrant to her new home. Council instructed the volunteer to ask a series of questions to ensure the girl's continued safety. One Council guide sheet noted that it was especially important to see "that a girl is living with older persons who may be able to exercise some control over her," continuing that the importance of this supervision would be obvious to "any woman."[39] Just in case it might not be obvious, however, the guidelines explained that young women, especially those who earned their own keep, often refused to accept the supervision of younger relatives and were likely to end up in trouble.

To make certain that settlement would continue to go smoothly, the volunteer would "adopt" the entire family, directing them to available employment, health care, educational opportunities, and even entertainment. These "friendly visitors," would return to the household on a regular basis to check on their clients' progress, offer explanations of American customs, help bring other family members to the United States,[40] and sometimes simply offer encourage-

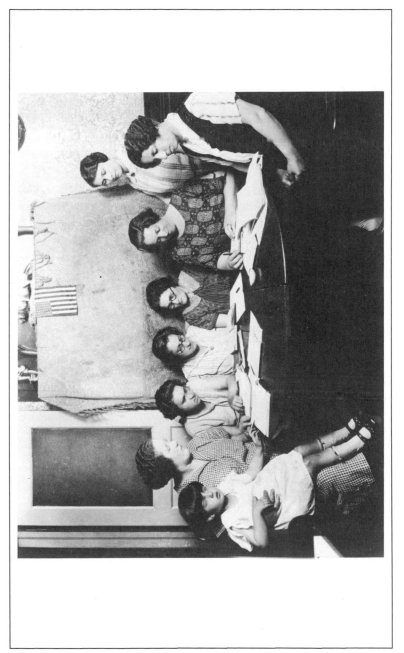

Typical of Council's immigrant aid efforts, members of the Newark Section Committee of Service to the Foreign Born conduct English and Americanization classes for women in the familiar surroundings of the immigrants' own kitchens. (Photo courtesy the National Council of Jewish Women)

ment. The friendly visitor would then report back to the Section in the port of entry, assuring the agents that the client had arrived safely and was appropriately cared for. Contact between client and friendly visitor would continue until aid was no longer needed or after three years, the period of time by which U.S. law differentiated between an immigrant and a soon-to-be citizen. [41]

Even Council's personal attention from dock to door could not keep all clients out of trouble. According to Council, the immigrant, confronted by desperate surroundings, driven by hunger, and convinced that she had no other opportunities, often resorted to crime. [42] Council, like most Progressive Reform agencies after 1900, [43] was quick to attribute delinquent behavior to circumstance rather than a lack of morals, explaining that poverty was "the parent of vice, ignorance, mendacity, [and] crime." [44] In Council's view, elimination of poverty would put an end to most criminal activity.

Popular women's club analysis traced poverty to a chain that began with ignorance, which could be eliminated through universal public education. [45] While NCJW generally agreed with this assessment, its own analysis borrowed again from settlement house philosophy to go beyond this simple view to explain poverty not as a lack of drive or knowledge but as an outcome of America's political and economic system. Because it viewed the problem as systemic, NCJW concluded that changes would need to be wide-ranging and would not likely come voluntarily. Yet, if it could not change the system that produced poverty, the rest of its efforts ultimately would be worthless. Therefore, like the settlement house movement, in addition to social welfare work NCJW demanded governmental legislation and began an extensive lobbying effort to see that its demands were met. Eventually many women's clubs would be counted among those that had "polished modern methods of pressure-group politics." [46] In the meantime, the realities of immigrant life demanded more immediate action than was likely to be forthcoming from the government. Following recommendations based on Council's national research, local Sections developed supplementary programs to aid immigrants from infancy through adulthood.

Again basing its approach on motherhood, NCJW believed that upstanding adults did not appear miraculously but had to be carefully shaped from earliest childhood days. Provisions for needy infants started with the basics. To ensure that no child would be born that might be an unbearable financial burden to the family, Council was an early advocate for birth control, pointing out problems caused by overpopulation in countries like India and China and noting that several European nations permitted its dissemination without negative consequence.[47] On the local level for example, in 1927 Detroit Section vice-president Elsie Sulzberger founded the "Mother's Health Clinic," reputedly the only source for birth control between Chicago and New York. In her autobiography, Margaret Sanger credited NCJW with being the first organization in the United States to demand publicly the legalization of birth control,[48] though it was not until 1931 that Council passed an official resolution calling for decriminalization of mailing materials "by properly authorized agencies, relative to birth control."[49] In keeping with Council's self-image as benefactor rather than client, no Council material on birth control mentioned that legalization might also benefit NCJW members.

Once the child was born, preservation of its health was of primary concern. In the first several decades of its existence, Council's day-to-day work was interrupted regularly by the illness or death of a member. How much more precarious, then, did the health of immigrants living in slums seem. Always focused on prevention, Council emphasized hygiene and nutrition in the hope that fewer children would succumb to illness. Members lobbied local politicians to implement public sanitation programs and campaigned for national governmental assurance of food purity. Sections provided free milk, penny lunches, and instruction on personal hygiene to public school children. Recreation and exposure to the outdoors were also important in Council's plans, so it financed outings and several Sections ran summer camps or vacation schools. Council women pressured municipalities to build parks and install sanitation systems. In addition to group programs, Council hired public health nurses to visit clients, provided free medical examinations, and when necessary, free medicine. Health care concerns also led NCJW to become a sponsor of Denver's National Hospital for Consumptives, which provided free services to the needy.

Once Council had done its best to guard the health of the children, it proceeded to provide for their religious and secular education. Since its inception, NCJW had been immersed in a struggle to protect Jewish homes against Christian intrusion, from providing religious education for members and their children to questioning the practice of adorning Jewish homes with Christmas decorations.[50] Extension of this work into the immigrant community flowed naturally. Christian missions were active in immigrant ghettoes, and Council was justifiably concerned that pressure from missionaries combined with the apparent rewards of assimilation would turn young Jews away from their heritage. Though many Council members certainly hoped to coax immigrants away from traditional Jewish practices that they viewed as embarrassing, the Jewish education they offered was no more monolithically Reform than was Council's membership. Council's commitment to uniting Jewish women from all denominations kept them from trying to "convert" immigrants to Reform Judaism. Instead, as with their own membership, Council fought to preserve Jewish identity without defining what that meant. Its purpose was not to promote or denigrate a specific interpretation of Judaism, but rather to "continue with unabated zeal to contend against the wholesale conversion of Jewish children."[51] Moreover, because Council ideology proclaimed family strength as the key to the preservation of Judaism, it was careful to avoid religious persuasion that might endanger familial ties: "Nothing should be presented to the child antagonistic to the belief and observance of the parents, as it would create a spirit of resentment in the home and respect for religious beliefs must be fostered."[52]

Its pluralistic approach to religious practice sometimes led NCJW to conduct activities that supported traditional Judaism. For example, out of respect for clients' Sabbath observance, on Saturdays Council Houses shut down all but essential programs or programs that conformed to traditional observance, such as Sabbath story hours or similar activities designed to keep children off the streets.[53] Council also took on the responsibility of distributing Jewish calendars to all social service agencies so they could facilitate their clients' observance of Jewish holidays,[54] and some Sections provided immigrants with necessary holiday provisions, such as matzah on Passover.[55] NCJW pressed the rabbinic community to provide religious services for Jews incarcerated in prisons and reformatories and for shut-ins. It also demanded that no Jew be turned away from a synagogue for lack of membership dues, [56] and it supported the growth of American rabbinic seminaries of all denominations so that congregations would have an ample supply of English-speaking rabbis who, shaped by the same cultural changes experienced by their congregants, were more likely to appeal to children being raised in America. [57]

Other Council programs seemed to support traditional Judaism on the surface, but in fact, reflected ambivalence. When one Talmud Torah needed sanitary plumbing, Council funded the repair, but out of concern for the welfare of the children, not out of support for the school's curriculum. [58] Still other programs actually encouraged religious observance but appeared to be anti-traditional. For example, Council religious schools rejected the traditional *cheder,* not so much because Council women felt uncomfortable with its values, but because they believed its teaching methods to be outdated and ineffective. In a similar contradiction, NCJW demanded that traditional Jewish schools go against custom and welcome girls as well as boys, not as part of any fight for equality or radical change, but because Council women knew from personal experience that girls who did not receive religious training did not become "good" Jewish mothers and would accordingly be unable to pass Judaism on to their children. The changes Council proposed to traditional Jewish education were based in the desire to slow assimilation rather than an attempt to criticize immigrant religious practice.

On one point NCJW was never ambivalent: religious education was not enough. Council supported immigrant access to quality secular education with great vigor. In addition to pressing for improvements in public school facilities and better teacher training, it ran free kindergartens and endowed public libraries. In a pioneering effort, NCJW recommended instituting preschool programs as well. [59] To ensure that children stay in school, Council participated in the 1909 White House Conference on Child Welfare and President Taft's 1911 Child Labor Committee. For Council, the outcome of that conference was a strong Congressional lobbying effort in support of child labor laws and protective legislation for women.[60] Because most Council members had raised or were raising children themselves, they knew from experience that entertainment was an important counterbalance to the demands of educational programs. Council's economical solution was the creation of "toyeries," libraries that lent toys rather than books.[61]

Council members nonetheless knew that as children reached adolescence toyeries would not divert teenage attention from the corrupting influence of the street. Again relying on the belief that education was the "preventive medicine of all living,"[62] Council promoted sex education as a prophylaxis against the white slave trade and sexually transmitted disease. Like the Female Moral Reform Societies that preceded it,[63] NCJW accepted the popular notion that women were responsible for upholding the morals of their children, and it encouraged mothers to take on the burden of this education. Council, however, was also realistic. Recognizing that "the majority of parents are disinclined or incompetent to give this instruction judiciously and effectively," NCJW was among the first proponents of sex education in the public schools.[64] By declaring parents incompetent on the subject, Council was not only pointing out a real gap in education but also creating an otherwise unavailable opportunity to infuse immigrant families with its own ideology, or as it would have termed its efforts, to "Americanize" the immigrants. In addition to lessons on biology, Council encouraged frank discussion of the values surrounding sexual behavior, especially regarding the differing standards applied to boys and girls. No one who was familiar with the white slave trade could have failed to notice that while prostitutes were prosecuted vigorously, their customers rarely suffered any consequences. Boys could easily conclude that "vice on their part was a comparatively innocent thing."[65]

Here, again, Council's critique of America's sexual double standard reflected attitudes expressed as early as the 1830s by Female Moral Reform Societies.[66] The significant difference, of course, was that Council needed to develop the justification for its position out of Judaism rather than Christianity. Guided by traditional Jewish attitudes, NCJW celebrated sexual intercourse as an expression of love but only within marriage.[67] It objected to the sexual double standard not because that standard demanded unfair chastity for girls but because, it argued, promiscuous boys endangered the community by feeding the white slave trade, weakening family commitments, and carrying sexually transmitted diseases. Council's sex education materials observed that families could as easily be destroyed by a father's sexual transgressions as by a mother's, and that there had never been "a physical or moral reason for maintaining two standards as regards chastity, one for men and the other for women."[68] Council pamphlets consistently debunked traditional "scientific" arguments attributing the double standard to biology.

Yet, unlike feminists who rejected notions of complementary gender roles and argued for equality as a logical expression of the claim that, biologically, males and females were not significantly different,[69] NCJW continued to stress natural differences between the sexes in every area except sexual promiscuity. Council readily accepted America's division of labor that made care of home and children the central task of womanhood while holding man responsible for the financial support and public representation of his family. Council never explained why it could use innate sexual difference to justify leaving scholarly pursuits to men, for example, but would not accept similar justifications when examining sexual behavior.

Council never acknowleged this internal ideological contradiction, nor did it provide convincing arguments that society should not apply its widely accepted notion of divinely ordained separate spheres to chastity. However, its failure to change attitudes toward sexual behavior did not deter Council from addressing the problems of promiscuity from another angle. Recognizing that they were not likely to eliminate temptation, Council women sought to provide distractions. They organized social activities, arranged for free tickets to cultural events, sponsored athletic competitions, screened movies, brought in lecturers, and volunteered as Big Sisters.[70] They also sought to protect children from corruptive influences by pressing authorities to bar minors from risqué movies, dance halls, and vaudeville shows.[71] Even these comprehensive programs, however, could not keep away subversive influences, and some youths ended up in the court systems. Repeating their belief that delinquency resulted from circumstance rather than from innate character flaws, NCJW insisted that with proper supervision, defendants would not likely repeat youthful offenses. In order to arrange for that supervision, Council members were instrumental in setting up a separate court system for juveniles, often volunteering as probation officers.

In Council's opinion, however, no form of court supervision could replace firm parental guidance. To help ensure a strong home life, Council offered parenting and Americanization classes. Aside from the obvious goal of teaching immigrants about their new country and preparing them to become citizens, NCJW saw their courses as a way to mitigate the gap between first generation children and their parents. Sadie American explained, "We see many tragedies because there are children who show dis-respect to their parents who do not know English."[72] Parents who depended on their children to ease interaction with American culture were easily manipulated by those children, and such parents found it difficult to enforce discipline. Council's course offerings, from housekeeping to English, were designed to provide parents with "street smarts" as well as more conventional information so they could better supervise their children.[73]

Though such education was important to immigrant family life, it was irrelevant without some semblance of financial stability. To that end, Council offered comprehensive vocational training to women. The Department of Immigrant Aid conducted careful studies to determine which fields were most likely to employ women, what kind of wages women might earn at those occupations, and what skills were required.[74] It offered training based on the results of those studies, so the education tended to perpetuate existing sexual divisions of labor and place women in the lowest-paying jobs.[75] It also perpetuated class divisions by assuming that immigrant girls could not or would not enter the professions or the arts.

In addition, Council training emphasized etiquette and domestic skills because they believed "each girl should receive training fitting her for the discharge of duties in the home."[76] Thus, Council's training reinforced traditional gender roles that ultimately led women back into the home. Like settlement house workers, Council women viewed themselves as educators and interpreters of American culture, "and even leaders, but never rebels."[77] Thus, despite Council's extensive vocational training programs, members had mixed feelings about women in the workplace. They recognized the need for single women to work, and a few supported women's entrance into the professions,[78] but most believed that childcare was ultimately woman's primary duty and that labor outside the home interfered with that duty. So deep was the ambivalence that, during World War I when military needs led many to call for the suspension of protective legislation, Executive Board member Estelle M. Sternberger questioned whether women were being duped by patriotic rhetoric to take otherwise inappropriate factory jobs, claiming the shortage of male workers was a myth.[79] By 1905 Hannah Solomon had concluded that Council's encouragement of women to enter the workforce was a "big mistake. Because we were afraid of pauperizing," wrote Solomon, "we have made criminals and lonely outcasts; we have wrecked homes which should have been conserved."[80] Reiterating her own class expectations, Solomon insisted that "No mother has a right to leave her home and the care of the young children unless she can delegate these responsibilities to someone whom she can pay or trust for their proper discharge during her absence."[81] Solomon was not alone. Annie Nathan Meyer openly opposed suffrage because she believed "the vote would enshrine the economically independent woman as an 'equal' when she should be regarded as 'an exception or a misfortune.'"[82] Another member, also relying on the notion that women's and men's roles were meant to remain distinct, observed that "the woman in modern industry is engaged in occupations for which nature seemingly did not fit her."[83] Council's support for working women was ultimately limited by its hope that women would leave the workforce when they became pregnant. Where they could have established childcare programs, Council members looked for ways to free the immigrant mother from the workplace so she could care for her own children.

Most Jewish women who did work were either single or working out of economic necessity (or both), giving NCJW grounds on which to reject the notion of women pursuing careers, while still developing policy designed to help those "unfortunate" women who had to work. Typical of that policy was NCJW's attempt to provide a more "feminine" alternative to factory work by giving immigrant women use of Council thrift shops as a sales outlet for goods produced at home.[84] Also typical was Council's cooperation with organizations like the National Consumers League,[85] which promoted protective legislation because "The *girls* of today are the *mothers* of the future; if they are overworked the children will pay the penalty."[86] This support for protective legislation, however, often put Council and their allies at odds with workers. For example, on the surface, calls for an eight-hour day seemed positive, but no one could guarantee that hourly workers would have any way to make up for the resulting lost income. One frustrated worker exclaimed, "The sooner that society women understand that they must keep their hands off the working woman, the sooner the working woman will be better off."[87]

NCJW's national board had laid out an idealistic approach to immigrant aid geared toward preventing dependence while preserving the dignity of the client. To many immigrants, however, Council's good intentions were overshadowed by members' desire to keep their distance. Though friendly visitors were admonished to treat the immigrants as neighbors, the fact is they were not neighbors. This actuality was Council's major departure from settlement house philosophy. Members had no intention of residing in the communities they served, seeing Eastern European Jews as clients rather than fellow citizens. Nor were immigrants encouraged to move into German communities. As author Ande Manners pointed out, Chicago's German Jews held gala balls to benefit Russian immigrants, but no Russian was ever invited.[88] Nor did Council women intend for their clients to become Council members. Though Council set its dues "at the lowest possible amount so that even the poorest woman need not be excluded," meetings were held in the afternoon, effectively excluding working women.[89]

Though official NCJW policy stated that friendly visitors should treat immigrants as family, the national board had no way of supervising the work of local Sections or individual members. While these volunteers undoubtedly believed they offered help to those they visited, it was easy for immigrants to interpret frequent visits as tests, a patronizing way of checking up on clients to make sure they were following Council's wishes. Some immigrants saw Council's support for protective legislation and child labor laws as further uninvited meddling. The *Jewish Daily Forward* sneered at Council women, claiming they put on unearned aristocratic airs and tossed out pennies "with their bediamoned hands more to show their delicate alabaster fingers with well-manicured nails than really to save the unfortunates."[90] Although the *Forward*'s description was overly harsh, it underscored the fact that the best of intentions did not substitute for genuine respect. Recognizing that Council schools provided valuable education, distinguished historian Oscar Handlin nevertheless correctly concluded that, "With the best intentions in the world, these institutions could not help giving the implication that the old ways were not truly American and were to be discarded."[91] Immigrants often saw Council efforts as an assault on their traditions, and they resented the pressure to assimilate.

Council never denied that it intended to help Russian immigrants Americanize and that Americanization meant becoming more like German Jews. But they also recognized and in many cases came to respect the values and traditions of the immigrants, a compassion produced by personal contact.[92] Council's ambivalence is well illustrated by the topics for a Council-sponsored essay contest. While one option was "American Customs and Ways of Living I Have Found Most Helpful," the other was "Old World Customs I Should Like My Children to Preserve."[93]

Council members were not alone in their ambivalence. Russian immigrants, desirous of retaining their cultural and religious identity, knew that they had no place else to go if they could not make America home. Thus, even though the immigrants might have chosen to do it more slowly or in a different way, they wanted to acculturate every bit as much as the German Jews wanted them to.[94] Immigrants willing to vocalize that sentiment also voiced appreciation for Council's efforts. One housebound immigrant reported that the Council volunteers who came to teach her English did, indeed, treat her as a friend.[95] A small, but significant number of Council's younger clients would later join NCJW and work as volunteers helping other immigrants. These clients-turned-members did not indicate a change in Council's relationship with immigrants in general but rather were accepted because they fit the profile of Council membership. A typical example was Hilda Satt Polacheck, a Hull House girl. Polacheck's father was a tombstone carver who, because he could carve the Hebrew lettering common on Jewish headstones, was always fully employed, so Polacheck was

not raised in poverty. At Hull House Polacheck showed a special
talent for writing, and with Jane Addams' help, attended University
of Chicago, though she would eventually forgo a career to raise a
family. Her husband's career led the family to Milwaukee where
Polacheck, as the new middle-class Jewish woman in a relatively
small community, was recruited into NCJW. Immigrants like Polacheck eventually would help change the composition of Council
from a predominantly German group to a thoroughly mixed
membership.[96]

Though sometimes enacted out of a patronizing sense of superiority, Council's intricate weave of social welfare programs substan-
tially benefited thousands of Jewish immigrants. Between 1904 and
1907, NCJW helped approximately 20,000 Jewish women and girls
make it through customs and settle in America.[97] Undeterred by a
series of governmental restrictions on immigration begun in 1921,
they continued to play a decisive role in immigrant aid work until
after the successful settlement of World War II refugees in the
1940s.[98]

In addition, Council undertook a series of projects as spin-offs of
their immigrant aid work. In 1923, under the chair of Rose Brenner, NCJW extended its social welfare services to Jews in rural
communities. Though other Jewish organizations had helped Jews
to settle outside urban centers, only NCJW provided for their ongoing religious, health, and educational needs.[99] Council hired
itinerant Hebrew teachers, nurses, and lecturers assigned to specific
rural districts to share information on everything from Jewish history to sex hygiene. Council also sponsored observances of Jewish
holidays, providing necessary foods and ritual objects. By 1928,
Council's Department of Farm and Rural Work had contacted
2,500 farms in eight states and had provided religious school classes
for 700 Jewish children in rural areas. They had also taken their
preventive health care programs into 115 rural communities.[100]

Council's most acclaimed spin-off project was its work on behalf of
the blind. Blindness was often caused by sexually transmitted disease,
and Council may have first undertaken the work as part of their fight
against the white slave trade. In the context of the Jewish community,
Council's assessment of the problem was innovative. It was the first
Jewish philanthropic organization to approach blindness as a health

Council's farm and rural work included hiring visiting nurses (top) and sponsoring Jewish activities outside urban areas. The sign on the wagon says "This way to kosher picnic." (Photos courtesy the National Council of Jewish Women)

issue rather than as a charity issue. While other philanthropies assumed that the blind could not earn a living and therefore must be supported by charity funds, Council implemented an extensive vocational training program.[101] They urged public schools to mainstream blind children rather than institutionalizing them and provided free eye exams, glasses, and educational programs on how to avoid loss of eyesight to all schoolchildren, again reflecting Council's emphasis on prevention.[102] That education included the still familiar (and "all-American") warning for children to stay away from firecrackers on the Fourth of July. NCJW also led the way in meeting the needs of the Jewish blind, printing the first Braille prayerbook[103] and volunteering to read aloud Yiddish newspapers so the sightless could keep abreast of events in the immigrant Jewish community.[104] Council's success in helping the blind led them to establish similar preventive and service programs for the deaf. Both programs earned NCJW wide acclaim from health, government, and social welfare agencies.

Another spin-off project was Council's Committee for Purity of the Press, which was established five years before B'nai B'rith created the Anti-Defamation League. Council members volunteered to act as watchdogs, endeavoring to "eliminate objectionable [anti-Semitic] matter from the Press."[105] In an effort to protect both the immigrant community and themselves, Council representatives met with newspaper editors to complain about anti-Jewish language and articles. The Portland Section succeeded in getting their paper to stop using the word "Jew" in reference to criminals unless they designated the religion of all criminals.[106] Other Sections wrote letters to the editor countering attacks against Jews.

Perhaps more important to public relations than this specific effort at defending Jews was the respect that Council's programming earned from non-Jewish social welfare agencies. NCJW exhibits won awards at the 1907 Jamestown and Paris International expositions, and their social welfare newsletter *The Immigrant* was so widely respected it was adopted as a text in college classrooms.[107] One reporter, impressed by its diversity and innovation, concluded that "The Council is nothing if not original."[108]

Rose Brenner exaggerated only slightly when she assessed the immigrant aid work of the organization over which she presided: "Just as Council has enabled the immigrant Jewess to become an intelligible and intelligent part of her American community, so it has given to our native American Jewesses the opportunity to translate their precious Jewish heritage into terms of American service. In this land of commissions and committees, I venture to assert that there is no group of earnest social-minded citizens, concerning themselves with the great educational, legislative and civic questions of the day, which does not include in its membership some representative, acting as such, of the Council of Jewish Women."[109] Council's immigrant aid work was an intricate weave of mothering, professional social work, and self-defense. The resulting fabric would form the core of Council's programming for decades to come. There is no way to estimate the numbers of lives touched by NCJW's extensive programming, though clearly no other organization wielded more influence over the life of immigrant Jewish girls than did NCJW.[110]

NCJW's leadership in social welfare work, particularly within the Jewish community, is directly attributable to the fact that Council was a woman's organization. Jewish and American separation of gender roles meant that men and women grew up in essentially different worlds, raised with differing expectations and visions of the society around them. In the case of German Jewish philanthropy, these differences between the sexes led men and women to have significantly different relationships to social welfare work.[111]

Unlike their husbands, Jewish women were not expected to center their lives around paid labor. According to prevailing American standards, women worked only when their families were in financial need. Popular notions said female paid laborers were lower class, married to failed men, spinsters, or young women waiting to get married. (Appendix A, Chart 9, confirms Council women's adoption of these notions.) In a Jewish community striving to be accepted by America's wealthier families, none of these situations was enviable. Jewish women understood expectations that "proper" women would be dependent on men and committed to domesticity as expressions not only of True Womanhood but also as truly American, a roadmap that would guide them into America's uppercrust. While Jewish men measured success by how well they could support their wives, Jewish women measured success by how well they fit the mold of True Womanhood, accomplished not only through conduct in one's own home but also by traveling in the "right" social circles.[112] Thus, while their husbands worked, Jewish women attempted to ensure their family's success by cultivating the proper social contacts.

Jewish women, however, had few regular opportunities to meet women outside their small circle of relatives and friends. Entertainment frequently took place by invitation only in the privacy of one's home. Strangers, especially immigrant strangers, rarely received such invitations. Because piety was an integral part of True Womanhood, the church was also a site of social interaction. One could meet the "right" people by joining the "right" church, but obviously church membership was not an option for Jewish women looking to acculturate but not assimilate. As a result, the primary intersection of Jewish and non-Jewish women's activities occurred in volunteer philanthropic projects. As Council vice-president Lizzie T. Barbe explained, philanthropy was the best way to bridge the gulf between Jewish and Gentile women because "when we get into the realms of endeavor, of trying to help, then we soon forget all our shadowy divisions. Need and want and sorrow know no boundary lines."[113]

Philanthropy accomplished through volunteer work was an especially effective means of acculturation. A declining birthrate, new technologies, and the availability of inexpensive domestic help meant that caring for the home did not require a woman's full-time efforts.[114] Idleness, however, was viewed as a character flaw, so women needed to find acceptable activities to fill their new-found free time. Voluntarism was respectable because it reinforced notions of woman as benevolent and nurturing, because it signified wealth, and because it had been adopted as proper by America's wealthiest women.[115] Outside of churches, the easiest place for women to participate in volunteer philanthropic work was women's clubs, and German Jewish women eagerly joined the secular women's organizations that would admit them as members. As they served side by side with Gentile women on hospital, library, or similar boards and auxiliaries, the boundaries did slowly begin to dissolve. Although Jewish women were never fully welcomed into "high society," their limited acceptance generated invitations to become members of some prestigious women's clubs, as exemplified by the invitations

Hannah Solomon and Henrietta Frank received to join the Chicago Woman's Club. These clubs are best understood not as parallel with men's fraternal lodges, most of which provided leisure time entertainment with other members of one's own class and ethnic group, but rather as parallel with men's paid labor. Just as the responsibility to earn a living was central to American definitions of manhood, women's clubs exemplified the best expression of True Womanhood.

Even when their philanthropic efforts became so sophisticated as seemingly to require participation in untraditional and even taboo activities, such as politics, women's clubs retained their attachment to "proper" womanhood by adopting domestic feminism.[116] If it was woman's duty to care for the sick, then she should be appointed to hospital boards and sanitation commissions. If it was a woman's responsibility to care for and protect her children, then she should also take responsibility for society's children. If that meant pressing politicians to implement a juvenile justice system, or running a summer camp, or going into the immigrant ghettoes to give parenting classes, then so be it. By using domestic feminism to justify social reform work, clubwomen were able to expand their sphere of influence outside the home without challenging traditional gender roles. Moreover, they were able to argue that this seeking of greater power in society was actually the duty of every responsible True Woman. As Rebekah Kohut summarized, "My sisters and I had always felt that while women's interests ought to begin at home and ought to end there, they need not necessarily confine themselves to it alone."[117]

NCJW's founders initially modeled Council's philanthropic efforts on the secular women's organizations to which they belonged (see Appendix A, Chart 20), embracing this domestic feminist philosophy in the process. Thus, unlike male-run Jewish philanthropies, which were founded in response to specific societal problems,[118] NCJW's philanthropy was undertaken as an expression of American and Jewish womanhood.[119] Council's philanthropy functioned as much to supply a previously absent female voice in the Jewish community and Jewish voice in women's clubs as it served to provide immigrant aid. So significant was it to Council's identity that even if there had been no poor Jews, Council would have made philanthropy central to its activities. The same cannot be said for male-run Jewish philanthropies.

Philanthropy as expression of American Jewish womanhood also produced several other features of Council philanthropy that differentiated its efforts from male-run organizations. First, NCJW took great pains to define its philanthropy as an expression of Judaism.[120] Though male-run organizations also would come eventually to see their work as specifically religious,[121] such a definition would not contribute to fulfilling the demands of American manhood, which rejected religious expression as too emotional to be appropriately masculine. It was not until after the turn of the century that male-run Jewish philanthropies began to question seriously the role of specifically Jewish content in their agencies.[122] For Jewish women, on the other hand, defining the act of philanthropy as a religious obligation provided a previously forbidden public role in Judaism without infringing on the traditional male domain of public religious ritual. Moreover, Council could justify its work as part of the long-standing custom for Jewish women (who often managed household finances) to offer "tzedakah"[123] to poor students or beggars. National board member Carrie Benjamin depicted "tzedakah" as the very essence of Jewish womanhood:

> Woman's fitness for the work of charity is emphasized throughout the old Hebrew writings. According to their idea the perfect woman must possess energy, strength of purpose and active zeal in ministering to the poor at her door, giving them her time, her trouble, her loving sympathy. She *may* open her mouth to wisdom, but her tongue *must* know the law of kindness. As the needle to the pole, so should a true woman's heart turn to deeds of charity. If man's proper study is man, woman's proper study is charity. This is the work that lies nearest her, and should be dearest to her. She herself was a gift of God's compassion for man, when God saw that it was not good for man to be alone. Hence she is an attribute itself of divine charity.[124]

While NCJW was founded to "renew Jewish womanhood" and "serve the best interests of Judaism," it is no coincidence that most of what the organization actually did was social reform and welfare work.

Because NCJW's charity work was undertaken as an expression of a religious ideal, not merely in response to a specific situation, Council emphasized that while it would always take care of its own, its programs would never be limited to Jews because "the problems of the general community are no less ours, and . . . they demand our whole-hearted interest."[125] The practice of serving all in need regardless of religion, ethnic background, or race had been common in disaster relief situations (like the San Francisco earthquake),[126] and for individual philanthropists like Jacob Schiff, but NCJW was a leader in making it standard organizational policy. This approach was based largely in the fact that women's social reform efforts across the United States emphasized the creation and improvement of public facilities providing health care, recreation, and education. Thus, unlike their male counterparts, Council women found themselves initiating campaigns to build parks and sewers or to install water fountains and garbage receptacles, all of which benefited the general public.[127]

Even Council programs directed at the Jewish community took a different approach than did those of male charities. Until NCJW was founded, no Jewish philanthropy addressed the needs of a national clientele. Jewish Federations and organizations like the United Hebrew Charities of New York City (UHC) served only a single metropolitan area. Because Council's outlook was national, it never faced the same dilemma as organizations like UHC, which attempted to preserve scarce local resources by encouraging Jews to settle elsewhere.[128] Nor did NCJW ever support suggestions such as that made by a spokesperson for United Hebrew Charities of Rochester that "all who mean well for the Jewish name should prevent them [Russian Jews] as much as possible from coming here."[129] For the women, such a position amounted to an abdication of the obligations of religion and womanhood. Several historians have noted that calls to prevent Jews from entering the United States changed with the passage of anti-immigrant laws in the 1920s, attributing the shift to "fraternal concern for the welfare of their Russian brethren in need of the asylum America could provide, and out of understanding that an attack on any segment of the Jewish community threatened the larger community as well."[130] Although these motives certainly fostered the change toward openness in the Jewish community, they should be evaluated in comparison to Jewish women's organizations, in particular NCJW, which had been pressing for such change for more than a decade.

Male-run Jewish philanthropies also differed from NCJW in that they did not develop any coherent program of legislative action to help their clients. Individual leaders, like Rabbi Stephen Wise, called for government intervention, but most organizations did not see active participation in politics as essential to their social welfare work. Council women, however, used philanthropy specifically to combine religious and political expression, in large part because as women they had few other means of participating as leaders in either politics or their religious community. In contrast, a man had the power of the vote and could exercise power by running for office (or in the Jewish community by becoming a rabbi). Thus men did not share women's need for social reform work as a pathway to participation in American public life.

That absence of need was demonstrated by the slow-paced adoption of Progressive stances by male-run Jewish philanthropies.[131] A few outspoken male Jews championed the causes of labor and social reform, but like Louis Brandeis and Jacob Schiff, they often focused on behind-the-scenes contacts, a method not available to most men and suggestive of a danger to the Jewish community requiring the cloak of secrecy. The prominent exceptions were Stephen Wise of New York City's Free Synagogue and Emil Hirsch. As early as the 1880s, Hirsch delivered sermons on behalf of rights for labor and women, against corrupt government, for prison reform and peace. Wise's most publicized efforts began with his first pulpit in 1900. But male organizations did not follow this lead until well after NCJW had established itself as an internationally recognized advocate of social reform. While the Central Conference of American Rabbis was generally sympathetic to Wise's and Hirsch's pleas for social justice, "many of its early efforts were timid and ineffectual because it did not have the experience, personnel, funds or even the mandate and structure to deal with the problems."[132] It did not begin passing social justice resolutions until the second decade of the twentieth century.[133] The Union of American Hebrew Congregations was similarly afflicted, sidetracked by internal debates over religious policy.

Even Hirsch's and Wise's positions were likely influenced by women's special attachment to Progressive issues. Both leaders counted significant numbers of Council women as supporters and congregants. Among Hirsch's followers were Hannah Solomon and Sadie American. Wise was aided in staffing the Hebrew School at his first pulpit by members of Council's Portland, Oregon Section.[134] In addition, as has been noted previously, many more women than men attended synagogue. Although it is impossible to know precisely why rabbis chose certain sermon topics, it is also impossible to deny the fact that those sermons were delivered to audiences composed largely of women.[135] It is likely that the rabbis chose to speak about certain issues specifically because they were of concern to women. This situation mirrored women's economic position, in which women exercised power indirectly as consumers. Of course, the real power lay elsewhere. Congregational grapevines would ensure that the men who controlled the synagogue purse strings heard the message, so despite female support, a rabbi might not dare speak on a topic he feared would offend his synagogue board. Nevertheless, rabbis like Hirsch and Wise built their reputations on taking radical stands. It was well within their characters to have risked male disapproval by articulating issues that had been of concern to Jewish women for several years.[136]

NCJW also stood out from other Jewish agencies in its development of a family framework for its philanthropic work. In both form and language, Council's social welfare programs reflected its emphasis on motherhood. Council women did not merely help families, they "adopted" them. They battled the white slave trade to protect immigrant "daughters." They shared their skills with immigrant mothers through parenting classes.

In addition to this family framework, NCJW was recognized by all Jewish agencies as the special champion of women.[137] That situation was left unchallenged in part because Council did such a good job and because many male organizations thought it appropriate that a woman's organization address women's concerns. This attitude did not in any way reflect Council's view of its own work. It serviced women's needs not because it limited its scope to its own sphere but because no other organization provided the necessary programs. At the 1908 Triennial Council reaffirmed this position, declaring: "the

Council and its Sections shall take up work not done by other associations and which at the moment is called for. . . . where there may be a crying need for some place of work, which no one else is ready or willing to take up, it should be done irrespective of sex."[138] This gap in services for women existed in large part because other Jewish agencies approached the family through male eyes. Expecting men to earn their family's keep, the male-run Jewish philanthropies acted as employment agencies for men, providing necessary training and contacts.[139] These organizations tended to address women's needs directly only if they became widows, when the agency could provide financial help as a surrogate male head of household. Council members, on the other hand, recognized that women needed to work out of economic necessity, and they tailored their vocational training to the specific demands of the female labor market.[140]

Council projects also emphasized direct contact with clients. The demands of the workplace meant that few Jewish men had the leisure to implement philanthropic programs themselves, so like their non-Jewish counterparts, they hired expert employees to conduct the work. Most Jewish men participated in philanthropy as donors or fund raisers—they had little, if any, face-to-face contact with the people they helped. Women, because they had more time than men, not only raised funds but actually implemented programs themselves.[141] Council members went into the homes of the needy, where they saw firsthand the problems confronting the poor in America. This personal contact inspired women to "undertake the task of humanizing the rapidly growing industrial society,"[142] which, in Council circles, translated into social reform work.

Council members were by no means exempt from the patronizing attitudes toward immigrants common in the German Jewish community, but their personal contact with those in poverty elicited a sympathy from Jewish women that their husbands sometimes found difficult to share. Like men's organizations, NCJW's Department of Immigrant Aid analyzed its work with statistics, but Triennial reports frequently were dominated by personal stories. The experiences of individual "friendly visitors" humanized the numbers and significantly influenced policy. For example, in 1926 NCJW commissioned a survey from the Bureau of Jewish Social Research to assess immigrant aid projects. Based on declining immigration statistics, the survey recommended that NCJW give up Ellis Island work. Several members spoke against the recommendation, prefacing their remarks with reference to their personal attachment to the work. The recommendation was rejected.[143] Where the personal experience of the many German Jewish men who had centered their lives in the work world and prospered confirmed the belief that any individual who worked hard enough could succeed in America,[144] women saw the details of personal circumstance that often kept the hardest-working, best intentioned people from breaking the barriers of poverty. As Anne Firor Scott has written, women as outsiders were able to provide a critique of the status quo not likely to come from men engrossed in the system.[145]

Perhaps the most significant result of Jewish women's face-to-face contact with the poor was the forging of a tenuous alliance with moderate labor groups such as the Women's Trade Union League (WTUL). When women looked for the causes of poverty, they frequently found that the business practices of their husbands, including seasonal hiring, low wages, and unhealthy working conditions were at fault. Chicago, where many Council members worked closely with Jane Addams, exemplified the potential for conflict resulting from women's concern.

Several Chicago members volunteered at Hull House and developed solid friendships with Addams. Hannah Solomon declared, "I consider Jane Addams the greatest woman of our century."[146] The affiliation with Hull House would become particularly problematic for one Council member, Sara Hart. In 1910 with the encouragement of the WTUL (to which many NCJW members belonged), the largely Jewish immigrant workers at Hart's husband's company, Hart, Schaffner, & Marx, went out on strike. Strike meetings were held at Hull House. Sara Hart, a frequent Hull House volunteer, heard the strikers' grievances firsthand. Unwilling to accept the strikers' picture of her husband as evil and greedy, she concluded that Harry was a fair man who had put executives between himself and his workers and had consequently lost touch with the realities of the workplace.[147] Convinced that the workers had legitimate grievances, she appointed herself unofficial representative of the strikers and asked Harry to give in to their demands. Harry, facing pressure from other businessmen who feared that any settlement would set a

Jane Addams (second from left) in 1933 wishing Hannah Solomon (second from right) a happy seventy-fifth birthday. Joining her was Fanny Brin (far left), then NCJW national president, and national secretary Mrs. Gerson Levi (far right). (Photo courtesy the National Council of Jewish Women)

precedent that would also bind them, refused. Sara continued volunteering at Hull House. We can only imagine the effects of this conflict on the Harts' marital relations—Sara does not recount such personal details. She does, however, describe her joy when, after several weeks of her own pleading and over the objections of other businesses, Harry decided to enter into arbitration.[148]

Sara Hart's situation illustrates the differences between the worlds of Jewish women and Jewish men. In another instance NCJW called for a boycott of stores, including some owned by Jews, where employees were treated poorly. Owners argued that they could not afford the sought-after changes. Assuming their lower-class clients would not shop at the same stores in which they worked, Council answered that if money was all the owners needed, its members would gladly pay higher prices. Rather than explore whether or not Council's concerns for these employees were valid, the *American Hebrew* printed a patronizing response that chided NCJW for being too idealistic, claiming it would learn with age and perhaps someday earn the right to be taken seriously.[149]

Though the *American Hebrew* may have approached Council's attempts at social reform condescendingly, history would prove women's organizations vital to the social reform movement. With their pressure to build parks, sewers, health programs, and the like, women's organizations changed the face of America's cities.[150] NCJW was able to lead the way in the Jewish community on Progressive social welfare efforts such as initiating preventive philanthropy, battling the white slave trade, and taking a national approach precisely because everything in the Jewish woman's world validated her choice to participate in social reform. It fulfilled American notions of womanhood, provided an opportunity for social advancement, and gave her otherwise unjustifiable access to power. Jewish men had no comparable reasons to support social reform, and in some cases, they had ample reason to believe it threatened their hard-won success.

As they became more aware of the horrors of persecution in Russia, as they faced increasingly more vocal immigrants and a growing Jewish labor movement, as they learned from their mistakes, and as they learned from NCJW's successes, German Jewish men, too, came to champion preventive philanthropy and build comprehensive national social welfare programs. By the 1920s, Jewish Federations, the Conference of Jewish Communal Service, the National Conference of Jewish Social Service, Jewish Family Services, and a myriad of similar organizations provided social welfare services. In fact, Jewish men donated hundreds of thousands of dollars to philanthropic causes, and the organizations they founded grew to overshadow NCJW both in numbers and in influence. Yet, though NCJW had not been the first Jewish organization to aid immigrants (who started arriving en masse a dozen years before Council was founded), subsequent Jewish service organizations borrowed heavily from Council's innovative methods. Many of these organizations still bear traces of Council-style philanthropy, and at least in part, all are the legacy of Council's renewed Jewish womanhood.

6.

The Rest of the Story

CJW would continue
its immigrant aid work well into the New Deal era. To facilitate this
continuation, Council developed contacts throughout Europe.
During World War I, it used those contacts to aid the efforts of the
Red Cross in providing humanitarian aid to civilians. Following the
war, many Europeans, including thousands of Jews, were displaced.
Council quickly mobilized its contacts to serve the needs of those
refugees. It sent Rebekah Kohut to supervise creation of a Reconstruction Unit to provide training, medical care, and hope to the
refugees so that eventually they might meet new U.S. immigration
requirements. Most important, Council began training European
Jewish women to carry on the work for themselves.

Sparking European Jewish women's activity was not new for
NCJW. In 1899, Sadie American attended a conference in London
during which she shared Council's self-education techniques.
Shortly after her visit, Jewish women in London organized their
own study circles and in 1902 founded the Union of Jewish Women
Workers.[1] In 1904, when Sadie American and Hannah Solomon
traveled to Europe as delegates to the International Council of
Women conference, they took along copies of Council's constitution in German translation. The Jüdischer Frauenbund was

founded later that year.[2] In 1923, as an outgrowth of their Reconstruction Unit, Council convened the first International Conference of Jewish Women (ICJW) and helped organize nine of its affiliates. As the ICJW's first president, Rebekah Kohut represented over a million Jewish women.[3] In addition, Council stretched its influence beyond Europe, establishing a Sheltering Home for Girls in Havana, Cuba, and informing Jewish women in several South American countries of white slave trade operations in their midsts.[4]

World War I also brought a series of American laws limiting immigration. The Johnson Act of 1921 and subsequent restrictive legislation did not immediately curtail the need for port work. Between 1920 and 1923 Council aided more than 65,000 immigrants, but by the middle of the decade the numbers would fall sharply.[5] The decreased numbers accompanied by increased hostility toward anything that might be construed as foreign or communist led many organizations to curtail their social welfare work in the immigrant community.[6] Council, however, continued its campaign to aid the needy, though it was careful to portray its efforts as counter to rather than in support of any "radical element." As the president of the New York Section observed, Americanization work took on new meaning because the presence of some communists in the Jewish immigrant community led some people to think that all Jews were dangerous "Bolsheviks." She called for Council members actively to defend their patriotism explaining, "We owe it to ourselves, to our people, and to our country to disprove such insinuation by the practice as well as the preaching of real Americanism."[7]

Eventually the decline in new arrivals allowed NCJW to lighten up on its dock work and concentrate on further development of programs it had initiated in immigrant communities. Council also continued its legislative fight against "anti-foreign prejudice."[8] Under the auspices of the League of Women Voters, Council representatives testified in behalf of the Cable Act before the House Committee on Immigration and Naturalization. NCJW also lobbied heavily for repeal of laws restricting immigration (see Appendix D). Despite Council's long record of support for America's democratic values, its continuing advocacy of Russian immigration propaganda led some government officials to eye the organization with suspicion and eventually to place it under FBI scrutiny.

Council was unaware of this scrutiny and used the resources and time freed by the decline in immigration to concentrate on strengthening the organization itself. The first step in this effort was identification of problem areas. Drawing on the Bible for inspiration, the Galveston Section humorously set forth its perception of the most serious challenges facing local sections:

Ten Commandments

1st. I am the Council who brought the Jewish Women before the eyes of the world—who opened the doors of Universal Service to Humanity.

2nd. Thou shalt have no other organizations before me. For I am a zealous body—desiring the co-operation of every individual member.

3rd. Thou shalt not hold lightly the obligations which thou hast assumed upon becoming a member of the Council of Jewish Women. For the Council will not hold thee guiltless shouldst thou fail her.

4th. Remember the Council Day to keep it surely. Many days hast thou for bridge, Mah Jong or movies—but the second Tuesday is thy regular meeting day, and on it thou shalt have no other dates.

5th. Honor thy Council, that the Council may forever be a power for good in the community in which thou livest.

6th. Thou shalt not withold [sic] thy dues or pledges from the Treasurer, but pay promptly, lest ye be dunned.

7th. Thou shalt not adulterate too much the business of the meetings, by side remarks to thy neighbor on extraneous matters.

8th. Thou shalt not be a kill-joy, nor a wet blanket, but enter heartily into any schemes for the filling of the Council's coffers.

9th. Thou shalt have no sidewalk conferences, but thou shalt fight it out in open meeting.

10th. Thou shalt not covet, even the Third Vice-Presidency, Chairman on Telephone, Rummage, or Home Economics, but serve in any capacity, however humble, for the good of thy Section.[9]

Circulated nationally, these "commandments" highlighted concerns that affected most organizations, like making meetings more productive, collecting dues in a timely fashion, finding volunteers to perform unglamorous tasks, minimizing interpersonal conflicts, and raising adequate funds. Named, as well, were several long-standing

Council problems, including competition with other organizations and with charm school–style entertainments. Other Sections reported tension between Reform and Orthodox members, a scarcity of qualified leaders (especially Jewishly educated leaders), and difficulty recruiting outside the small social circle that formed the core of the group. [10]

The national board responded by initiating a campaign to expand membership and thereby bring new energy into the Sections. It began publication of *The Jewish Woman*, a Council newsletter/magazine (in the 1940s renamed the *Council Woman* and currently called the *Council Journal*). It also undertook a major publicity campaign to see that its work was covered by the press. In 1923 the publicity committee reported that in the preceding three-year period, 7,957 articles had appeared in the Jewish press and another 10,900 had appeared in secular newspapers throughout the country. [11] The publicity campaign, the involvement of women in volunteer work during World War I, and Council's growing reputation for innovation and success all contributed to a significant increase in membership. Between 1920 and 1927, more than 15,000 women joined NCJW, taking its membership total from 36,500 to 51,000. This jump in membership reflected a similar trend in secular women's associations, whose popularity in America peaked in the years between the world wars. [12]

As with many other women's organizations, Council's growth came to an abrupt halt with the beginning of the Great Depression in 1929. [13] That year 9,000 women left the organization. Though understandably concerned, Council leaders did not panic. They lowered dues from $5.00 to $3.50, indicating that most Council members tightened budgets during the Depression, but they were far from indigent. [14] Council preserved its own resources by providing for the newly poor with programs already in place rather than by undertaking new projects. It reemphasized its nonsectarian approach to philanthropy, opening the doors of Council Houses to all those in poverty, helping with job placement where possible, and encouraging women with gardens to can surplus food, which it then distributed. Consistent with established patterns, Council focused on caring for needy children, encouraging them to continue their educations (rather than enter the work force) by providing free meals

THE·JEWISH·WOMAN

OFFICIAL ORGAN OF
THE COUNCIL OF JEWISH WOMEN

Vol. I No. 1   *October, 1921*

A NEW YEAR'S WISH

May God   May Its
Strengthen   Fulfillment
Every Noble   Bring Peace
Resolve In The To Womankind
Heart of Woman Everywhere

CIVICS

PHILANTHROPY

RELIGION

EDUCATION

"WHAT DOTH THE LORD REQUIRE OF THEE
BUT TO DO JUSTICE, LOVE MERCY AND WALK
HUMBLY WITH THE LORD THY GOD."

NEW YEAR'S   *NUMBER*
5682   1921

The cover of the first issue of NCJW's newsletter offers members a woman-identified Rosh Hashanah greeting. It also shows Council's motto and seal (bottom center), as well as what the editors saw as the pillars of Council experience: civics, philanthropy, religion, and education. The newsletter, after several name changes, now exists as the *NCJW Journal*. (Photo courtesy Jewish Division, The New York Public Library, Astor, Lenox, and Tilden Foundations) in public schools.[15] These efforts would be the "last stand" for most settlement houses, as respected movement leaders like Jane Addams passed away and government and private monies were withdrawn from programs that could be labeled "controversial" because they dealt with immigrant communities, which might harbor "subversives."

NCJW had been running many of these programs for more than thirty years. Although they required local volunteer efforts, they did not necessitate supervision by the national board. It turned its attention inward, looking for ways to improve Council's structure. In 1926 Council had funded an internal survey to determine how the organization could work more efficiently. By 1928 the board had begun implementing the recommendations of that survey. One of the most significant changes was the decision to centralize NCJW offices in New York City. Because immigrant aid work involved many cities, offices had been scattered across the country. The board decided that while the diversity placed national representatives in many places, thus making them more accessible, it impeded communication and was an unnecessary expense. Many local Sections retained their own Council offices, but except for the Washington, D.C. office, which coordinated Council's lobbying activities, all national functions were moved to New York.

Council also began to organize state and regional conferences, to share information more readily with those who could not attend national conventions and to facilitate cooperation between Sections in close proximity to one another. These conferences also provided increasing numbers of individual members with access to the kind of training previously available only at national Triennials. In addition, Council created regional and state board positions, forming a ladder that members could climb as they gained more experience in the organization, preventing boredom and frustration at being stuck in low-level offices. These new positions also provided an additional training ground for potential national board members. At the same time, they allowed members to serve in leadership positions without having to be on the national board. This step was especially important because the number of national board positions was limited, and as the organization grew, the percentage who could serve nationally would shrink. These structural changes allowed for Council's growth in the 1930s and beyond, but they did not address the uneven nature of that growth.

In the decade when Babe Didrikson symbolized the expanding boundaries of women's potential, and the best-known woman, Amelia Earhart, was famous because she disappeared, Council Sections continued to play very different roles in different communities. In some cities the Section was primarily a study or social club, leading several Jewish publications to list NCJW as a social organization along with groups like B'nai B'rith. Such listings, however, obscured Council's role in other locations, where it was a comprehensive social welfare agency or was easily mistaken for a synagogue sisterhood. Council's power and influence also varied by community. In many cities, NCJW representatives on community boards were often the only women's voices contributing to local decisions. Sometimes that voice was strong enough to act as a veto, or at least to prevent men from speaking for the entire community.[16] In other cities Council was viewed condescendingly as an elitist coffee klatch, undeserving of serious attention. This tremendous variation left a confusing public impression. Even in the Jewish community, a significant number of people were unsure of NCJW's purpose or what differentiated it from the organizations with which it frequently cooperated. In cities with small or no local Sections, NCJW was often invisible altogether. The national board did not offer a way to counter these consequences of diversity, and the problems caused by variations in Section practice persist today. Thus, though Council hoped its efforts to restructure would promote unlimited growth, the confusion produced by diversity would limit membership gains, and Council's numbers would quickly be surpassed by the more focused Hadassah. NCJW membership peaked around 100,000 in the 1950s and has remained fairly constant since then (see Appendix C).

Council's rebound in membership in the mid-1930s coincided with the rise of Hitler in Germany and the resulting resurgence of American Jews' interest in Judaism and Jewish history. European anti-Semitism sparked new immigration to America, and Council, which had never fully given up its immigrant aid work, quickly geared up to deal with the situation. It pressed for legislation to allow refugees fleeing Europe to enter the United States and provided comprehensive settlement and Americanization aid once the refugees arrived. This effort was not without its problems. Council's programs had been designed to accommodate poor Eastern European immigrants, not well-educated, middle-class Germans, leading to misunderstandings and in some cases hostility.[17] Nevertheless, most refugees expressed gratitude for Council efforts that, even as early as 1936, had provided services for more than 4,000 people seeking to escape the Nazi net.[18]

As the situation in Europe deteriorated, other Jewish organizations had also initiated immigrant aid programs, sometimes in competition with Council efforts. Conflicts between NCJW volunteers and paid social workers from other Jewish agencies were not infrequent. Professionals feared that female volunteers threatened their job security and prestige while also complaining that volunteers were incompetent.[19] In part, this conflict was eased by the 1934 merger of eighteen social service agencies into the National Coordinating Committee (NCC). "An office was opened in one room at the Clara de Hirsch Home and the NCJW lent the executive director of its Service to the Foreign Born, Cecilia Razovsky, to take charge. . . . This was the beginning of an organization which eventually developed into the second largest voluntary social agency in America."[20] Razovsky brought the skills and methods developed by NCJW to the new organization, effectively giving Council extraordinary influence over the development of Jewish social welfare work in the United States. She also instituted a training program for volunteers, most of whom were NCJW members, and acted as their supervisor, placing them in specific positions and assigning specific tasks.

The diversity and skill requirements of those tasks were impressive. Volunteers at ports of entry welcomed newcomers, acted as interpreters, helped fill out paperwork, provided meals, arranged for transportation to final destinations and made sure a greeter was at that destination, escorted immigrants to temporary shelter, explained immigration laws, and helped locate family members. Additional volunteers worked in communities across the United States to help new immigrants find housing, obtain necessities such as furniture and utensils, locate jobs or start businesses, learn English and American customs, get to places of worship and social gatherings, find medical care, and prepare for citizenship examinations. Many volunteers also helped with public relations work, acted as researchers, and served on policymaking boards of immigrant aid agencies. One Council volunteer found herself preventing murder when recently settled immigrants in her community recognized a newcomer as being a concentration camp informant.[21] Hundreds of NCJW members met the enormous challenges this volunteer work entailed, most earning the respect of the professional caseworkers with whom they cooperated.

Razovsky's organizational skills combined with the commitment of both volunteers and professionals to produce an effective organization, but though NCC performed its work successfully, the enormity of the emergency quickly overwhelmed the agency. To ease the overload, the National Refugee Service was created in 1939, but rather than complement the work of the NCC, it often competed for scarce resources. Once again, a merger solved the conflict, this time in 1946 to form the United Service for New Americans, an organization that would merge eventually with its international counterparts to form the United HIAS Service. Razovsky remained a major player throughout, but the various mergers did not always go smoothly. On several occasions other (largely male-run) organizations attempted to take over programs established by Council. They viewed NCJW's role in the coalitions as trainer and provider of volunteers to aid the paid staff of other member organizations. Council's leadership rejected this restricted view and rejected most attempts to supplant its immigrant aid programs, especially on the national level.[22] Ultimately NCJW won recognition as "the only agency at the time which followed through from reception on arrival to Americanization."[23]

NCJW was also one of the few American organizations informed of the secret settlement of Jews at Oswego, New York. There it shared expertise in the Americanization process. In addition to underwriting English classes financially, Council had a national network of personal and business contacts that enabled the organization to obtain basic supplies, scarce in wartime America.[24]

As it had after World War I, NCJW sent provisions to European refugees following World War II. In 1945 it instituted the Ship-A-Box program, a system of providing educational toys and materials to young European children and their teachers. In 1946 it established homes for girls in Paris and Athens, aided displaced persons in locating lost property and relatives, and offered college scholarships so that European Jewish students could study in America and then return to home communities desperate for social workers and medical personnel.

As Europe tried to put itself back together the Jewish community began the arduous process of trying to heal its wounds. A major step toward that healing was the creation of the State of Israel in 1948. Despite its Reform reputation, NCJW had never been anti-Zionist. Henrietta Szold's first public speech on Zionism was delivered before Council's Baltimore Section.[25] As on religious issues, Council's membership was divided on its opinion of Zionism and kept the subject off its agenda so that debate would not become divisive to the entire organization.[26] With the founding of Hadassah in 1913, those women who held strong pro-Zionist sentiments shifted their activity to the new organization. Until World War II, NCJW remained officially neutral, though individual Sections occasionally cooperated with Zionist groups.

In the emotional atmosphere of 1948, however, Council could no longer maintain its neutrality. NCJW never explored the deep theological justifications for the Jewish State, nor did it debate the issue. It did call for unrestricted Jewish immigration to Palestine after the war, and in 1946 Council resolved to support the creation of the State of Israel as a place of refuge and a source of general Jewish culture. All of Council's subsequent Israel programs focused on aiding the State's educational and childcare system, beginning in 1948 with the extension of the Ship-A-Box program to Israel. Within a year Council had raised the funds to establish a library for the School of Education at Hebrew University. Eventually NCJW would create Hebrew University's High School (1963) and the Center for Research in the Education of the Disadvantaged (1968). In 1972 it introduced the HATAF (Home Activities for Toddlers and their Families) program to train Israeli mothers in skills that would stimulate intellectual growth of their children. NCJW also pioneered the Home Instruction Program for Preschool Youngsters (HIPPY/HaETGAR), implemented nationally by the Israeli government in 1975. That project was followed almost immediately by the

This story hour at Beth Hayeled, a Council-sponsored model nursery school at Jerusalem's Hebrew University, typifies NCJW's focus on children and education in its many Israel programs. (Photo courtesy the National Council of Jewish Women)

kickoff of the MANOF program, a residential support service for delinquent adolescents. NCJW has continued its strong support for Israel in the form of funds for education, childcare, and cultural exchanges to foster the training of Israelis in the methods of social work and education developed by NCJW in the United States. Most recently, NCJW's Research Institute for Innovation in Education at Hebrew University in Jerusalem has focused its attention on aiding the settlement of Ethiopian Jews in Israel. Council's Department of Israel Affairs is one of its largest efforts, operating on a yearly budget in the neighborhood of $600,000.

Though most of Council's immigrant aid work focused on social welfare programs and physical aid to the needy, Council also examined the causes of displacement. In the turbulence of twentieth-century Europe, war was obviously a major factor, in Council eyes second only to anti-Semitism. NCJW founded its Committee on Peace and Arbitration in 1908 to study the causes of war and recommend a course of action,[27] more than a decade before other national Jewish organizations took formal action on the issue.[28] Under the indefatigable leadership of Fanny Brin, the committee placed articles on pacifism in Council publications, proposed resolutions calling for the outlawing of war, and brought the prominent Carrie Chapman Catt and Jeanette Rankin to give keynote addresses before Triennial assemblies.[29] As a result of these efforts, NCJW affiliated with several peace organizations, including the Women's International League for Peace and Freedom and the National Council for the Prevention of War. These affiliations would earn NCJW the label "un-American" from Congress's Dies Committee[30] and draw the attention of the FBI. Council briefly halted its peace work during World War I to avoid accusations that NCJW was unpatriotic,[31] but despite the Red Scare, the committee had resumed its efforts full-force by 1920.

In 1925, Council was one of nine American women's organizations to participate in a national conference on the "Cause and Cure of War." Its purpose was to discover the false assumptions that allowed the world to think of war as an appropriate means to solve conflicts. They developed a comprehensive outline detailing psychological, economic, political, and social causes for war.[32] Interestingly, Council never used arguments based on gender; that is, they did not attribute war specifically to the male psyche, nor did they suggest that women's capacity for nurturing made them natural peacemakers. This type of gender-based analysis would have complemented Council's vision of womanhood, but it cast men as an enemy and therefore was unacceptable. Though Council often cooperated with liberal women's peace groups, it remained silent on their warning that women's rights could not advance under threat of war.[33] Instead, Council supported its arguments for peace with Jewish texts provided by prominent social reformer Rabbi Abraham Cronbach of Hebrew Union College.[34] To NCJW, peace was a religious obligation, not an issue of feminism or woman's nature.

Though it recognized that a society must begin with peace education at the most elementary level, Council's choice of action emphasized legislative work. NCJW demanded that the United States endorse the World Court and the League of Nations, that it work to make war illegal under international law (including prohibiting the use of self-defense as a justification for military action), and that it tax war profiteers.[35] In cooperation with the Women's International League for Peace and Freedom, it supported the People's Mandate to Governments to End War and sought the ban of chemical and biological weapons, an end to compulsory military training at state colleges, and the passage of a law that would require a national referendum before the United States could declare war. NCJW also favored arms embargoes to nations at war and consistently pressured the government to reduce military budgets. Ironically, Congresswoman Florence Prag Kahn, a Council member, held office during the 1930s and might have acted as Council's advocate on these issues, but she represented a district with a strong military presence and opposed NCJW's position on military issues.

NCJW did much of its legislative lobbying through the Women's Joint Congressional Committee (WJCC). Affiliation with that group landed Council on the infamous Spider-Web Chart. Prepared by officials of the Chemical Warfare division of the U.S. Department of Defense, the chart graphically linked twenty-nine women's organizations in an effort to demonstrate their conspiracy to bring "International Socialism" to American shores. Circulated throughout the Red Scare era of the 1920s in government agencies like the FBI and

Henry Ford's notoriously anti-Semitic paper *The Dearborn Independent*, the Spider-Web Chart accused women activists of being communists, citing not only their peace work but also their social welfare agenda, including opposition to child labor.[36] Intimidated by the government document, the General Federation of Women's Clubs and the PTA withdrew from the WJCC, but NCJW's support for the organization's peace and social welfare policies remained steadfast.

With hindsight, it is easy to expect that Council's peace work would be undermined by the events of the Holocaust. Yet, Council never entirely relinquished its commitment to peace even at the height of World War II. A 1935 special edition of the *American Hebrew* on NCJW was also filled with stories of anti-Jewish repression in Nazi Germany, so NCJW was aware of the Nazi threat (though certainly not of the magnitude of that threat) well before the war began.[37] Council's first response was to explain the situation of Jews under Hitler as an outcome of the war, arguing that therefore Jews had all the more reason to do peace work.[38] In 1936, despite opposition by important moderates in the American Jewish establishment, Council lent full support to an economic boycott of Germany and called for the United States to withdraw from the Berlin Olympics.[39] As late as 1941, Council urged the U.S. government to remain neutral, recognizing that national defense was a legitimate concern but still believing there were realistic alternatives to fighting. Council urged the government to undertake "a study of those democratic institutions which we are preparing to defend" in the hopes that such a study would reveal ways to strengthen those institutions that did not require use of the military.[40]

Few Council records exist for the war years. Like the rest of the country, Council members seemed to have been consumed by the patriotic fervor ignited at Pearl Harbor. They grudgingly declared support for military aid to Europe[41] and actively served as Red Cross volunteers, air raid wardens, nurses, rationing board members, and the like. Yet, even after the war ended, and the horrors of Hitler's regime were revealed, Council never officially reversed its anti-war stand. Peace work would never again dominate Council programming, but the influence of Council's initial discussions would continue to surface in the organization's policies.

This 1947 poster, part of a typical NCJW exhibition display, illustrates the organization's pacifism, political involvement, and strong support for the United Nations. (Photo courtesy the National Council of Jewish Women)

As the Cold War set in, Council urged the government to combat communism by supplying the developing nations with economic aid rather than weapons, arguing that a satisfied populace would not succumb to Soviet takeover. They praised programs like the Peace Corps as exemplary of the alternative vision to militarism. NCJW was also a major proponent of the creation of the United Nations. Present at the UN's founding, Council took its status as official observer seriously, developing institutes and UN kits to help Sections educate members on international issues. Council maintained its tie to the UN through its accredited observer, a position held by Ann Robison from 1947 to 1960. Not surprisingly, NCJW has been a particularly ardent supporter of UN programs for children, even testifying before Congress in behalf of UNICEF.[42] Like much of the Jewish community, Council was forced to reconsider its support for the UN after the 1974 resolution equating Zionism with racism. Commitment to UN ideals, however, and an optimistic belief that the UN will become increasingly more effective in its pursuit of those ideals have led NCJW to continue its close relationship through its Non-Governmental Organization representatives.

As World War II came to an end and soldiers returned from Europe, America searched for stability. In the absence of the international political stability the war was supposed to have achieved, white America found constancy in the one area of life they could most directly manipulate: the family. Books like Farnham and Lundberg's *Modern Woman: The Lost Sex* (1947) popularized the notion that "normal" women desired only to be wives and mothers and that women who attempted anything else threatened the "natural" separation of gender roles on which the healthy family presumably depended. These were familiar and generally comfortable ideas to most Council members, and as the country turned its focus toward family life, so did NCJW. However, the organization found that its traditional area of emphasis, child welfare, was well covered. The baby boom produced not only children but also a variety of programs to serve those children. In the Jewish community, new suburban synagogues provided religious schools, and the movements with which they affiliated concentrated on developing the educational materials and personnel needed to run them. Council saw no point in duplicating existing efforts, so as most of

NCJW established America's first nationwide program of Golden Age Clubs in 1946. Here, a rhythm band is the source of social interaction and recreation for New York City senior citizens. (Photo courtesy the National Council of Jewish Women)

American Jewry was becoming increasingly child-centered, NCJW looked to other segments of the family. It found that the needs of the elderly had been largely ignored. To respond, in 1946 NCJW established its Golden Age centers, the first national program in the United States to provide recreation for seniors.[43] Council continued its efforts on behalf of the elderly by participating in the Meals on Wheels program in the fifties and by instituting the Retired Senior Volunteer Program in 1963.

In addition to witnessing the baby boom, postwar Americans also experienced a resurgence of religion. President Eisenhower made "In God We Trust" the country's motto, and unbelievers were associated with the atheism of the communist enemy. Jews consecrated themselves to denying Hitler a posthumous victory by joining synagogues in order to provide their children with a religious education. Council members also affiliated with synagogues, but they did not bring a renewed religious spirit to their own organization. Rather, most Sections came to function as civic clubs. The Madison, Wisconsin Section was typical. It held fund-raising events like fashion shows and luncheons and ran a thrift shop. These activities provided funds to support NCJW programs, such as Ship-A-Box, and local services, such as hosting holiday parties at the VA hospital (for which Section members furnished homemade favors). The Section also made significant financial contributions to the Madison General Hospital, local mental health programs, United Jewish Appeal, and education programs for the children of migrant workers. Other Section activities included sending clothes to Korea, running a revolving loan fund, conducting bingo games for hospital patients, supporting the Freedom Campaign against McCarthy and Madison's Clean-Up Campaign, and saving magazines to be sent to India to fight communism there. Self-education efforts continued through Council publications and speakers at the Section's monthly meetings. As one Section member remarked, "it's hard to distinguish between Council service and community service, the two merge so."[44] In other words, on a local level, Council was a civic group to which Jews belonged more than it was a Jewish group that did civic work.

Council's most notable change following World War II was an increasing sophistication in legislative work. The Holocaust underscored the importance of legal protection for minorities, leading NCJW to pay closer attention to the processes of government. Beginning in 1958 with the Council Leadership Training Program (CLTP), an effort to improve Council leadership on the local level, and continuing in 1963 with the School for Community Action, a program to train women in lobbying techniques, NCJW developed an intricate system of political action. To inform members about political events of import, NCJW published two newsletters, *Spotlight* and *Council Platform*. Each issue detailed a single piece of legislation under consideration by Congress. If Council had taken a specific position on a bill, such was noted with an explanation of the reasons for support or rejection. Most often, however, the newsletters ended with a series of questions intended to spark debate in local Sections, encouraging members to become aware of political issues and act in whatever ways their consciences directed. For editors of Section bulletins, Council also published a special newsletter, *Across the Nation*, that provided synopses of national news to be included in local publications.

Underlying Council's approach to legislation was the belief that self-protection for Jews required the protection of all minorities and the preservation of individual freedoms. In the 1950s NCJW viewed McCarthyism as the most serious threat to those freedoms. Council vociferously opposed any attempt to curtail free speech. Even after McCarthy was censured, Council's newsletter in an article with the ominous headline: "Are Your Phones Being Tapped?"[45] warned of the threat an interfering government could pose. Council publications also discounted the threat of communism, disassociating the philosophy from its supposedly corrupt practice by the Soviet Union. Council leaders were never called before McCarthy's committee, though unbeknownst to them, they were under surveillance by the Chicago office of the FBI.[46] Contained in that FBI file was a portion of a Council pamphlet, "Rightwing Retreat From Freedom," which had been read into the Congressional Record in 1962.[47] The pamphlet warned that right-wing Christian extremist groups were "reviving the McCarthy era of fear" by running so-called Anticommunist schools that encouraged vigilante action against "liberal campaigns." Such materials earned NCJW its reputation for political liberalism, a label that still applies.

NCJW members continued their fight to protect individual liberty by working as advocates for patients in mental institutions and by setting up halfway houses so those patients could be reintegrated into society.[48] That work, however, would be overshadowed quickly by the explosion of demands for Black civil rights at the end of the fifties. Though far from being without flaw, NCJW's track record on race relations compared favorably with most other women's organizations. Though it did not vocally oppose racist attitudes or attempts to exclude Blacks from women's organizations, neither did it support such racism, perhaps because racist expressions were often accompanied by anti-Semitism and because the absence of Black Jews in the United States meant that NCJW never had to debate whether to admit Blacks to their own organization. Council was also somewhat unusual in the degree to which it had cooperated with the Black community. In Chicago, it had joined with Black women's clubs under the leadership of Ida B. Wells to work briefly for civil rights in response to the city's race riots in the first two decades of the century.[49] In the 1920s, several local Sections donated funds to the Pro-Falasha campaign, despite debates over whether Ethiopian Blacks were actually Jews or not.

By the 1940s, the Holocaust had revealed to Jews the dangers of prejudice in an incomparable and starkly painful way. Council responded with increased resolve to work for civil rights in the United States. NCJW worked to abolish poll taxes that effectively kept Blacks from voting and, in 1945, was a member of the Coordinating Committee to Build Better Race Relations under the direction of Mary McLeod Bethune. FBI records also show Council as a member of the Civil Rights Federation. Such affiliations, though often limited to middle- or upper-class segments of the Black community, were not routine for women's clubs, though it is unclear how cognizant NCJW was of the degree of risk involved in such affiliations. For example, the FBI unjustly suspected the Civil Rights Federation of being a communist front, a promoter of espionage, and a threat to internal security, but there is no indication that Council members ever knew they were under investigation.[50] Still, some of the organization's positions clearly went against the grain of what most Americans had come to expect from an elitist women's club. Lest there were any who doubted the sincerity of Council efforts, the national board solidified its position in 1955 with a national resolution to support integration.[51]

Not surprisingly, individual Council members were not as free from racist attitudes as organizational resolutions might indicate, but the national board challenged them to think about whether "we are as open-minded as we pretend to be" and recognized that closer scrutiny of individual attitudes would disclose "a point where we each stop, beyond which we are unlikely to act on our principles." The Board then suggested that "We each need to move ahead to expand our area of action and personal commitment to civil rights."[52] Council's commitment to civil rights as a moral issue and as being in the best interest of Jews overpowered individual racism. Even Southern Sections, which reported some dissent over national civil rights policy, did not experience any substantial loss in membership.[53] Overall, though its analysis of racism did not extend to groups other than Blacks and though it did not argue for anything beyond equality according to white standards, NCJW was unwavering in its advocacy of civil rights legislation proposed by Black leaders.

Support for the Black community also led Council to focus once again on child welfare issues. Just as they realized that immigrant children needed help on many levels to overcome their poverty, so too they recognized that legal changes alone would not improve the life of Black children. Council members launched a comprehensive program to help the children of the ghettoes of the 1960s, from urban renewal to literacy programs. They fought for improvements in public schools and turned over ownership of several of Council's old settlement houses to the Black community. They also launched a campaign to ensure improved treatment for domestic workers, most of whom were Black women.[54] It is perhaps a further indication of how deeply liberal Jews related to the civil rights struggle and associated it with their own self-interest that despite the lack of Jewish content in Council work of the 1950s and 1960s, NCJW was given the William J. Schroder Award by the Council of Jewish Federations and Welfare Funds for "superior achievement in the advancement of social welfare."

As the turbulence of the 1960s spilled into the 1970s, NCJW briefly resumed its peace work by opposing the Vietnam War.[55] Its primary emphasis, however, was not on the strength of America's foreign policy but on the strength of its families. In 1972 Council commissioned the "Windows on Day Care" report, America's first survey on the quality, effectiveness, and availability of day care facilities. NCJW followed that report with a 1975 survey of the juvenile justice system and moved from there to programs designed to detect and prevent child abuse. Council acted on the surveys by testifying before Congress in an effort to spark government action. It also founded the NCJW Center for the Child in 1985. Thus far the Center has involved more than 1,000 volunteers in a three-faceted program to improve childcare, help working mothers, and assist abused children. [56]

The emphasis on programs for children would continue throughout Council's history. A 1951 headline in Council's newsletter proclaimed, "We Give Child Welfare Top Priority." [57] In the 1960s, Council's major civil rights program was an attempt to boost the quality of education received by ghetto children. In the 1970s, NCJW would be among the first American organizations to address the needs of abused children and battered wives.

Council's efforts on behalf of children in the 1970s were accompanied by a reconsideration of what was in the best interest of mothers. In the mid-1950s, Jews joined other upwardly mobile Americans in the flight to suburbia. Suburban women, many with college educations, often pursued careers until they married (or until they finished putting their husbands through school), and then dropped out of the work force to bear and raise children. By the 1960s, many of these women were beginning to discover that the happiness promised by the "Dick and Jane" family was missing from their lives. Betty Friedan, a Jewish woman with much the same background as NCJW members, gave voice to this disillusionment in her classic book, *The Feminine Mystique* (1963). Like women's club leaders before her, Friedan told women to return to adult intellectual pursuits as a counterbalance to days spent speaking only to toddlers, urging women to get involved in the world outside the home through career or politics. The women who took Friedan's advice were labeled second wave "feminists." They demanded increased political rights, equal pay for equal work, the right to choose abortion, and an opportunity to succeed in America parallel to that available to men. Theirs was not a movement to topple American economic and political systems but a fight for the right to participate in those systems.

In Friedan's suburban context it was possible to see NCJW as a feminist organization. For nearly eighty years Council built itself on the need for women to act both in and outside of the home. Several years prior to the publication of Friedan's work, NCJW reprinted the text of a speech by Mrs. Theodore Wedel, Deputy Director of Volunteers for the American Red Cross. Council members enthusiastically received the address because Wedel reminded her audience that activities outside the home made a woman "a more interesting person to come home to." Wedel also cited the importance of a woman's outside activities to the well-being of her children, noting: "Modern psychology tells us that probably more American children—at least in the middle class—are harmed by over-possessive and protective mothering than by neglect. Yet, if a woman has no interest in life except her children, how can she help becoming possessive?"[58]

According to NCJW, volunteer work was an integral part of a high standard of motherhood. Council consistently exacted the highest professional standards from its volunteers and leaders. One member described the results of a 1950s Council leadership course in terms strikingly similar to Friedan's encouragement of women to speak their minds, recalling "how timid little women, mousey, seemingly afraid to open their mouths, emerged from our 12-week courses strong, out-going people, with firm convictions—real leaders."[59] The success of these local workshops led NCJW to initiate the Council Leadership Training Program in 1958.

NCJW was far from the only organization vying for the time of Jewish suburban housewives, but unlike PTAs and local charities, NCJW programming encompassed international issues and encouraged thought and debate over the political events of the day. A remarkable number of Council leaders in the 1950s reported that what initially attracted them to the organization was the high level of discussion at meetings. Viola Hymes, National President from 1959 to 1963, first joined NCJW because "although it was wonderful to be a young bride, there was one thing I really missed—being part of a lively and stimulating group of like-minded people."[60]

Another Board member declared, "There's nothing I enjoy more than sitting down with a group of intelligent women, with strong opinions on important social issues, and thrashing out a program of action." She found NCJW's "diverse program so interesting and useful and its leaders so full of stimulating ideas, that [she] decided to devote [her]self to Council" instead of to her career as a professional accompanist.[61]

Both these women were typical Council leaders. They had college degrees, worked before marriage, raised children, and participated in Council events primarily when their children were at school. They joined NCJW because it offered much of what Freidan claimed was lacking in women's lives. Council valued a woman's educational training, encouraged her to stretch intellectually and to apply her talents to solving issues of great social and political import. It offered high-quality leadership training and provided a place for the woman to act as a leader once she completed that training. It taught her the "ins and outs" of the national political machine, involving her in lobbying efforts and political organizing. Council's top leadership testified before Congress and the United Nations, rubbed shoulders with dignitaries, and met regularly with their counterparts in other national and international organizations.

In the early 1960s, NCJW even seemed to be a leading proponent of feminism's political agenda. After participating in President Kennedy's 1962 Commission on the Status of Women, NCJW was convinced it needed to reconsider its stand on the Equal Rights Amendment. Several major organizations, like the General Federation of Women's Clubs, had already voiced support for the legislation, and NCJW joined the Commission cautiously, believing that it had been organized to put through the Amendment.[62] In fact, the opposite was probably true, but the information made available to Commission members and the discussions that ensued served as a kind of intensive consciousness-raising session. By 1970, Council members had concluded that preservation of women's individual liberties was more important than any benefits that might come to women through protective legislation, and they resolved to support passage of the ERA. That resolution has been reaffirmed by every national convention since 1970.

NCJW was also an early supporter of woman's right to choose abortion, seeing the issue as an extension of their support for birth control, Planned Parenthood, and efforts to combat poverty. Today NCJW approaches abortion as a matter of individual liberty and of health. Some NCJW work in this area has been recognized nationally, such as Jeri B. Cohen's establishment of the Women's Emergency Network. Supported in part by her home Section in North Dade, Florida, the fund helps poor women pay for abortions not covered under restrictive federal Medicaid policy.[63] In 1989, NCJW President Lenore Feldman affirmed her organization's position in a speech before hundreds of thousands of pro-choice supporters at the Washington, D.C. "March for Women's Equality/ Women's Lives," and in 1992, Joan Bronk did the same in her role as NCJW president. Council work also has included exposing bogus clinics[64] and keeping an eye on legislation that might limit woman's right to choose. The key to Council's support for abortion rights and the ERA was its addition of individual liberty arguments to its history of domestic feminist arguments. This addition was essential to the organization's continued success in the 1970s and 1980s because it allowed NCJW to value motherhood while also valuing pursuit of a career, an increasingly common choice among Jewish women.

Despite Council's feminist veneer, it did not bill itself as a feminist organization, and Council women still hesitate to label themselves feminists. At the end of the 1980s the national board members considered Council's program goals to be in the best interest of women, and all were committed to achieving equality for women, but most noted that in many Council circles, the term "feminist" carried negative connotations. Because many women saw early feminists as opposed to motherhood, a significant percentage of Council's membership opposed any association between NCJW and the term "feminism." That Council virtually ignored calls to move the 1977 convention out of Virginia because the state had not yet ratified the ERA exemplified the conflicts between Council ideals and its policies.[65]

There is still no agreement within NCJW about how extensive a feminist agenda should be. Some Sections still address members according to marital status and husbands' first names, an issue first

In the last two decades, Council members have taken on many feminist issues. On the left, members demonstrate in support of the Equal Rights Amendment. On the right, 1989 NCJW president Lenore Feldman (right) and Anna May Ross deliver 16,000 pro-choice petitions to Attorney General Richard Thornburg. Earlier, Feldman had addressed several hundred thousand marchers at a pro-choice rally in Washington, D.C. (Photos courtesy the National Council of Jewish Women)

debated in 1896.[66] Other Sections have initiated active campaigns to support civil rights for lesbians, despite opposition from other regions that see the issue as peripheral to or in conflict with NCJW goals. Historically, Council has been committed to obtaining rights for mothers, but it has not been interested in making critiques on notions of womanhood that center on motherhood. The extent of Council's future feminist agenda will depend largely on how far it is willing to stray from this agenda.

In addition to the challenges of feminism, the 1970s also brought a renewed focus on Judaism. It would be inaccurate to say NCJW was ever a secular organization. At every convention at least one leader has risen to implore women to pay more attention to religious observance. Council consistently promoted American Jewish culture, endowing the first scholarship for the study of American Jewish life (now administered by the National Foundation for Jewish Culture), providing Jewish books to public libraries, and sponsoring lectures and conferences on topics of Jewish interest. It repeatedly pressed for higher standards in Jewish education, demanding and sometimes funding the adoption of the most modern facilities, materials, and teaching methods.[67] Just as Council insisted on professional training for social workers, it demanded training and proper pay for religious school teachers.[68] Council also attempted to assist teachers by introducing into religious schools the concept of "mothers' meetings" (now referred to as PTAs)[69] and by encouraging Jewish observance in the home. Through its newsletter, NCJW initiated a dialogue on how best to help Jewish children understand Christmas and on how far public school celebrations of Christmas could or should go before Jews object. Some Sections acted as a local welcome wagon, bringing new families in the community a challah and flowers on their first Sabbath in their new home. Such programs were pushed into the background in the 1950s and 1960s perhaps because members' religious needs were met by the growing number of suburban synagogues.[70]

In the 1980s, Council's religious goals were strikingly similar to those expressed in 1896. The following are NCJW's 1987 resolutions in the area of Jewish Life:

> The National Council of Jewish Women believes that Judaism bequeaths to every Jew a rich legacy of ethical and religious values, a

cultural heritage and a strong sense of individual, family and community responsibility. Transmitting this legacy through education and implementing its principles strengthen Jewish identity, the Jewish community and our commitment to Jews throughout the world.

We Therefore Endorse and Resolve to Work for:
1. The unity of the Jewish people by promoting mutual respect and understanding among all branches of Judaism.
2. Jewish community support of   ,
    a. Quality Jewish education by encouraging and supporting life-long study of Jewish religion, history, culture, and contemporary issues.
    b. Programs for Jewish individuals and families in need of services.
3. Strengthening the Jewish identity of youth through educational and social programs in the community and on the college campus.
4. The study of the Holocaust as part of the regular curriculum in all schools.
5. The acceptance and participation of women in all phases of Jewish life.
6. Rabbinic reinterpretation which will eliminate inequities experienced by women under Jewish law.
7. The elimination of anti-Semitism.
8. The attainment of religious and cultural freedom and the human rights of Jews wherever they are denied or abridged.[71]

With the exception of resolutions #5 and #6, NCJW's position on religion has come full circle. Council is still dedicated to unifying the Jewish community (#1), to supporting religious education for adults (#2a), and to combating assimilation by providing quality religious education to youth (#3). It still defines community and social action as religious expression (introduction and #2b), and as do all Jewish organizations, NCJW continues to be concerned about eliminating anti-Semitism and the discrimination against Jews which inevitably results (#7, #8). Finally, NCJW continues to think about how it can teach non-Jews about the Jewish community (#4).

Significantly, Council's religious work has returned to its foundations at a time when the Jewish community is again deeply divided and when the feminist movement has again suggested that feminists can solve problems that have thus far gone unsolved by men. Just as in the 1890s, when ignorance of Judaism acted as a common denominator between Jewish women from various backgrounds, leading them to participate in study circles, modern feminism has united women from different denominations in questioning Judaism's teachings on womanhood. Council has found it can encourage that questioning, using feminism as a common ground without favoring one interpretation over another. In the 1980s NCJW sponsored the Jewish Women's Resource Center and several conferences on Judaism and sexism. Unlike its turn-of-the-century religious policies, Council now unhesitatingly backs diverse efforts to make Judaism egalitarian, whether through support for the ordination of women, independent efforts to develop nonsexist liturgy, or Orthodox feminist attempts to improve the conditions of divorced women within a *halakhic* (Jewish legal) framework.

Though the national board attributes Council's religious resurgence to grassroots interest, the return has also been helped by circumstance. In an effort to attract working women to the organization, Council moved its national conventions from weekdays to weekends. That meant the convention had to provide in some way for Sabbath observance. Conventions now regularly begin with Sabbath dinners and include services written and conducted by members. Issues on which most Jews agree, including support for Israel and Soviet Jews,[72] have also provided a common ground on which women from diverse Jewish backgrounds could begin religious dialogue.

Heading into the Twenty-First Century

As in other women's organizations, Council's greatest immediate challenge is to find ways to appeal to young women. Demographically, the available pool of Jewish women has shrunk over the past generation. At the same time, more Jewish women are entering the work force, effectively limiting the time they might devote to volunteer work. In contrast to the decrease in potential members is the increase in membership options open to women. Major Jewish organizations, like the United Jewish Appeal, once exclusively male, are now beginning to accept women in their higher ranks. These factors make it likely that competition to recruit Jewish women for voluntary work will continue to be stiff for several decades.

To meet this challenge, NCJW has begun to add to its traditional programming in significant ways. Council has not de-emphasized its programming for Israel, for children, or for political change, but all its programming has been infused with modern feminist thought. In addition to supporting basic feminist issues, like ERA and the right to choose abortion, Council has begun to develop a notion of equality that requires taking on traditionally male roles. This approach is distinctly different from Council's tradition of domestic feminism, which emphasized expansion of the responsibilities of motherhood but insisted on a clear separation of gender roles.

Council's 1985–87 Biennial Report provides an example of the new philosophy. The title of the Report, "Women in Power," was explained by Sandra Goldberg in a slide show presentation designed to circulate among local Sections:

> Many of us have been loath to aspire to power because we see it in a negative context. The difference between men's and women's view of power is best illustrated by training sessions I've conducted. In one part of the session, we play the "values game." Values like "happiness," "love," and "power" are marked on cards and given to the participants. They can trade them or discard them—according to how much they want each value. When the participants are women, the card marked "power" is usually discarded, left over, unwanted. No one wants power. When the participants are men, the power card is the first card everyone wants! There is a lesson we can learn from men. The ability to have and use power is essential—it is vital if we are to act on our beliefs and use our influence to change minds and lives.[73]

Goldberg's scenario tells much about Council and where it is headed. As in NCJW's history, there is a clear recognition that men and women live in significantly different worlds. Yet, rather than finding sources of power in women's traditional roles, Goldberg suggests that Council women must adopt traditionally male values if they expect to achieve their goals. The implicit assumption here is that Council's onetime dependency on influencing others is not working and must be replaced by the exercise of direct power. This position is consistent with Council's attempts to work within American systems rather than topple them. The irony is that what Council once viewed as a threat to the system, namely, women's entrance into traditionally male domains, it now sees as less radical than the idea that true power lay outside the system altogether, in the supposedly female values of "happiness" and "love."

One consequence of Council's new approach is its support for women in the work force. Although NCJW still places a high value on motherhood, it no longer sees raising children and pursuit of a career as mutually exclusive. Council has accompanied this change in attitude with concrete actions designed to attract working women, like adjusting meeting times to fit work schedules. In 1989, NCJW volunteers conducted a national survey of pregnant working women that demonstrated the importance of supportive supervisors to employees with children. Borrowing from long-standing practices once reserved for fraternal organizations hoping to appeal to heads of households, NCJW offers members life insurance and credit opportunities. In 1986, NCJW was the first Jewish women's organization to offer its members a credit card. Council's advertising campaign for its MasterCard Gold Card emphasized the opportunity for women to establish their own credit histories independent of husbands' incomes. In an innovative move, a Council task force on voluntarism suggested that Sections keep "Personal Career Portfolios" to document members' skills and activities, which can then be used to provide job references.[74] The transition from volunteer work in NCJW to paid careers is no longer unusual, perhaps sparked by such success stories as Mara Guilianti, mayor of Hollywood, Florida, who gained political acumen serving as NCJW's Florida State Chair for Public Affairs.[75]

While courting the increasing number of working women, Council has had to take care not to alienate its nonworking members. This delicate balance is illustrated brilliantly by excerpts from the text of the final segment of the "Women in Power" slide show:

> Women in power—they hold gavels and microphones—
> they hold babies and they hold purse strings . . .
> Women in power—carry doctor's kits and sewing kits . . .
> Women in power—fix cars and they fix dinner . . .
> In Council eyes, homemaking and pursuit of career are
> both worthy of glory in equal measure.

The major programming change brought by Council's concern for attracting new members is self-help programming. For most of its history, NCJW has been an organization of volunteers helping clients. Led by efforts in Los Angeles, several local Sections have begun a transformation into "women's centers," offering as many (if not more) programs for Council members themselves than programs for others.[76] Such programs include support groups and counseling for divorced women, single parents, and substance abusers. Now, in addition to implementing a Golden Age program, for example, NCJW offers information to aid members caring for elderly parents. Along with advocating better public health programs, Council provides workshops on combating health problems which Council members themselves are likely to face. In its most recent budget, expenditures for "Services to Members and Sections" nearly equaled funds spent on "Program Services."

This shift in programming has not come without dissent. To some longtime members it is an anathema for Council members to be both deliverers and recipients of Council services. Nor has the change taken place uniformly across the country. One leader explained that Council fosters such deep attachment to its programs that it is often difficult for women to let go and move on to something new.[77]

The new emphasis on programs to benefit members also fails to address two important problems facing NCJW. The first problem is one of image. For nearly a century, Council has been depicted as an elitist organization. This reputation is so pervasive it has even seeped into American Jewish fiction. In Jo Sinclair's *Wasteland*, the working-class protagonist is jilted by a wealthy young woman whose parents stereotypically expect her to marry a professional. He later reads a newspaper announcement that the woman has been elected president of the Junior Council of Jewish Women, which he interprets as a confirmation of her snobbishness. [78]

In part, the reputation of elitism is based on reality—Council members always have been counted among America's wealthiest Jews. Following the pattern of many American Jewish organizations, wealth has been an important factor in determining Council's leadership. [79] In many cities, the higher your rank in the organization, the more money you are expected to give. [80] Council has done nothing to alter significantly this pattern, which limits leadership positions to those who can afford them. It is possible that this situation might not seriously hurt the organization. As more women return to the work force, they have more funds at their disposal. Wealth, however, does not guarantee quality leadership, and continued exclusion of women who cannot match contributions in time with contributions in dollars could put the organization in a precarious position. As long as Council members are expected to demonstrate wealth through substantial donations, Council's reputation as an elitist organization will not abate.

The second problem is also a financial one. Given the high level of skills required to hold Council office and administer its programs, it has become increasingly difficult to draw the line between volunteer and paid positions. As more members bring skills to the organization from the workplace, and as more members seek paid positions, the determination of which jobs NCJW can expect members to perform voluntarily and which it will pay for becomes increasingly complicated. To date, NCJW has developed no clear guidelines on what types of Council work should be compensated, nor has it determined who should make that decision. It also has yet to establish a clear policy on the hiring of members over outsiders for Council positions.

In contrast to these troubling issues, Council's strength is highlighted by the traditional benefits it offers to members. For example, in a society that is often alienating and isolating, especially to people who are single or divorced (an increasingly common situation for Jewish women), Council provides a sense of community. In addition to providing lifelong friendships, Council has programs that offer the equivalent of graduate-level training in social work and political science. Thus it offers a member (who usually has a college degree) an opportunity to further her education as well as providing a place that values and encourages use of the education she already has. Council's national clout and strong record of achievement also provide members with a sense of accomplishment.

Ultimately, Council sells itself by giving the members a sense of self-worth. As one newsletter article summarized, "there should be nothing startling in the ego-centered conviction that Council gives a woman top returns on . . . the investment of self. . . . In exchange for precious capital of energy and time, the Council woman collects priceless returns of self-knowledge, growth, skill, confidence and the well-being which is the by-product of creativity and usefulness."[81] This emphasis on individual worth has proved to be moderately successful in attracting women to Council.

In the last several decades Council's membership has hovered around 100,000, with a national budget of approximately $3.5 million.[82] As throughout Council's history, some cities have stronger Sections than others, and that pattern is not likely to change. At its centennial, NCJW continues its struggle to strike a balance between willingness to experiment and adherence to old ideals. As in the past, Council's future will likely be determined by how skillfully its leadership can walk that tightrope.

Appendixes

APPENDIX A

The Women

HO were the women who molded Council in its early years? If one accepted Council's depiction by the turn-of-the-century Jewish immigrant press, NCJW was an elitist club of wealthy German women who, if they practiced Judaism at all, practiced the bare minimum of ritual common among Reform Jews. This perception was rooted in resentment by Eastern European Jewish immigrants toward all American Jews who offered paternalistic aid to the newcomers. Because the immigrants were hardly an unbiased source, it was necessary to investigate the accuracy of their perception.

The policies and character of NCJW were shaped by its leaders. Therefore, investigation began by exploring, in detail, the lives of 200 national and local board members. Although this exploration led to certain numerical conclusions, it was conducted as a biographical study rather than a formal statistical analysis. The board members were divided into two categories. Group A was most active in Council's first twenty years, 1893–1913. Group B was most active in the subsequent twenty years, 1913–1933. Such a division was necessary because 1913 marked a major transformation of Council's focus from religion to philanthropy, and it was important to determine whether this change was accompanied, or caused by, a change in the makeup of the organization's leadership.

The process of choosing which women to examine began with the compiling of names from reports, minutes, convention proceedings, and Council newsletters. Of approximately 700 names of board members collected, over 400 were eliminated immediately for lack of adequate data. Several other factors narrowed the remaining field to 200. Care was taken not to have any single Section or any geographical region grossly overrepresented. In particular, several names from New York City were eliminated. This Section is still slightly overrepresented in the sample, but because the New York City Section did the yeoman's share of Council's work at Ellis Island, and because that immigrant work was one of Council's major projects, the slightly high numbers reflect New York's extraordinary influence on Council rather than give a false picture of Council's leaders.

Information on the subjects frequently came in clumps according to family. So, if data were available for one family member, they were also likely to be available for other family members. One theory I hoped to test was that NCJW was made up of a small network of relatives, either by blood or through marriage. So as not to skew the results in favor of this theory, I eliminated many names of those with obvious relatives in Council.

I also eliminated the names of many women who were married to rabbis. In most cities, the wives of prominent Reform (and occasionally traditional) rabbis were active in NCJW. Because they were married to public figures, information on their lives was frequently available. Thus, an inordinate number of rabbis' wives made the first cut. While their influence was extremely important, these women were not the majority of Board members, and I did not want the sample to indicate otherwise.

The names of the 200 who survived the cuts and the Sections to which they belonged are listed in Charts 1 and 2. A variety of sources provided information on these women, most importantly, *Who's Who in American Jewry* (1926, 1928, 1938). Subjects provided their own biographies to this publication, so I considered it the most accurate. To supplement this source I consulted the *American Jewish Yearbook*, obituaries, memoirs, letters, census records, newsletters, and a variety of periodicals and newspapers. The results of the survey largely confirmed early perceptions of Council members.

Several factors indicated the German heritage of the women in Group A. Seventy-nine percent of Group A were born in the United States prior to the influx of immigrants from Eastern Europe. Another 11 percent were born in Western Europe (see Chart 3). In addition, most of their surnames, both maiden and married, are Germanic rather than of Eastern European origin. Actual parentage was difficult to determine, but of those for whom information was available, only 7 percent were born in Eastern Europe, compared to 18 percent of German or Sephardic heritage (see Chart 4).

The heritage of Group B was more difficult to ascertain. Eighty-three percent were American born, but unlike Group A, it was impossible to determine when the parents of Group B had arrived in the United States. Again, surnames indicated German background, and affiliation with Reform synagogues also indicated descendance from the earlier wave of immigrants. Still, 11 percent of Group B were born in Eastern Europe, so while the group was dominated by women from German families, those from Eastern Europe constituted a significant and growing minority (see Chart 3).[1] However, these Eastern European members were not from the ranks of Council's poor immigrant clients. As Council itself described, "among the colonies of Russian Jews there residing, there are always a few who have the leisure, refinement and education which would guarantee them as desirable members of our organization."[2] The class standing of these Russian women matched that of their German counterparts and did not significantly change the character of the organization.

The image of Council women as genteel married ladies was also, for the most part, accurate. Most members of Group A were between the ages of thirty and sixty (see Chart 5). Most of them married in their twenties and were married before they joined NCJW (see Chart 6). In 1900, only twenty-six of the subjects in Group A were single, and ten of those later married (see Chart 7). At least half of the married women were raising an average of 2.34 children while they were active in Council (see Chart 8).

The picture for Group B is slightly different. Like Group A, Group B tended to marry in their twenties. Only 8 percent remained single.

This reduction in unmarried leaders contradicts general American trends for college-educated women, whose rate of singlehood was usually double that of noncollege women.[3] More than twice as many of Group B than Group A graduated from college, leading one to expect more, not fewer single women (see Chart 12). The high marriage rate is likely due to the entrance of many single women into professions like teaching and social work. Unlike most of their married sisters, single women often needed to earn a living. Many single Jewish women were employed as social workers or teachers by NCJW, and several were members, but the demands of full-time jobs made it unlikely that they would hold leadership positions in the organization. In addition, Council's endorsement of the community's expectation that all Jewish women would marry and its emphasis on motherhood were more attractive to married than single women.[4]

The 78 percent of Group B who were mothers bore an average of 2.17 children while they were active in Council. However, the average age is almost ten years younger than Group A, with most between the ages of twenty and fifty. This discrepancy in ages is due to the creation of Junior Sections, which included teenagers in their membership. In smaller towns, Junior and Senior Sections were actually combined, so that women in their late teens and early twenties could have served on the adult Section board.[5] In addition, the Junior Sections familiarized girls with Senior Section activities and provided sure acceptance into the Senior Section at the time of marriage. For many of the women in Group A, Council simply did not exist in their early years of marriage. The high percentage of married leaders with children in both groups would foster Council's emphasis on renewing Jewish motherhood.

Not only were most Council leaders married, but they were married to economically successful men. For both groups, occupational information was available for only half the spouses, but of those studied, all worked as professionals or in business (see Chart 11).[6] Though exact figures were difficult to obtain, there were ample indicators that Council women were economically well off. They frequently formed the core of their city's elite Jewish social club (like the Ravisloe Country Club in Chicago), a significant minority attended private schools, many reported having servants,[7] and their publications highlighted fashion, travel, and upper-class cultural events.[8] Few women in the study had to work to earn a living, and 63 percent of Group A and 75 percent of Group B had the luxury of being full-time volunteers (see Chart 9). Those who entered the labor force did so in acceptable upper-class positions. Some ran family businesses in lieu of absent husbands or fathers. Others were writers, or entered social work or educational positions through their Council activities. A few were professionals.

In addition to being well off, Council leaders were also well educated. In Group A, over 80 percent of the women completed at least a high school education with 20 percent earning bachelors or advanced degrees.[9] In Group B the figures are even higher. Over 90 percent of Group B completed high school, and 54 percent went on to complete college or earn advanced degrees (see Chart 12).[10] The higher numbers for Group B are attributable to the growth of America's public schools and the late nineteenth-century proliferation of colleges open to women.[11] As economist Julie A. Matthaei noted, women's pursuit of higher education in the mid-1800s was an outgrowth of the movement to make homemaking into a science.[12] Because Council women strongly backed this "modernization" of domesticity, it is not surprising that they pursued higher education when it became available. College education was an expensive undertaking, and its pursuit was also consistent with German Jewish desires to enter America's upper class. The percentage of Council women attending college seems to be high, but comparative figures for the general Jewish community or for comparable classes of non-Jewish women are not available.[13]

Despite their high level of secular education, few Council leaders had formal religious training.[14] Two indicated private studies with rabbis and at least five attended synagogue religious schools, but most women did not list attendance at religious school among their accomplishments (see Chart 13). While slightly more than the 11 percent of Group A and 8 percent of Group B may actually have received some formal instruction, the women clearly did not view religious education as a significant part of their lives. The few who displayed knowledge of Bible or Hebrew tended to be daughters of rabbis and, no doubt, were taught in their homes. Even Hannah Solomon admitted that most of Council's founding members were woefully ignorant of the tenets of Judaism.[15] Given the lack of qualified teachers and adequately funded religious schools in the United States before Council's founding, the deficiency of Council leaders' religious education is not surprising.

Though their Jewish education may have been lacking, Council leaders' commitment to the Jewish community was not. In addition to their Council activities, 65 percent of Group A and 52 percent of Group B served on the Board of another Jewish organization (see Chart 17). These other organizations included charity federations (where the women might be official representatives of NCJW), hospitals, lodges, and similar groups. In addition, many Council leaders staffed religious schools and contributed articles of Jewish interest to Jewish and secular publications, usually without pay (see Chart 10).

Council women were also active in synagogues (see Chart 16). Information on synagogue membership was available for 63 percent of Group A. Of those, only 2 percent did not belong. In Group B, all of those for whom information was available were synagogue members (75 percent). In both groups, roughly two-thirds of the women who belonged to synagogues affiliated with Reform institutions,[16] but a significant minority, 13 percent of Group A and 20 percent of Group B, affiliated with more traditional synagogues.[17] Though Reform practice would clearly dominate Council activities, the traditional minority was vocal and would consistently force Council to examine its approach to religious issues. The minority was also strong enough to block financial support for Reform institutions, as in 1916, when it defeated a proposal to celebrate NCJW's twenty-fifth anniversary by donating a building to Hebrew Union College.

One interesting observation is that information on synagogue membership was not available for the single women in either group (with the exception of Rose Brenner). It is impossible to determine whether single women really stayed away from the synagogue, viewing it as a family affair, or whether single women's participation was simply not recorded because most synagogues recognized women only through the membership dues their husbands paid.

Likewise, single women's participation in synagogue sisterhoods was difficult to assess. However, 34 percent of Group A and 41 percent of Group B did participate in sisterhoods (see Chart 14). This percentage is quite high considering that sisterhoods, especially in their early years, competed with NCJW for members, resources, and money. Sisterhood membership, however, symbolized commitment to one's synagogue, and NCJW's high membership rate in sisterhoods was a further sign of their allegiance to these religious institutions and sometimes to the individual rabbis who led those institutions.

Somewhat less appealing to NCJW members was membership in Hadassah. Only 8 percent of Group A and 21 percent of Group B were members of Hadassah (see Chart 15). That this Zionist organization was not founded until 1912 accounts for the extremely low percentage in Group A, especially because at least 18 percent of Group A considered themselves Zionists (see Chart 18). Of Group B, 24 percent declared themselves to be Zionists. These figures hovering around 20 percent seem to be an accurate reflection of Zionist sentiment within Council prior to World War II. This relatively low number (compared with figures near 100 percent today) likely reflects the influence of the rejection of Zionism by many Reform Jewish leaders at the turn of the century.

In addition to their Jewish affiliations, Council leaders were also active in secular organizations, especially women's organizations. Chart 20 lists some of those groups. These organizations depended on voluntarism and were composed largely of upper-class, gentile women and were a ticket to respectability and acceptance in the eyes of many Jewish women. The most popular groups were the General Federation of Women's Clubs and the League of Women Voters. These groups were politically neutral, a safe alliance for Jews hoping to avoid controversy and its potential for anti-Semitic backlash. Few Council members belonged to suffrage organizations, though many professed sympathy for the cause (see Chart 21). Overall, at least 71 percent of Group A and 82 percent of Group B belonged to one or more secular organizations.

Like many of the secular women's clubs, NCJW was made up of a network of women who participated in non-Council activities together and knew each other well. At least 16 percent of Group A and 23 percent of Group B had relatives in Council (see Chart 22). However, because obvious family groups were eliminated from the study, and because it was impossible to trace all relations through marriage or distant blood relatives, it is likely the actual percentages were much higher.[18]

Council leaders were also a mobile group. Thirty-eight percent of Group A and 49 percent of Group B were active in a Section other than in the city of their birth (see Chart 23). Many more subjects lived in another city for a significant length of time but later returned to the city of their birth. The connections to Jewish women in many cities would be crucial to the rapid establishment of Sections in those cities in Council's early years.[19]

Many Council members also had shared membership in local organizations before they joined the local NCJW section. Though data on this question were insufficient to draw conclusions for Group B, at least 24 percent of Group A belonged to a local Jewish benevolent society, lodge, sewing circle, or literary society before they became members of Council (see Chart 19). Frequently, these local groups gave up their independent status, and the entire group would become a Council Section.[20]

A clear picture of Council leaders emerges from this survey. They were married with children, well educated, and economically well off. Most were German Jews—all were devoted to the survival of Judaism in America. That devotion was equaled by their devotion to Council itself. Most remained active in NCJW for more than a decade, many giving a lifetime of service.

Chart 1: Subjects of Study—Group A
NCJW Leaders: The First Twenty Years, 1893–1913

Sadie American	Carrie S. Benjamin
Esther M. Andrews	Meta P. Bettman
Miriam K. Arnold	Sarah Bienstock
Jeannette L. Arons	Madeleine Borg
Harriet Asher	Frances A. Cohen
Sophie Axman	Jessica Cohen
Minnie Baldauf	Mary M. Cohen
Goldie Bamber	Nina Morais Cohen
Reba C. Bamberger	Alma D. Cowen
Lizzie T. Barbe	Dora Cohen Davis

Jeannette I. Davis

Emma Eckhouse

Julia Eshner

Theresa B. Ezekiel

Lottie Feibelman

Julia Felsenthal

Leah R. Fielding

Jane B. Fischel

Ida Zenobia Frazier

Isabella Freedman

Stella Freiberg

Hanna Friedenrich

Hattie Friedenthal

Ida Weis Friend

Bird Stein Gans

Jeanette Goldberg

Rosa H. Goldenberg

Edna Goldsmith

Lillian Goldsmith

Selina Greenbaum

Belle Loeb Hanauer

Janet S. Harris

Rachel H. Hays

Laura B. Hurix

Anna Hillkowitz

Fanny B. Hoffman

Belle Levy Johnson

Rebecca R. Judah

Hattie Kahn

Rachel L. Kauffman

Fanny Kempner

Rose Kohler

Rebekah Kohut

Alice Z. Lazaron

Kate Levy

Alice Lewi

Sarah M. Lewis

Belle Loewenstein

Miriam D. Louis

Bertha Lubitz

Babette Mandel

Louise Mannheimer

Jean Wise May

Grace Mendes

Annie Nathan Meyer

Fannie S. Miller

Marion Misch

Laura Mordecai

Belle L. Moskowitz

Maud Nathan

Carrie Oppenheimer

Seraphine Pisko

Ernestine S. Prager

Bella Ney Printz

Jennie F. Purvin

Henrietta Radzinski

Bertha Rauh

Hattie Rauh

Julia Richman

Myra Frank Rosenau

Pauline Rosenberg

Esther Ruskay

Julia Scheeline

Emma W. Schloman

Flora Schwab

Hattie H. Sloss

Hannah G. Solomon

Rosa Sonneschein

Flora Spiegelberg

Pauline Steinem

Sara Messing Stern

Rosetta Stone

Hennie Strouse

Carrie Taubenhaus

Sadie T. Wald

Isabel R. Wallach

Cassie Ritter Weil

Esther Weinshenker

Bella Aub Wiener

Dora K. Wile

Subjects of Study—Group B
NCJW Leaders: The Second Twenty Years, 1913–1933

Nima H. Adlerblum
Mrs. Benjamin L. Abraham
Ella Kahn Alschuler
Rose Haas Alschuler
Grace Baer Bachrach
Miriam Epstein Bamberger
Florence Dorfman Banen
Dorothy Walter Baruch
Corinne Bernheimer Bauman
Helen Berkman Blumenthal
Berthe Weil Born
Rose Brenner
Sylvia Freehof Brenner
Fanny Fligelman Brin
Mollie Rothenberg Brudno
Fannie Dushman Budson
Bessie Schwartz Cohen
Reba Blustein Cohen
Bessie S. Cone
Miriam Marlin Cosel
Sadie J. Crockin
Ida Davis
Sadie Eichenbaum
Ethel Rose Feineman
Irma Cain Firestone
Sayde Gorchov Frankel
Rosina Mandelberg Freedman
Lillian A. Myers Freund
Henrietta Schwartz Fried
Blanche Pearl Gilman
Clara Stern Gilman
Blanche Bauman Goldman
Edith Joseph Goldsmith
Luba Robin Goldsmith
Rebecca Fischel Goldstein
Rosa Zuckerman Goldstein
Rose Z. Goldstein
Reva B. Gordon

Flora Woog Hart
Jennie Hecht
Madeleine Stiefel Heilbrunn
Adele Bluthenal Heiman
Rosalie Nathan Hendricks
Bertha Beitman Herzog
Hannah Hirshberg
Sara Sarason Jackson
Dorothy C. Kahn
Sayde Ascheim Kantrowitz
Sadie Fischel Kass
Rosalie Heller Klein
Florence Frank Kohn
Sally Oram Krauss
Marion S. Kreiner
Rose Fink Krohn
Eleanor Klein Lapowski
Florina Lasker
Loula Davis Lasker
Sadie Braham Lefkowitz
Lizzie Davies Levenson
Elma Ehrlich Levinger
Jeannette Victor Levy
Minna T. Livingstone
Sadie R. Loewith
Evelyn Kate Aronson Margolis
Esther Epstein Marowitz
Rose Lillian Marvin
Blanche Strauss Marx
Edna Rice Meissner
Mosette Levaur Morganstern
Josephine M. Munchweiler
Blanche Beitman Ottenheimer
Nettie Podell Ottenberg
Tamar de Sola Pool
Cecilia Razovsky
Nannie Ashenheim Reis
Belle Zemansky Reynolds

Eva Halpern Robin
Sophia Moses Robison
Rosalind Labovitz Rosenbloom
Phoebe Jane Ruslander
Frances Mary Schermer
Yetta Baumgarten Schoenfeld
Sara X. Schottenfels
Rosalind A. Schwab
Bertha Gottlieb Shane
Anna Silberman Shapiro
Rachel Frank Skutch
Sonia Cheffetz Smith

Clara Rosenfeld Sommerfield
Constance Sporborg
Estelle M. Sternberger
Sadie Fraley Stix
Birdye Spier Stodel
Lillian Johanna Strauss
Anne Dorothea Sugarman
Beatrice I. Sulzberger
Elsie K. Sulzberger
Rachel Hays Sulzberger
Julia Swett
Carrie Stein Weyl

Chart 2: Section Membership of Subjects

	Group A	Group B
Albany, NY	1	
Atlanta, GA	1	
Augusta, GA	1	
Baltimore, MD	2	6
Boston, MA	5	
Bradford, PA	1	
Bridgeport, CT	1	
Brooklyn, NY	2	5
Charleston, WV	1	
Chattanooga, TN	1	
Chicago, IL	11	3
Cincinnati, OH	4	2
Cleveland, OH	5	3
Columbus, OH	2	
Dallas, TX	1	
Dayton, OH	1	
Denver, CO	5	
Detroit, MI	1	
Duluth, MN	2	
El Dorado, AK	1	
El Paso, TX	1	
Hartford, CT	1	

(continued)

Chart 2: (continued)

	Group A	Group B
Houston, TX	1	
Indianapolis, IN	2	1
Jamaica, NY	1	
Kansas City, MO	3	1
Lafayette, IN	1	
Little Rock, AK	3	
Los Angeles, CA	2	2
Louisiana, MO	1	
Louisville, KY	2	1
Milwaukee, WI	1	
Minneapolis, MN	1	3
Mt. Vernon, NY	1	
New Castle, PA	2	
New London County, CT	1	
New Orleans, LA	1	
New York City, NY	23	18
Peoria, IL	1	
Philadelphia, PA	6	4
Pittsburgh, PA	6	3
Portland, OR	1	
Providence, RI	1	
Richmond, VA	1	
Rochester, NY	1	
San Antonio, TX	1	
San Francisco, CA	2	2
Savannah, GA	2	
Seattle, WA	1	
Spokane, WA	2	
Springfield, MA	2	
St. Louis, MO	3	5
St. Paul, MN	1	
Trenton, NJ	1	
Toledo, OH	1	
Utica, NY	1	
Vancouver, Canada	1	
Virginia-Eveleth, MN	1	
Waco, TX	1	

(continued)

Washington, D.C.	2	1
Worcester, MA	1	2
Yonkers, NY	1	

Region	# Sections	# Members
NORTHEAST	11	18
MIDWEST	11	15
SOUTH	2	7
WEST	5	9

Chart 3: Place of Birth

Place	Group A	Group B
United States	79	83
Western Europe	11	2
Eastern Europe	6	11
Other	1	2
Unknown	3	1
Of U.S. born members, those born in major urban center	58	56
	73.7%	67.46%

Chart 4: Parents' Birthplace

	Group A	Group B
United States	2	insufficient
Western Europe	14	data
Eastern Europe	7	
Other	2	
Unknown	75*	

*The majority of these have German, rather than Eastern European, surnames.

Chart 5: Date of Birth

Group A

Year of Birth	Age in 1900	#
1820–29	71–80	1
1830–39	61–70	1
1840–49	51–60	3
1850–59	41–50	20
1860–69	31–40	38
1870–79	21–30	20
1880–89	11–20	6
Unknown		12

Group B

Year of Birth	Age in 1920	#
1850–59	61–70	2
1860–69	51–60	2
1870–79	41–50	15
1880–89	31–40	34
1890–99	21–30	31
1900–09	11–20	7
Unknown		9

Chart 6: Age at First Marriage

Age	Group A	Group B
17–19	5	6
20–25	31	55
26–29	7	13
30–35	4	3
36–39	1	2
40	1	0
Unknown	33	13

	Chart 7: Marital Status	
	Group A	*Group B*
Married	61	88
Widowed	12	4
Divorced	1	0
Single	26*	8

*Ten of these women were single in 1900 but later married.

Chart 8: Children

In Group A, at least 43 women had children. Information was unavailable for another 34 women. The remaining women were single.

In Group B, 78 women had children with information missing for only 2 subjects.

# of Children per Mother	*# of Mothers*	*# of Mothers*
	Group A	*Group B*
0	*6*	*11*
1	*11*	*16*
2	*11*	*27*
3	*11*	*23*
4	*5*	*7*
5	*2*	*4*
6	*2*	*0*
7	*1*	*1*

Average # of Children per Mother: Group A: 2.34; Group B: 2.17

Chart 9: Occupation (full-time)		
	A	B
Artist/Musician	1	2
Business	1	4
Cleric	5	1
Educator	6	7
Government Appointee	2	0
Librarian	1	0
Physician	2	2
Politician	1	0
Professor	0	2
School Administrator	5	0
Social Worker	2	5
Writer/Journalist	6	2
Volunteer*	63	75
Unknown	5	0

*Of the volunteers, approximately 10% of each group worked before marriage, but not after.

Chart 10: Work in the Jewish Community (Volunteer or Paid but Part-time)		
Served as religious school principal or teacher	15	5
Wrote on Jewish subjects	16	6
Director or staff for Jewish organization	8	10

Chart 11: Husband's Occupation

	Group A	Group B
Architect	2	1
Builder	1	0
Business	11	5
Finance	1	3
Jewish Professional (rabbi, cantor, etc.)	7	6
Lawyer/Judge/Politician	9	13
Physician/Dentist	6	10
Professor	1	1
Unknown	46	52
Related to Jewish Professional		
wife	7	5
daughter	9	2

Chart 12: Education

Highest Level Achieved	Group A	Group B
Elementary	1	4
High School or Finishing School	38	19
Some College	22	18
College, Graduate Degree, or Advanced Fine Arts Training	21	54
Unknown	18*	5

*All but 4 of these had at least an elementary school education, but information on further schooling was unavailable.

Chart 13: Formal Religious Education
(Other than in Council Study Circles)

	Group A	Group B
Yes	11	8
No		
Unknown	89	92

Chart 14: Synagogue Sisterhood Membership

	Group A	Group B
Member Synagogue Sisterhood	34*	41**

*10 belonged to Reform groups, 4 to traditional
**30 belonged to Reform groups, 10 to traditional
Note: none of the single women belonged to a sisterhood

Chart 15: Hadassah Membership

	Group A	Group B
Member Hadassah	8*	21

*Hadassah was not founded until 1913.

Chart 16: Synagogue Membership

Yes	61	75
Reform	48	55
Traditional	13	20
No	2	
Unknown*	37	25

*Most single women fall into this category.

Chart 17: Activity in other Jewish Organizations

	Group A	Group B
Board Member other Jewish Organization (hospital, orphanage, lodge, federation of charities, etc.)	65	53

Chart 18: Commitment to Zionism

Zionist	18	24
Anti-Zionist	2	
Unknown	80	76

Chart 19: Member of Jewish Organization Prior to Joining NCJW

Yes	24	insufficient data
Benevolent society	14	
Lodge (Order of Eastern Star, True Sisters, etc.)	6	
Literary society	2	
Sewing society	3	

Chart 20: Secular Affiliations		
	Group A	*Group B*
Member Woman's Club:		
Yes	71	82
Unknown	29	18
Civic	53	72
Social	33	36
Professional	9	21
Specific Organization:		
Big Sisters	2	2
Consumers League	7	3
Council of Women		
(national or international)	5	1
Federation of Women's Clubs		
(general or international)	26	19
Girl Scouts	1	5
International League		
for Peace & Freedom	5	6
League of Women Voters	10	27
Mothers Congress/PTA	4	6
Red Cross	4	12
WTUL	1	1

Note: This list is representative, not comprehensive. It is likely that many more women participated in or gave money to these or similar organizations, but did not list such affiliations in sources available to the author.

Chart 21: Support for Woman Suffrage		
Suffragist		
(member of suffrage		
organization, published		
pro-suffrage articles,		
delivered pro-suffrage paper)	9	2

Note: Most members seemed to be sympathetic to the struggle for suffrage, but they did not join suffrage organizations.

Chart 22: Relatives in NCJW		
	Group A	Group B
Yes	16	23
Daughter	3	0
Daughter-in-law	0	1
Mother	3	3
Mother-in-law	0	2
Sister	7	5
Sister-in-law	3	0
Other	2	14

Chart 23: Section Member in Location Other than Place of Birth (Of U.S.-born members only)		
Yes	38	49
No*	41	33
Unknown	3	3

*Moving to a suburb of the city of birth counts as a "no." Additionally, many of the "no's" lived in another city for a significant period of time but later returned to their place of birth.

Biographical Sketches

Fanny Rosenberger Adler. Born in Kansas City. Graduate of St. Mary's College (Davenport, Iowa). Secretary of committee that planned the 1893 Jewish Women's Congress. Married Henry Adler. They had one son. Lived in Chicago where she was a visiting nurse for Associated Jewish Charities and president, Chicago Young Ladies Aid Society in the 1890s. Members of this group were Jewish, but their work was exclusively civic, such as providing penny lunches to schoolchildren. Member of Woodlawn Women's Club, Women's League, Personal Service Society.

Ella Kahn Alschuler. Born 16 September 1880 in Mattoon, Ill., to Carrie (Kaufman) and Felix Kahn. Educated at University of Chicago. President, NCJW Chicago Section, national board member (1923–26). Married Judge Samuel Alschuler (1923). Served on Cook County Civil Service Committee, Chicago-Winfield Tuberculosis Sanitarium. Director of Service Council for Juvenile Court Girls. Member of National Conference of Social Work, American Association of Social Workers, Women's International League for Peace and Freedom, League of Women Voters, Woman's City Club, Congregation Kehilath Anshe Ma'ariv (Reform).

Sadie American. Born 3 March 1862 in Chicago to Amelia (Smith) and Oscar L. American. Educated in Chicago public schools. Also received some religious education and taught at the Reform Temple Sinai Sunday School (1894–99). NCJW founder, its first national secretary, president of the New York City Section, and inspiration behind NCJW's immigrant aid work. Also known for founding Chicago's vacation schools, playgrounds, and juvenile court, for fighting the white slave trade, and for peace work. Helped found London's Jewish Study Society (1899) and Union of Jewish Women Workers (1902) and the Jüdischer Frauenbund (1904) in Berlin. Board member of numerous organizations, including the Council of Women of the U.S. (1895–1904) and the New York Consumers League (1895–1906). Frequent speaker at national and regional conventions of women's organizations. Papers published include two on vacation schools and playgrounds in the *Journal of Sociology* (November 1898 and January 1899). Died 3 May 1944 in New York City.

Esther M. Andrews. Born 15 December 1861 in Manchester, England, to Rebecca (Vogel) and Marcus Myers. Education in public and private schools, including some coursework at Radcliff College. Married Julius Andrews (1881). They had one daughter. Served on NCJW national board 1902–08, was national chair for Council Juniors (1909), and president of Boston Section for eleven years. Also legislative chair of Mass. State Federation of Women's Clubs. Appointed to several Mass. government advisory boards: Minimum Wage, Prison, War Council Commission. Appointed by Governor Alvan T. Fuller as first woman on Mass. Governor's Council. Trustee of Boston Psychopathic Hospital. Volunteer probation officer. Member Business and Professional Women's Clubs, Republican Party, Council of Women and Children in Industry, Committee on Appointments in Public Service.

Lizzie T. Barbe. Born 1856 in East Liberty, Ohio, to Caroline Frances Hamlin (a Quaker) and Colonel Marcus M. Spiegel (a Civil War hero). First cousin to Hannah Solomon (whose mother was Marcus' sister). Family had two black servants, one of whom

Barbe described as an older sister. Educated in Akron, Ohio, and Chicago. Married Martin Barbe (1876). Had two sons and two daughters. NCJW founding member, longtime national officer, and board member of Chicago Section (president 1902–05). Conducted NCJW's Vacation Sewing School. Officer of Jocannah Lodge-United Order of True Sisters; secretary of Hebrew Union College Auxiliary; president of Temple Sinai Sisterhood and active in National Federation of Temple Sisterhoods; board member of Jewish Training School.

Carrie Shevelson Benjamin. Born 1861 in Russia (other sources say Poland). Came to U.S. as child. Mother Anne Shevelson's father was rabbi. Educated in public schools and Syracuse University (1881). Read paper at 1893 Jewish Women's Congress "Woman's Place in Charitable Work—What It is and What It Should Be." Also read paper at first convention (1896). First president of NCJW Denver Section. National chair Alpha Phi Sorority (1883). Taught high school in Syracuse. Married Maurice Benjamin (1890). They had three children (Maurice, Barets, and John). Founder of Denver Woman's Club. Appointed by governor to Colorado Board of Charities. Returned to New York City at turn of century and, with sister, established the Benjamin Deane School for Girls, which she headed until 1926. Died 26 December 1951.

Rose Brenner. Born 3 April 1884 in Brooklyn to Louise (Blumeneau) and Jacob Brenner (a judge). Earned B.A. from Adelphi College (1908). While in college, her mother died, and she cared for five younger siblings. Remained single, though had lifelong companion, Fannie R. Cohen. NCJW Brooklyn Section president (1912–18); national vice-president (1915–16); national president (1920–26). During her presidency, national membership went from 30,000 to 52,000. Served on Brooklyn School Board. First woman on executive board of trustees of Beth Elohim Temple (Brooklyn) and past president of its sisterhood. Died suddenly on 5 April 1926.

Fanny Fligelman Brin. Born 20 October 1884 in Berlad, Roumania, to Antonette (Friedman) and John Fligelman. Immigrated to U.S. when she was three months old. Phi Beta Kappa graduate of

University of Minnesota (1906). Married Arthur Brin (manufacturer, Brin Glass) in 1913. They had three children. NCJW national president (1932–38). Also national chair of Committee on Peace and Arbitration and president of Minneapolis Section. Best known for her peace work. Worked with Carrie Chapman Catt to found National Committee on Cause and Cure of War (1923), renamed Woman's Action Committee for Lasting Peace (1942). First woman on Minnesota State Teachers College Board. Appointed by Eleanor Roosevelt to Women's Committee to Aid Social Service Work. Served as alternate consultant to U.S. delegation to conference at which United Nations was founded (1945). Member College Women's Club, Woman's Club of Minneapolis, League of Women Voters, Women's International League for Peace and Freedom, Hadassah, American Association of University Women, National Conference of Christians and Jews. Grandmother of Rabbi Deborah Brin, Canada's first female rabbi. Died 4 September 1961.

Mary M. Cohen. Born 26 February 1854 in Philadelphia to Matilda (Samuel) and Henry Cohen. Educated in Philadelphia private schools. NCJW founding member, national and Philadelphia Section board member. Corresponding secretary for Jewish Publication Society. Superintendent of Mickve Israel Religious School. President, Mickve Israel Association, Hebrew Sunday School Society. Follower of Sabato Morais and committed to Orthodox Sephardic practice. Published fictional short stories, articles on religion and on social economy. Sometimes wrote under pen name "Coralie." Was first woman to read a paper before the Philadelphia Social Science Association (1884), to which she was inducted. Founder of Browning Club (1888), New Century Club. Member of Contemporary Club, Fairmount Park Association Board of Directors, Pennsylvania Museum and School of Industrial Art. Worked for seven years as private secretary to editor of *American Journal of Medical Sciences*. Also known as a talented artist, woodcarver, stenographer, and teacher.

Nina Morais Cohen. Born 6 December 1855 in Philadelphia to Clara (Weil) and Rabbi Sabato Morais. Educated in Philadelphia public schools. Married lawyer Emanuel Cohen (1885). Household employed two female servants. Organizer, president (1894–1907) and Study Circle leader of NCJW Philadelphia Section. Frequent contributor to Jewish and secular press. Completed father's work on the prophet Jeremiah for JPS. Delivered lectures on Ibsen, Dante, and Homer as well as on Jewish subjects to Jewish and Christian audiences. Supported suffrage. Died 19 February 1918.

Alma D. Cowen. Born 13 December 1872 in Kalamazoo, Michigan, to Bertha (Schuster) and Bernard L. Desenberg. Educated at University of Michigan and Kalamazoo College. Longtime NCJW national board member and Chicago Section president (1911–16). Was one of the national officers who traveled the country speaking and helping to organize many Council Sections. Married Cook county Judge Israel Cowen (1897). They had two children. Served as vice-president of National Federation of Temple Sisterhoods, president of Kehilath Anshe Ma'ariv Sisterhood, and trustee of the National Jewish Hospital (Denver). Also active in Chicago Committee for Palestinian Welfare. Served as president of local PTA (1920–25) and League of Religious Fellowship (1919–20). Member Chicago Woman's Club.

Julia Felsenthal. Born 1867 in Chicago. Daughter of Rabbi Bernard Felsenthal. Member of the original planning committee for the 1893 Jewish Women's Congress. Spoke at that event on "Jewish Religion in the Home." NCJW national chair of Committee on Religion (1894–95). Worked as religious school teacher and superintendent, social worker and settlement house resident. Director, Associated Jewish Charities of Minneapolis. President, Chicago Section-Conference on Jewish Women's Organizations. First president of Minneapolis chapter, Hadassah. Member, Women's International League for Peace and Freedom. Died 22 October 1954.

Ray (Rachel) Frank. Born 10 April 1866 (other records say 1864/65) in San Francisco to Bernard Frank, an Indian agent who claimed descendancy from the Gaon of Vilna. Educated in California's public schools and University of California-Berkeley. Sat in on courses at Hebrew Union College, but never sought ordination. Founder of NCJW, speaker at the Jewish Women's Congress, and frequent speaker at subsequent Council events. Helped organize

Oakland Section (1895). Worked as teacher, journalist, and orator. At a time when women rarely occupied Jewish pulpits, Frank preached regularly in synagogues throughout the West and Midwest, and refused many requests that she stay on as rabbi. Opposed woman suffrage, though once women had the vote, organized Champaign, Ill. League of Women Voters. Married University of Illinois Economics Professor Simon Litman (1901). Her activities on campus evolved into University of Illinois' Hillel. Helped found Champaign's first Reform temple and its Hadassah chapter. Died 10 October 1948.

Janet Harris. Born 19 November 1869 in Titusville, Pennsylvania, to Helen (Katz) and Abraham Hirsch Simons. Educated in Bradford, Penn. public schools and Loretto Abbey (Toronto). Original NCJW national board member, and national president (1913–20). Helped organize many Sections. Also active in International Council of Jewish Women. Married Nathaniel E. Harris (1896). Taught in Bradford public schools. Served as vice-president, National Council of Women, including chairing Quinquennial Commission that arranged for massive women's convention in Washington, D.C. (1925). Also board member of State Federation of Pennsylvania Women. Member: Women's International League for Peace and Freedom, League of Women Voters, American Legion Auxiliary, Veterans of Foreign Wars Auxiliary, and Temple Beth Zion.

Sara Hart. Born 9 November 1869 in Chicago to Henry and Theresa Spiegel (of Spiegel catalog fame). Cousin (through mother) to Hannah Solomon. Educated Chicago public schools. Married Harry Hart (of Hart, Schaffner, & Marx). They had one daughter. Family was wealthy, and the presence of servants freed her to do volunteer work at Hull House and Juvenile Court. Member of Sinai Temple where she taught religious school. Member Board of Trustees Women's and Children's Hospital, Order of Eastern Star, and twenty-five other committees.

Hattie Kahn. Born 12 November 1870 in Maryville, Missouri, to Amalia (Sanders) and August Oppenheimer. Educated in Missouri public schools. NCJW national treasurer (1908–11) and president of Washington, D.C. Section. Married Adolph Kahn (1896). Especially active in care of delinquent girls. Director of Jewish Community Center and Summer Outings Committee. Organizer of Jewish Foster Home. On advisory board of Juanita K. Nye House. Member: Citizens Committee on Public Recreation, Citizens Committee on Commitment of Feeble-minded, District Council of Social Agencies, Juvenile Protective League, United Hebrew Relief, Hebrew Home for Aged, Hadassah, Washington Hebrew Congregation. Director of Monday Evening Club.

Rebekah Kohut. Born 9 September 1866 in Kaschau, Hungary, to Henrietta A. (Weintraub) and Rabbi Albert Bettelheim. Paternal ancestors were rabbis, physicians, or both for seven generations. Mother was Hungary's first Jewish woman schoolteacher. Came to Philadelphia in 1867. By age nine had moved to San Francisco. Educated San Francisco High School and Normal College. Coursework at University of California and Columbia. Received honorary D.H.L. from Jewish Institute of Religion (1934). First president of NCJW New York Section, director of NCJW's Reconstruction Unit following WWI, and first president of the World Congress of Jewish Women (1923–WWII). Married Rabbi Alexander Kohut (1887), who died in 1894, leaving her alone in New York City to care for eight stepchildren. To provide for the family, she founded and ran the Kohut School for Girls (1899–1904) and later served as executive director of the Columbia Grammar School. Served on innumerable committees and boards, mostly those providing services for immigrants. As a result, Kohut became involved in politics, first as a municipal appointee to committees dealing with unemployment, and then campaigning for Mayor Seth Low (1897 and 1901). Supported suffrage and was early advocate for national unemployment insurance. Founding member of National Women's Republican Club and National Congress of Mothers. Also founded several synagogue sisterhoods, supported Zionism, and worked with her stepson George to preserve the scholarly work of her husband in a special collection at Yale University. She frequently delivered papers before women's organizations, published articles (especially in women's and Jewish periodicals), and wrote four books. Died 11 August 1951.

Minnie D. Louis. Born 1849 in Philadelphia to Fannie (Zachariah) and Abraham Dessau. Educated Packer Collegiate Institute, Brooklyn. Speaker at 1893 Jewish Women's Congress and at Women's Building. NCJW National Board member (1893–95). Organizer NCJW New York Section (1894). Married businessman Albert H. Louis (1866). Known as poet and essayist and served as editor for Personal Service Department of *American Hebrew* (1891–93). Also worked as District Inspector for New York public schools (1895–97), resident director of Clara de Hirsch Home for Working Girls (1897–98), and field secretary of Jewish Chautauqua Society (1899–1901). Founder Louis Down Town Sabbath and Daily School, which became the Hebrew Technical School for Girls (the first school of its kind). On board of kindergartens of Hebrew Free School Association, Mount Sinai Training School for Nurses. Volunteer teacher at Temple Emanu El's Sunday School for eighteen years. Introduced New York's first vacation school (1890). Died 12 March 1922.

Babette Mandel. Born 25 October 1848 in Aufhausen, Wuertemberg, Germany, to Elise (Reese) and Emanuel Frank. Educated in Chicago Public Schools. NCJW's first national vice-president. President, NCJW Chicago Section. Married Emanuel Mandel (1871). They had one son, Edwin. Family's wealth allowed her to volunteer and to donate generously to several causes. Founder, Maxwell Street Settlement, West Side Dispensary, and Jewish Training School. Trustee, Jewish Orphans' Society (which her mother had founded and endowed) and director, Chicago Lying-in Hospital and Dispensary. Died 1945.

Louise Mannheimer. Born 3 September 1845 in Prague, Bohemia, to Katherine (Urbach) and Joseph Herschman. Educated at St. Tiene School, with private tutors, Prague Normal School, and University of Cincinnati. Speaker at 1893 Jewish Women's Congress and Congress of History. Founding member NCJW. Married Rabbi Sigmund Mannheimer. Had two sons who became rabbis and a daughter, Jane (Jennie), a noted dramatist. Served as Sabbath School teacher and contralto in husband's congregations. Composer, essayist, and prize-winning poet in German and in English.

Inventor, Pureairin Patent Ventilator. President German Women's Club (Rochester, N.Y.). Founder and president Boys' Industrial School (Cincinnati). Member Mother's Congress (Cincinnati).

Evelyn Aronson Margolis. Born 19 January 1878 in San Francisco to Carrie (Goldwater) and Philip Nathan Aronson. Maternal grandfather was one of first white settlers in Arizona. Earned B.A. from University of California and did graduate work at Universities of Berlin and Pennsylvania. NCJW national board member (1905–27), board member San Francisco Section (1903–06), and Philadelphia Section (1918–38). Married Dropsie College and Hebrew Union College professor Max Leopold (1906). They had three children. Served in several government-appointed positions in Philadelphia: Gov. Sproll's Advisory Committee, City Dept. of Public Welfare, Board of Censors. Organizer of Philadelphia chapter Hadassah. Director of Hebrew Sunday School Society. Member of Congregation Mickve Israel. During WWI, served as lieut. in Red Cross canteen.

Alice Davis Menken. Born 4 August 1870 in New York City to Michael Marks and Miriam (Peixotto) Davis. Educated Gardner Institute and graduate work at New York School for Community Workers. Member and frequent speaker for NCJW. Married Mortimer Menken (descendant of Rabbi Gershom Seixas) in 1893. Well known for social work. Founder, Jewish Big Sister Movement, and was President, Society for Political Study (1911–13). Worked with Women's Court. Trustee, Institute for Instruction of Deaf Mutes. Director, Florence Crittendon League. Especially noted as expert on prison reform. Appointed by Gov. Alfred Smith to board of managers N.Y. State Reformatory for Women (1920). Served on National Committee on Prisons and Prison Labor. Author of several pamphlets, articles, and a book on prison reform. Served in Women's Motor Corps (WWI). Trustee, Federation of Jewish Philanthropies and Women's Branch of Union of Orthodox Jewish Congregations. Served for twenty-seven years as sisterhood president of Spanish & Portugese Synagogue (1901–28). Member Republican Party, Women's City Club, National Probation Association, Daughters of the American Revolution, Congregation Shearith Israel. Died 23 March 1936.

Annie Nathan Meyer. Born 19 February 1867 in New York City to Anne Augusta Florance and Robert Weeks Nathan. Sister of Maud Nathan and first cousin to Emma and Josephine Lazarus. Board member NCJW New York Section (1895). Chair, 1893 Literary Congress at Chicago World's Fair. Educated privately and at Columbia University. Married physician Alfred Meyer (1887). They had one daughter. Best known as founder of Barnard College (1889) and as author. Had three plays produced on Broadway: *The District Attorney, The Advertising of Kate,* and *Black Souls.* Also wrote several books and articles. Active in several philanthropic endeavors. Opposed woman suffrage. Died 23 September 1951.

Marion Misch. Born 13 May 1869 in Allentown, Penn. (other sources say Newark, N.J.) to Rachel (Pulaski) and Louis Benjamin Simon. Educated in public school and Normal School of Pittsfield, Mass. Also studied privately through correspondence with Rabbi de Sola Mendes. President, NCJW (1908–13). Also active in Providence, Rhode Island Section. Married Caesar Misch (1890). Had one son. Ran family department store after husband's death (1921), and was the only woman in New England operating such a business at the time. Served on several boards in Providence: National Federation of Temple Sisterhoods, Montefiore Ladies Hebrew Benevolent Association, Temple Beth El Sisterhood, Society for Organizing Charity, District Nursing Association, State Federation of Women's Clubs, Association for Blind, State Sex Hygiene Committee, North End Free Dispensary, Providence Public School Board (for fifteen years). First woman appointed to Providence Playground committee where she was in charge of purchasing all supplies. Reappointed by both Republican and Democratic mayors. Lectured internationally, taught religious school, and wrote "Children's Service for the Day of Atonement" and a compilation of "Prose and Poetry for Jewish Homes and Schools." Member of several Jewish and literary clubs in Providence. Died 19 January 1941.

Laura Mordecai. Born 5 June 1837 in Philadelphia to Sara Ann Hays and Major Alfred Mordecai (who resigned his post in protest of having to fight against fellow Americans in the Civil War). Great-niece of Rebecca Gratz. Educated in Philadelphia, Washington,

D.C., and France. President and Study Circle leader in Philadelphia Section during 1890s. President Philadelphia Needlework Guild. Superintendent, Sunday School Society (1872–83). Active in Congregation Mickve Israel.

Belle (Lindner Israels) Moskowitz. Born 5 October 1877 (some sources say 1878) in New York City to Esther (Freyer) and Isidor Lindner. Educated in Horace Mann School and Teachers' College (Columbia). Board member, NCJW New York Section and ran Section's Home for Girls. Married architect Charles Henry Israels. After his death in 1911, married Henry Moskowitz. She had three children. Best known for her political work as public relations adviser to Gov. Alfred E. Smith. Also served as chief clerk for Grievance Board of Dress & Waist Manufacturers Association, and on committees of Travelers' Aid Society, Hudson District Charity Organization Society, and Educational Alliance. Died 8 December 1933.

Maud Nathan. Born 20 October 1862 in New York City to Anne Augusta Florance and Robert Weeks Nathan. Sister of Annie Nathan Meyer and first cousin to Emma and Josephine Lazarus. Educated in private schools and public high school in Green Bay, Wis. Founding member of NCJW New York Section. Married Frederick Nathan (1880). Had child who died at age eight. Organizer and president, New York Consumers' League. Officer, Women's Municipal League. General Federation of Women's Clubs national chair of Committee on Industrial Conditions Affecting Women and Children. Gave speeches to: American Academy of Political and Social Science, International Congress of Women, National Council of Women, General Federation of Women's Clubs, National Woman's Suffrage Association, National Congress of Mothers, and many local groups. First woman invited to speak from the pulpit of Temple Beth-El in New York City. Also wrote articles in *New York Times, North American Review,* etc. Died 15 December 1946.

Bertha Rauh. Born 16 June 1865 in Pittsburgh to Pauline (Wertheimer) and Samuel Floerscheim. Graduated with honors from Pittsburgh Central High School. Longtime board member (including president) of NCJW Columbian Council (Pittsburgh Section). Married Enoch Rauh (1888). They had one daughter (Helen) and one son (Richard). Appointed by three mayors as director of Pittsburgh's Public Welfare. She was the first woman in the U.S. to serve in a mayoral cabinet. Founder of Pittsburgh Symphony Society and the Ladies Aid Society. President, Milk and Ice Association and the Juvenile Court Aid Society. On board of Gusky Orphanage, Allegheny Free Kindergarten Association, Civic Club, Soho Public Bath, Juvenile Court Committee, Allegheny General Hospital, Girl Scouts, Travelers' Aid. On advisory committees of Public Health Nursing Association, League of Hard of Hearing, Federation of Jewish Philanthropies, National Probation Association, Congress of Women's Clubs, National Child Labor Association, YM & YWHA, Historical Society, National Mental Hygiene Society, Municipal League, League of Women Voters, Republican Women, Humane Society. Also member of Business and Professional Women's Association, Women's City Club, Temple Rodef Sholom, and several literary clubs, including the Reading Circle, which she led for nine years.

Cecilia Razovsky. Born 4 May 1891 in St. Louis to Minna (Meyerson) and Jonas Razovsky. Secretary, NCJW Immigrant Aid Department (1920–32), editor of *The Immigrant* (1921–30), and on national board of directors through 1930s. Represented NCJW at 1932 World Conference of Jewish Women (Vienna) and on Joint Legislative Committee on immigrant legislation. Married Dr. Morris Davidson (1927). Education Washington University, Corlis School of Law, St. Louis School of Economics, and graduate work in sociology at University of Chicago. Worked as legal secretary (Judges Sale and Goldsmith, St. Louis), teacher of English to immigrants, probation officer, inspector for Dept. of Labor. Considered expert on Jewish immigrants, having done studies of Jewish refugees in European ports, Cuba, Mexico, Canada, Brazil, and Argentina. Appointed by Secretary of Labor Perkins to investigate conditions at Ellis Island. Active in several social work associations. Author of pamphlet, "Handicaps in Naturalization," which was entered into the *Congressional Record* in 1932 and helped influence Congress to reduce naturalization fees.

Nannie A. Reis. Born 28 December 1871 in Dresden, Germany, to Zerlina and Adolphe Ashenheim. Arrived in U.S. 1884. Active in NCJW Chicago Section. Married Ignace Reis (1895). They had two sons. Worked as translator and correspondent. Contributing editor to *Reform Advocate*. Director, Ill. League of Women Voters. President, Conference of Women's Organizations. Founder of Ill. Travelers' Aid Society and its secretary for twenty-five years. Also known for work for blind in Chicago. Died 14 October 1940.

Julia Richman. Born 12 October 1855 in New York City to Theresa (Mellis) and Moses Richman. Educated in New York City Public Schools, Normal College (later renamed Hunter College), and graduate courses at NYU. NCJW founder and national board member. Started career as public school teacher in New York City. Then first Jewish principal and ultimately New York's first female district superintendent. Known as school reformer, introducing parents' meetings, eye exams for students, and tracking. Also interested in athletics. Director Hebrew Free School Association, Educational Alliance, and Jewish Chautauqua Society. First president of New York City's YMHA. Established Teachers Settlement House. Edited a Jewish periodical for children, *Helpful Thoughts*, and wrote two books: *Jewish Ethics* and *Good Citizenship*. Also wrote articles on Jewish and educational topics for periodicals and newspapers. Died of appendicitis on a trip to Paris 25 June 1912.

Pauline Rosenberg. Born 1865 in Pittsburgh to Henrietta (Lehrberger) and Meyer Hanauer. Founder of NCJW and Pittsburgh Section (Columbian Council), NCJW's second national president and chair of several national committees. Speaker at 1893 Jewish Women's Congress. Helped organize Council Sections in Oil City (Penn.), Altoona, Scranton, Youngstown, and Washington, D.C. Educated in Pittsburgh public schools. Some coursework at Barnard and Columbia. Turned down opportunity to attend Smith to manage the family household in the place of her ailing mother. Married Hugo Rosenberg (1886). In Pittsburgh, served on board of Allegheny General Hospital Ladies Auxiliary, Pennsylvania Federation of Women's Clubs, Woman's Club, Civic Club, Needlework Guild, Free Kindergarten Association, Tenement House and Public

Bath Committee, Personal Service Society, Columbian Council School Settlement.

Esther J. Ruskay. Born 1857 in New York City to Goldie (Webster) and Abraham Baum. Educated in New York's public schools. Earned B.A. from Normal College (1875). Studied literature at Columbia for one year. Led Study Circle for NCJW New York City Section (1904–05). Married Samuel S. Ruskay. Taught in New York public schools for two years and worked as writer and journalist. Contributed stories, poems, and articles on Jewish life to newspapers and magazines. Published two books, *Book of Poems for Children* and *Hearth and Home Essays.*

Sara X. Schottenfels. Born in New York City to Minna (Ambrunn) and Julius Schottenfels. Completed coursework at Bryn Mawr. Secretary of NCJW New York City Section. Librarian at Maimonides Free Library. Published list of library's periodicals and Judaica collection. Delivered variety of papers before women's societies and clubs. Member, League of Women Voters, American Jewish Historical Society, Ivriah.

Flora Schwab. Born 1855 in Germany to Babette (Cohen) and Max Kahnheimer. President, NCJW Cleveland Section and national board member. Married Moses B. Schwab. Officer, Educational Alliance, Cleveland Federation of Women's Clubs, Consumers' League, Health Protective Association, Cleveland Novelist Club, Women's Temple Association. Also served on Cleveland's centennial commission and as vice-president of War Emergency Commission. Especially active in establishment of playgrounds.

Hannah Greenebaum Solomon. Born 14 January 1858 in Chicago to Sarah (Spiegel) and Michael Greenebaum. Sisters Henrietta Frank and Mary Greenebaum Haas were also involved in NCJW. Married Henry Solomon (1879). They had three children. The founder, first president, and guiding force behind the NCJW. Also active in Chicago Section. As representative of NCJW, involved in National and International Council of Women (attended 1904

Berlin convention as delegate with Susan B. Anthony), General Federation of Women's Clubs, International Council of Jewish Women, Associated Jewish Charities, and many similar organizations. Assisted in founding Chicago Juvenile Court and Ill. Federation of Women's Clubs. First Jewish member of Chicago Woman's Club (1877). Served on board of Chicago Civic Federation. Frequent public speaker as Council president, including being the first woman invited to speak on several American synagogue pulpits. Board member of Temple Sinai and follower of radical Reform rabbi Emil G. Hirsch. Died 7 December 1942.

Rosa Sonneschein. Born 12 March 1847 in Nagykansiza, Hungary, to Fannie (Sternfeld) and Oberrabiner Hirsch B. Fassel (rabbi of Hungary's wealthiest synagogue and decorated for his literary works). Graduated high school in Hungary. Came to U.S. in 1869. Supporter of NCJW primarily through coverage in the magazine she edited, *The American Jewess* (1895–99), America's first periodical for Jewish women. Married Rabbi Solomon H. Sonneschein, a radical Reform rabbi whom she divorced (after their four children were grown) because of religious disagreements and his alcoholism. Worked as a correspondent for German, American, and English periodicals, publishing short stories and covering World Expositions in Chicago, Paris, and St. Louis. Pushed Temple Isaiah (Chicago) to become world's first synagogue to admit women to full membership without restrictions. One of America's first Zionists, and one of only a handful of women to attend the first World Zionist Congress in Basle (1897). Sonneschein earned fame for her blunt editorial style and for the cigar she smoked daily after dinner. She died in 1932.

Flora Spiegelberg. Born September 1857 in New York City to Rosalia and William Langerman (a 49'er during gold rush and a soldier in the Colorado and California state militias). Educated in New York City public schools and private German schools. Founding member of NCJW's New York Section. Married Willi Spiegelberg, mayor of Sante Fe (1874). They had two daughters. Organized one of first playgrounds in U.S. Served on City Commission in Sante Fe and arranged the city's sanitary plan. She also wrote children's books.

Constance Sporborg. Born 11 July 1879 in Cincinnati to Rose (Winkler) and Louis Amberg. Educated University of Cincinnati. National NCJW president (1926). Married lawyer William Dick Sporborg (1902). They had two children. President, New York City and State Federations of Women's Clubs in late 1920s and early 1930s. On board of General Federation of Women's Clubs. Chair, East Coast Motion Picture Preview Committee, Women's National Exposition of Arts and Industries, Women's Exhibit at 1933 World's Fair (Chicago), Westchester County League of Women Voters. National recording secretary of Conference on Cause and Cure of War. Member, Jewish Center of Port Chester.

Pauline Steinem. Born in Bavaria to Bertha (Slisower) and H. Perlmutter. Earned teacher's diploma from Teacher's Seminary at Memmingen, Bavaria. President, NCJW Toledo Section and national chair of Sabbath School Committee. Married Joseph Steinem. Delegate to International Council of Women (1908). President, Ohio Woman's Suffrage Association. Testified before women's suffrage committee of U.S. Senate. Helped develop Ohio Juvenile Court and served for eight years on Ohio State Board of Charities. In Toledo, president of Hebrew Associated Charities and Loan Association and Federation of Women's Societies. First woman elected to public office in Toledo. Grandmother of feminist Gloria Steinem. Died 5 January 1940.

Estelle M. Sternberger. Born 6 July 1886 in Cincinnati to Hannah (Greeble) and Abraham Miller. NCJW national executive secretary (1920–23) and board member of Cincinnati Section (1918–19). Edited Council's newsletter, *The Jewish Woman*. Educated University of Cincinnati (1907–11) and Community School of Jewish Philanthropy (1907–14). Married Harry Sternberger. They had one daughter. Communal worker and nationally known radio commentator. Secretary, National Conference of Jewish Women's Organizations and World Conference of Jewish Women. Executive director, World Peaceways, Inc. National board member, National Council of Women and National Federation of Temple Sisterhoods. President, Reading Road Temple Sisterhood. President, Cincinnati Jewish Consumptives Relief Society (1914–19). Board member, National Farm School, Women's City Club, Hamilton County

Council of Defense, Jewish War Relief Appeal, National Conference of Christians and Jews. Regular contributor to various publications.

Rachel Hays Sulzberger. Born in New York City to Judith (Peixotto) and David Hays (descendant of colonial settler Jacob Hays). Graduated from New York's Normal College. Second president of NCJW New York City Section. Married merchant Cyrus L. Sulzberger. They had three children. Prior to marriage, taught public school. Later worked for JPS and served as Director of Recreation Rooms House for twenty-five years. Vice-president, United Neighborhood Houses and Women's Auxiliary of Educational Alliance. Also on board of Jewish Working Girls' Vacation Society and first woman trustee of Aguilar Free Library (later New York Public Library). As chair of Parks Anti-Litter Campaign, got trash receptacles placed in city parks. Member Urban League, Daughters of the American Revolution. Died 10 February 1938.

Elsie K. Sulzberger. Born 5 September 1884 in Hungary to Julia and Alexander Weissbrun. Courses at Hunter and Barnard colleges. Officer, NCJW Detroit Section. Married Mayer B. Sulzberger. They had one daughter. Founder, "Mother's Health Clinic," reputed to be the only birth-control clinic between New York and Chicago (1927). Associate editor, Detroit *Club Women Magazine* (1921–31). Author, several poems, stories, essays.

NCJW National Membership, 1893–1990

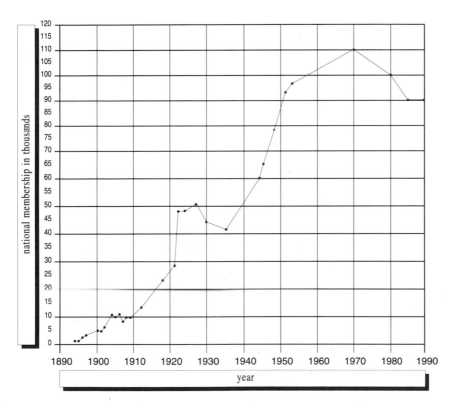

NCJW Positions on Selected Legislation

IN general, NCJW has consistently supported social welfare programs, civil rights, protective legislation for children, public health measures, ethics in government acts, peace efforts, and environmental protection. It has avoided taking stands on trade and agricultural legislation as well as on laws governing unions and business.

Opposed:

1917   Selective Service Act; Espionage Act; Sedition Act
1919   Volstead Act
1921   Johnson Act
1922   Equal Rights Amendment
1940   Alien Registration Act
1950   Internal Security Act (McCarren Act)
1952   McCarren-Walter Act
1953   Bricker Amendment
1986   Capital Punishment

Favored:

1906 Pure Food and Drug Act; Meat Inspection Act
1910 Mann Act (White Slave Trade Act)
1916 Federal Child Labor Law
1917 War Revenue Act (especially Section taxing war profits)
1919 join League of Nations
1921 Sheppard-Towner Act
1922 Cable Act
1926 Sterling-Reed Bill; Jones-Cooper Bill (Maternity and Infancy Act); World Court (establishment of and affiliation with)
1927 Kellogg-Briand Pact (outlawing war)
1935 Social Security Act; Neutrality Acts
1938 Ludlow Resolution; Food, Drug, & Cosmetic Act; Fair Labor Standards Act; Anti-Lynching Bill
1942 United Nations (establishment of and affiliation with)
1946 Atomic Energy Act; National Health Insurance Bill
1954 Housing Acts
1957 Civil Rights Acts
1961 Peace Corps (establishment of)
1963 Nuclear Test Ban Treaty
1964 24th Amendment; Equal Employment Opportunity Act
1965 Voting Rights Act
1969 Nuclear Non-Proliferation Treaty
1972 Equal Rights Amendment
1973 Roe v. Wade (legalizing abortion)
1985 Anti-Apartheid Act; Civil Rights Restoration Act

APPENDIX E

Council Presidents

1893–1905	Hannah G. Solomon
1905–1908	Pauline Rosenberg
1908–1913	Marion Misch
1913–1920	Janet Harris
1920–1926	Rose Brenner
1926	Constance Sporborg
1926–1932	Ida W. Friend
1932–1938	Fannie Brin
1938–1943	Blanche Goldman
1943–1951	Mildred G. Welt
1951–1955	Katharine Engel
1955–1959	Gladys F. Cahn
1959–1963	Viola Hymes
1963–1968	Pearl Willen
1968–1970	Josephine Wiener
1970–1975	Ellie Marvin
1975–1981	Esther Landa
1981–1982	Shirley Leviton
1982–1983	Helen Marr
1983–1987	Barbara Mandel
1987–1989	Lenore Feldman
1990–	Joan Bronk

Notes

Abbreviations

AJA   American Jewish Archives
JPS   Jewish Publication Society
(N)CJW   (National) Council of Jewish Women
(P)AJHS   (Publications) of the American Jewish Historical Society

Introduction

1. Sara L. Hart, *The Pleasure is Mine: An Autobiography* (Chicago: Valentine-Newman, 1947), 263.

2. Ibid. Also, Hannah Solomon Scrapbook, Box X-172, AJA; Rebekah Kohut, *More Yesterdays* (New York: Bloch, 1950), 36.

3. Kathryn Kish Sklar, *Catharine Beecher, A Study in American Domesticity* (New York: Norton, 1976), 156.

4. Theodora Penny Martin, *The Sound of Our Own Voices: Women's Study Clubs, 1860–1910* (Boston: Beacon, 1987), 18.

5. *American Hebrew*, 31 May 1895, 86.

6. Karen Blair, *The Clubwoman as Feminist: True Womanhood Redefined, 1868–1914* (New York: Holmes & Meier, 1980), 3.

7. Daniel Scott Smith, "Family Limitation, Sexual Control, and Do-

mestic Feminism in Victorian America," in *Clio's Consciousness Raised*, ed. Mary Hartman and Lois W. Banner (New York: Harper & Row, 1974), 119–36.

8. *Chicago Herald & Examiner*, 11 January 1938, clipping in the Hannah Solomon Scrapbook, Box X-172, AJA.

9. Ann Douglas, *The Feminization of American Culture* (New York: Knopf, 1977), 8–9.

10. Ibid., 6, 74.

11. Nancy Cott, *The Grounding of Modern Feminism* (New Haven: Yale University, 1987), 4.

12. Blair, *Clubwoman as Feminist*, 119.

13. Ibid., 41.

14. Annie Nathan Meyer, *It's Been Fun* (New York: Henry Schuman, 1951), 4–5.

15. Using the term *anti-Semitism* to mean "anti-Jew" is problematic because it obscures the existence of other Semitic peoples, especially Arabs. However, in an effort to reflect accurately NCJW's language and understanding (rather than current usage standards), this study will follow Council's pattern and use the term *anti-Semitism* to mean "anti-Jew."

1. The Founding

1. For details of the Women's Building and women's programing at the Chicago World Columbian Exposition, see Jane Madeline Weimann, *The Fair Women* (Chicago: Academy Chicago, 1981).

2. Hannah G. Solomon, *Fabric of My Life* (New York: Bloch, 1946).

3. Ibid., 80.

4. *Reform Advocate*, 22 July 1893, 442.

5. Mrs. Henry [Hannah] Solomon, *Jews of Illinois in Story and Tableaux* (Chicago: Chicago Section-Council of Jewish Women, 1919), 11.

6. Deborah Grand Golomb, "The 1893 Congress of Jewish Women: Evolution or Revolution in American Jewish Women's History?" *American Jewish History* 70 (September 1980), 52–67.

7. Though Solomon was not among them, even Chicago's militant suffragists opposed a separate women's building and argued that any woman who was worthy of inclusion should be given space in the appropriate general exhibition, so Solomon's position was, in fact, in accordance with her community's most visible feminists. Weimann, *Fair Women*, 39.

8. Hannah Greenebaum Solomon, *A Sheaf of Leaves* (privately printed, 1911), 50.

9. *Papers of the Jewish Women's Congress, 1893* (Philadelphia: JPS,

1894), 171–72; "The New Woman," *American Israelite* (December 1895), 4–5.

10. Quoted in Donna A. Behnke, *Religious Issues in Nineteenth Century Feminism* (Troy, N.Y.: Whitston Publishing, 1982), 189.

11. "Council of Jewish Women," *Reform Advocate*, 24 October 1896, 151.

12. Solomon, *Fabric*, 43.

13. Ellen Sue Levi Elwell, "The Founding and Early Programs of the National Council of Jewish Women: Study and Practice as Jewish Women's Religious Expression" (Ph.D. diss., Indiana University, 1982), 64.

14. Solomon, *Sheaf*, 50.

15. The original committee of sixteen included Vice-Chair Lillian (Mrs. I. S.) Moses, secretary Fanny (Mrs. Henry) Adler, Mary (Mrs. Charles) Greenebaum Haas, Julia Felsenthal, Carrie (Mrs. L. J.) Wolf, Etta Rosenbaum, Mrs. Charles Stettauer, Bertha Loeb, Sadie (Mrs. Max) Leopold, Flora Nusbaum, Lena (Mrs. Martin) Emmerich, Esther (Etta) Witkowski, Babette (Mrs. Emanuel) Mandel, Lena (Mrs. August) Frank, and Sadie American. Marital status and husband's names are included to aid in identification and because that is how the women addressed each other in print. The first name of Mrs. Charles Stettauer was not indicated in any Council sources.

16. Solomon, *Sheaf*, 48. For the actual notice, see *Reform Advocate*, 22 July 1893, 442.

17. Rose and Hortense Wolf and Ruth C. Feibel, *History of the Council (Cincinnati Section), 1895–1965* (Cincinnati: Cincinnati Section, NCJW, 1965), 1. Unfortunately, records do not indicate who received the letters or how recipients were chosen.

18. Solomon, *Sheaf*, 71.

19. Mrs. Hannah G. Solomon, "Report of the National Council of Jewish Women," *American Jewess* (April 1895), 27.

20. Ibid.

21. Mrs. Henry [Hannah] Solomon, "Beginnings of the Council of Jewish Women," *American Hebrew*, 12 April 1912, 725.

22. Ibid.

23. Solomon, *Sheaf*, 48.

24. Solomon, "Beginnings of Council," 725.

25. *Reform Advocate*, 22 July 1893, 442.

26. Solomon, *Sheaf*, 48–49.

27. Emil G. Hirsch, "Editorial," *Reform Advocate*, 29 October 1892, 214.

28. Solomon, *Fabric*, 82–83.

29. Mrs. Philip Angel, interview by Gerald Kane, 20 April 1970, Near-print File, AJA.

30. *Reform Advocate*, 22 July 1893, 442.

31. Solomon, *Sheaf*, 71.

32. *Reform Advocate*, 18 May 1891, 193–95. Other scholars included Kaufmann Kohler, Henry Berkowitz, and Adolph Moses. See Moshe Davis, *The Emergence of Conservative Judaism* (Philadelphia: JPS, 1963), 123; *American Hebrew*, 5 January 1900, 303–4; Adolph Moses, "The Position of Woman in America," *American Jewess* (April 1895), 15f.; Henry Berkowitz, "Woman's Part in the Drama of Life," *American Jewess* (May 1895), 66.

33. Solomon, *Sheaf*, 146.

34. Solomon, *Fabric*, 116.

35. *American Israelite*, 7 September 1893, 6.

36. *Jewish South*, 29 September 1893, 4.

37. *Papers*, 1893, 8.

38. Ibid., 11.

39. "Report on Jewish Women's Congress," *Jewish Messenger*, 8 September 1893, 3.

40. Mrs. E. M. [Ada] Chapman, "Influence of Jewish Religion in the Home," *Jewish Messenger*, 22 September 1893, 4.

41. *Papers*, 1893, 258.

42. Kohut, *More Yesterdays*, 120.

43. Sadie American quoted in *Reform Advocate*, 26 December 1896, 295.

44. Anne Firor Scott, *Making the Invisible Woman Visible* (Urbana and Chicago: University of Illinois Press, 1984), 37.

45. The rabbis were listed without first names as Moses, Stolz, Norden, and Levy.

46. By 1880, almost all U.S. Jews were represented by the Reform movement, so despite the absence of Orthodox leaders, the presence of so many rabbis really did indicate broad support. Ann D. Braude, "Jewish Women in the Twentieth Century: Building A Life in America," in *Women and Religion in America*, Vol. 3: *1900–1968*, ed. Rosemary Radford Ruether and Rosemary Skinner Keller (San Francisco: Harper & Row, 1986), 138.

47. Max Kohler, "German-Jewish Immigration to America," *PAJHS* 9 (1901), 87–105. Also Deborah Dash Moore, *B'nai B'rith and the Challenge of Ethnic Leadership* (Albany: SUNY-Albany, 1981), 6ff.; Naomi Cohen, *Encounter with Emancipation* (Philadelphia: JPS, 1984), 172.

48. Leon A. Jick, *The Americanization of the Synagogue, 1820–1870* (Hanover, N.H.: University Press of New England, 1976), 71–74.

49. Michael Meyer, *Response to Modernity: A History of the Reform Movement of Judaism* (New York: Oxford, 1988), 292.

50. By May 1894 Sections had been founded in Chicago, Quincy (Ill.), Baltimore, Pittsburgh, Denver, Newark, New York City, and Philadelphia. By January 1895 NCJW had added Sections in Duluth, St. Paul, Minneapolis, Kansas City, and Cincinnati.

51. *National Council of Jewish Women: Proceedings of the First Convention, November 15–19, 1896* (Philadelphia: JPS, 1897), 147 (hereafter cited as *Proceedings, 1896*). Council figures through the 1920s estimate that approximately 1/12 of all American Jewish women belonged to NCJW, but the organization gives no indication as to how it arrived at its assessment, making the conclusion unreliable. Moreover, the generalizations do not account for significant fluctuations in Council membership, nor do they account for such important factors as age or class. For Council's figures, see Estelle M. Sternberger, *Daily Readings in Human Service: A Handbook of Information on Council Ideals and Activities* (New York: NCJW, 1925), 23.

52. Sternberger, *Daily Readings*, 23.

53. Evelyn Aronson Margolis, "The Council Section: Its Relation to the Jewish Community," *Jewish Woman* (September 1922), 10.

54. Evelyn Bodeck, "Making Do: Jewish Women and Philanthropy," in *Jewish Life in Philadelphia, 1830–1940*, ed. Murray Friedman (Philadelphia: ISHI, 1983), 143–62.

55. *Proceedings, 1896*, 149.

56. Hannah Solomon Scrapbook, Box X-172, AJA.

57. Carrie Shevelson Benjamin, "A Paper on Philanthropy," *American Jewess* (January 1897), 181.

58. For example, Atlanta, Georgia's Section began as a synagogue sisterhood. See Beth Wenger, "Jewish Women of the Club: The Changing Public Role of Atlanta's Jewish Women (1870–1930)," *AJHS* (March 1987), 315. Madison, Wisconsin's Section was previously the Queen Esther Society. For additional examples see William Toll, "A Quiet Revolution: Jewish Women's Clubs and the Widening Female Sphere, 1870–1920," *AJA* (spring/summer 1989), 7–26; *Proceedings, 1896*, 79; Jennie Gerstley memoir in *The American Jewish Woman—Documents*, ed. Jacob Rader Marcus (New York: KTAV, 1981), 315 (hereafter cited as Marcus, *Documents*). Also see Appendix A, Chart 19.

59. *Proceedings, 1896*, 155.

60. At this convention Council formally dropped "National" from its name, perhaps in deference to the new Canadian Sections. "National" was not used again officially until 1924. No explanation of this name change was ever printed, though it may have been to clarify its relationship to the

International Council of Jewish Women, which was founded in 1923. Because the organization is now known as NCJW rather than CJW, the author has chosen to avoid confusion by using NCJW throughout the text, even when referring to years when "National" was dropped from the organization's name.

61. *Proceedings, 1896,* 49.

62. "Council's Triennial Convention," *Reform Advocate,* 28 November 1896, 231.

63. *Proceedings, 1896,* 278.

64. Ibid., 279.

65. Ibid. Frances Willard described the same position, saying that clubs and charities served as "school[s] for women in which they might learn how to take their place alongside men in the great work assigned to useful human beings." Quoted in Kathleen D. McCarthy, *Noblesse Oblige: Charity and Cultural Philanthropy in Chicago, 1849–1929* (Chicago: University of Chicago Press, 1982), 32.

66. *Proceedings, 1896,* 63.

67. Ibid., 392.

68. For ages of Council members, see Appendix A, Chart 5.

69. *Proceedings, 1896,* 315.

70. For an interesting elaboration of Council's opposition to prohibition, see "Sobriety in Jewish Life," in Esther Ruskay, *Hearth and Home Essays* (Philadelphia: JPS, 1902), 92–96.

71. Martin, *Sound of Our Voices,* 119. Also Scott, *Making the Invisible Woman Visible,* 345.

72. *Proceedings, 1896,* 305. Other suggestions included collecting proceeds from publishing and selling books of Jewish interest.

73. "The National Council of Jewish Women and Our Dream of Nationality," *American Jewess* (October 1896), 28.

74. *Proceedings, 1896,* 407.

75. For details of the organizations, see ibid., 215.

76. Weimann, *Fair Women,* 15. Also Hart, *The Pleasure is Mine,* 81–82; Solomon, *Fabric,* 226.

77. John W. Chambers, *The Tyranny of Change: America in the Progressive Era, 1900–1917* (New York: St. Martin's, 1980), 110.

78. Among the Council leaders whose Council experience helped garner them political appointments on the municipal, county, state, or federal level were: Sadie American (various commissions in Illinois and New York; FDR's Conference on Child Welfare), Esther Andrews (first woman appointed to Mass. Governor's Commission, administration of Alvan T. Fuller), Sadie Crockin (Governor Harrington's Preparedness &

Survey Commission, Maryland), Blanche Gilman (Mayor LaGuardia's City Commission working on increased milk consumption), Rachel Hays (School Board, Borough of Manhattan), Laura Hertz (appointed by Governor Stephens as trustee of Santa Barbara Normal School), Rebekah Kohut (Mayor LaGuardia's Commissioner of Welfare, offered when she was seventy years old), Loula Lasker (U.S. Advisory Commission on Conditions of Immigrants at Ports of Entry), Sadie Loewith (New York City Board of Recreation), Evelyn Margolis (California Governor's Advisory Commission under Governor Sproll), Cecilia Razovsky (chair of Secretary of Labor Perkins' Committee to Investigate Conditions at Ports of Entry), Pauline Steinem (first woman elected to public office in Toledo, Ohio), Julia Swett (Governor Meier's Commission for Investigation of State Institutions, Oregon). Many other Council leaders were appointed to various government committees organizing war work during World War I and World War II. This track record continues today. In Florida, for example, six Council activists have become state senators or assembly representatives, and former National Board Member Mara Giulianti attributed winning her campaign for mayor of Hollywood to the leadership skills she gained in NCJW. "NCJW Provides Training for Women in Power," *NCJW Journal* (Summer 1987), 12ff.

79. *Proceedings, 1896*, 216, 227.

80. Elisabeth Israels Perry, *Belle Moskowitz* (New York: Oxford, 1987), 34.

81. Ibid., 6.

82. Ibid., 220.

83. Ibid., 11.

2. Council Religion

1. Hannah Solomon quoted in *Reform Advocate*, 27 January 1894, 388.

2. Solomon, *Sheaf*, 124.

3. Rosa Sonneschein, "Editorial," *American Jewess* (January 1898), 192.

4. *Proceedings, 1896*, 281.

5. Ibid.

6. Richman has been commonly portrayed as an assimilationist because as superintendent of New York City schools she opposed the speaking of Yiddish on school grounds. Her Council activities, however, suggest that her attitudes toward Judaism and Orthodoxy were far from simple. A reassessment of her work is certainly in order.

7. For example, see William Toll, *The Making of an Ethnic Middle Class: Portland Jewry Over Four Generations* (Albany: SUNY-Albany, 1982), 56.

8. *NCJW Fifth Triennial Convention Proceedings—1908* (New York: NCJW, 1908), 56.

9. Minutes, National Council of Women of the United States (1897), 5, Gerritson Women's History Collection (microfiche).

10. *Proceedings, 1896*, 35.

11. Though NCJW took its inspiration from Reform Judaism, its definition of social reform work as a religious obligation preceded any such public expressions by Reform organizations. The Central Conference of American Rabbis, for example, had given lip service to social reform but did not take any official stance or action until the second decade of the twentieth century. See Cohen, *Encounter with Emancipation*, 195f. Also Leonard J. Mervis, "The Social Justice Movement and the American Reform Rabbi," in *Critical Studies in American Jewish History*, Vol. III, ed. Jacob R. Marcus (Cincinnati: AJA and New York: KTAV, 1971), 118–77.

12. Sue Elwell, "Council Judaism: The Failure of a Turn-of-the-Century Religious Expression" (unpublished paper, 1980), 7.

13. Janet Wilson James, ed., *Women in American Religion* (Philadelphia: University of Pennsylvania, 1980), 6–7.

14. Dianne Ashton, "Rebecca Gratz and the Domestication of American Judaism" (Ph.D. diss., Temple University, 1986), 61.

15. *Proceedings, 1896*, 205ff.

16. Kohut, *More Yesterdays*, 191.

17. Daniel J. Elazar, *Community and Polity: The Organizational Dynamics of American Jewry* (Philadelphia: JPS, 1980), 32.

18. Jick, *Americanization of the Synagogue*, 51.

19. Douglas, 144–45, confirms for American clergy in general between 1850 and 1895.

20. Jick, *Americanization of the Synagogue*, 71. Also, for example, Rev. Joseph Leiser, "Why the Young Men are Deserting the Synagogue," *Reform Advocate*, 8 April 1899, 212.

21. Michael Meyer, *Response to Modernity*, 283; Max Kohler, "German-Jewish Immigration," 94.

22. Carol Hymowitz and Michaele Weissman, *A History of Women in America* (New York: Bantam, 1978), 65.

23. Rosa Sonneschein, "Review of the National Council of Jewish Women," *American Jewess* (July 1895), 189.

24. Cohen, *Encounter with Emancipation*, 180.

25. Abraham J. Karp, *Haven and Home: A History of the Jews of America* (New York: Schocken, 1985), 363. Also true for nineteenth-century Christian men. Barbara Welter, "The Cult of True Womanhood: 1820–1860," in *Our American Sisters: Women in American Life and Thought*, ed. Jean E. Friedman and William G. Shade (Boston: Allyn and Bacon, 1973), 96.

26. Tobias Schanfarber, "News & Views," *American Israelite*, 11 December 1908, 5.

27. Sources providing evidence that the synagogue had been feminized include: Mary M. Cohen, "Symposium on Women in the Synagogue," *Reform Advocate*, 20 February 1897, 7, 8; Theresa Lesem in *Reform Advocate*, 27 March 1897, 90; Hannah Solomon, "Address to Omaha Convention," *Reform Advocate*, 5 November 1898, 182; "Council of Jewish Women," *American Hebrew*, 13 April 1900, 704; "Symposium: Women and the Synagogue," *American Hebrew*, 14 April 1916, 655ff.; Dr. Adolph Moses, "Women's Position in America," *American Jewess* (April 1895), 15; Norma Fain Pratt, "Transitions in Judaism: The American Jewish Woman Through the 1930s," in James, *Women in American Religion*, 216; Davis, *Emergence of Conservative Judaism*, 186. Though this study concentrates on non-Orthodox synagogues, there is evidence to suggest that Orthodox synagogues experienced a feminization process as well. For example, the fact that in the 1920s many Orthodox congregations splintered over the issue of placing women behind or next to a mehitza suggests that large numbers of women were attending worship services and were having a significant impact on synagogue practice. See Braude, "Jewish Women in the Twentieth Century," 139.

28. Lesem, *Reform Advocate*, 27 March 1897, 90.

29. Rebekah Kohut, "Symposium: Women and the Synagogue," *American Hebrew*, 14 April 1916, 656.

30. *NCJW Fourth Triennial Convention Proceedings—1905* (New York: NCJW, 1905), 129–30.

31. Michael Meyer, *Response to Modernity*, 379.

32. *Jewish Woman*, 4 October 1924, 11–12.

33. A more appropriate female parallel to B'nai B'rith would be the United Order of True Sisters.

34. *NCJW Ninth Triennial Convention Proceedings—1920* (New York: NCJW, 1920), 266. Boys were not eligible to join Senior Sections, so they were encouraged to join B'nai B'rith. *Cincinnati Section Bulletin* (May 1916).

35. Welter, "Cult of True Womanhood," 96.

36. See sources discussed in Blu Greenberg, *On Women and Judaism: A View from Tradition* (Philadelphia: JPS, 1981), 83–84.

37. Rev. Henry Berkowitz in *American Jewess* (May 1895), 66.

38. Kaufmann Kohler, *Hebrew Union College and Other Addresses* (Cincinnati: Ark Publishing, 1916), 2. Also, Simon Wolf in Marcus, *Documents*, 3995, and Rabbi C. H. Levy in *Jewish Comment*, quoted in *Reform Advocate*, 6 March 1897, 43.

39. *Proceedings, 1908*, 184.

40. Cohen, *Encounter with Emancipation*, 160; Oscar Handlin, *Adventures in Freedom: 300 Years of Jewish Life in America* (New York: McGraw-Hill, 1954), 75.

41. Emil G. Hirsch in *Reform Advocate*, 4 March 1899, 80.

42. Maurice Harris, a leading New York Reform rabbi at the end of the nineteenth century succinctly summarized rabbinic frustration asking, "Can we survive emancipation?" (Cohen, *Encounter with Emancipation*, 159). Half the rabbis who spoke at NCJW's First Triennial (1896) also echoed this concern, including Henry Berkowitz and Sabato Morais. Also see Kauffman Kohler quoted in Davis, *Emergence of Conservative Judaism*, 186; Rev. Joseph Leiser (Lafayette, Ind.) in *Reform Advocate*, 8 April 1899, 212–14; Karp, *Haven and Home*, 164; Handlin, *Adventures in Freedom*, 75.

43. "Council of Jewish Women," *Menorah* [B'nai B'rith] (November 1896), 318.

44. David Philipson, "The Ideal Jewess," *American Jewess* (March 1897), 257ff.

45. Similar disregard aided Rebecca Gratz's Sunday School Movement. Ashton, "Rebecca Gratz," 231.

46. "Do You Want Some Reasons for Enlisting New Members?" *Chicago Section Bulletin* (December 1923), 11.

47. For specific text references, see Judith Hauptman, "Women in the Talmud," in *Response* (Summer 1973), 161–65.

48. Rabbi Louis Grossmann in *The Union Bulletin* [UAHC], (March 1913), 9. Also Kaufmann Kohler, "Women's Influence on Judaism," *American Hebrew*, 5 January 1900, 304; Dr. Benderly in *American Hebrew*, 2 January 1914, 283.

49. Rebekah Kohut, "Jewish Women's Organizations in the United States," *American Jewish Yearbook, 1931–32*, vol. 33 (Philadelphia: JPS, 1931), 165.

50. *Menorah* (December 1896), 388.

51. For example, *Proceedings, 1896*, 109.

52. *Menorah* (December 1896), 405.

53. Ibid. (November 1896), 19. Also see *American Hebrew*, 31 May 1895, 86.

54. *Proceedings of the UAHC*, Vol. 8 *(1911–1915)*, 7698.

55. Cott, *Grounding of Modern Feminism*, 17.

56. Esther Ruskay in *American Hebrew*, 13 April 1900, 704.

57. "National Council of Jewish Women," *American Jewess* (June 1895), 129.

58. Sklar, *Catharine Beecher*, 160.

59. *Proceedings*, 1896, 195, 352.

60. *Papers*, 1893, 250.

61. Winnie Saltzman, Flora Rothenberg, Ann Robison, Jesse Brilliant interviews by the author, New York City, 2 September 1987. Also Judith Aronson, "The National Council of Jewish Women: A Study of the Los Angeles Section in Transition," in *Speaking of Faith*, ed. Diana L. Eck and Devaki Jain (London: Women's Press, 1986), 186.

62. Solomon, *Fabric*, 116.

63. For example, Rabbi Leo M. Franklin, "Woman's Noblest Work," *Reform Advocate*, 29 October 1898, 168; *American Israelite*, 23 November 1905, 5.

64. Lee Virginia Chambers-Schiller, *Liberty, a Better Husband* (New Haven: Yale University Press, 1984).

65. Mina Carson, *Settlement Folk: Social Thought and the American Settlement Movement, 1885–1930* (Chicago: University of Chicago), 93; Blanche Wiesen Cook, *Women and Support Networks* (Brooklyn. Out & Out Books, 1979), 22; Sarah Schulman, "When We Were Very Young: A Walking Tour Through Radical Jewish History on the Lower East Side, 1879–1919," in *Tribe of Dina*, ed. Melanie Kaye/Kantrowitz and Irena Klepfisz (Boston: Beacon, 1989), 271.

66. Review, "Well of Loneliness," *Jewish Woman* (April–June 1929), 50.

67. *Proceedings*, 1896, 116.

68. For example, Mrs. Henry Myers, "Woman's Work in the World," *American Jewess* (March 1898), 274.

69. *Chicago Section Bulletin* (December 1923), 2.

70. This possibility has been suggested by Sue Levi Elwell.

71. For example, Dr. E. Schreiber in *Reform Advocate*, 26 December 1896, 298.

72. Rebekah Kohut, *As I Know Them* (Garden City, N.Y.: Doubleday, Doran & Co., 1929), 253–54.

73. *Proceedings*, 1905, 178.

74. Solomon, *Sheaf*, 145.

75. *A Course of Study in Jewish Prayer in Eight Lectures* (NCJW Committee on Religion, 1923), 172.

76. *Proceedings, 1923*, 191–92.

77. Blanche Blumauer, "Woman in the Religious Life of Today," *Jewish Woman* (October–December 1929), 5. Also Margolis, "The Council Section," 11; Mrs. Carl Wolf, "Woman and Education," *Jewish Woman* (February 1924), 10f.; and *Council of Jewish Women Bulletin* (1908), 1.

78. *Proceedings, 1896*, 160.

79. Ibid., 159.

80. Ibid., 160.

81. Scott, *Making the Invisible Woman Visible*, 286.

82. Martin, *Sound of Our Voices*, 1.

83. See Chapter 1, n. 58.

84. *Proceedings, 1896*, 337.

85. Ibid., 187–88.

86. Martin, *Sound of Our Voices*, 45ff. Bodeck, "Making Do," 160, confirms this function for Philadelphia's Study Circle.

87. Martin, *Sound of Our Voices*, 3, 46.

88. Ibid., 105.

89. Ibid., 39.

90. *Proceedings, 1896*, 334–35.

91. Ibid., 190.

92. Florence Herst, "The Council Study Circles," *Chicago Section Bulletin* (November 1922), 16.

93. Davis, *Emergence of Conservative Judaism*, 123–24.

94. Martin, *Sound of Our Voices*, 26.

95. Douglas, *Feminization*, 59.

96. For example, Scott, *Making the Invisible Woman Visible*, 82.

97. Nahida Lazarus Remy, *The Jewish Woman*, trans. Louise Mannheimer (n.p., 1895; reprint New York: Bloch, 1916), 7.

98. *Papers, 1893*, 19.

99. *Proceedings, 1896*, 159.

100. Remy, *Jewish Woman*, 90.

101. Sarah Bentschner Visanska in *Jewish Messenger*, 23 April 1897, 4.

102. Remy, *Jewish Woman*, 165.

103. Wolf, "Woman and Education," 10. For a similar attitude, see Rose Kohler, "Woman's Position in Jewish History," *American Hebrew*, 15 February 1895, 435–36.

104. Martin, *Sound of Our Voices*, 37.

105. For example of this depiction of Esther see David Philipson, "The Ideal Jewess," *American Jewess* (March 1897), 257.

106. Nannie A. Reis, "The Modern Esther," *Jewish Woman* (January–March 1928), 4.

107. Arthur Vance, "A Purim Fantasia," *American Hebrew*, 16 March 1900, 577. Also Rosa Sonneschein, "Editorial," *American Jewess* (March 1898), 296.

108. *Council Newsletter* (March 1933), 4. Also Rose Brenner, "Council Sabbath," *Jewish Woman* (December 1924), 13.

109. Kohut, *As I Know Them*, 297.

110. *Proceedings*, 1896, 198, 210f.; *American Hebrew*, 29 March 1912, 641.

111. *Proceedings*, 1908, 247.

112. Solomon, *Sheaf*, 171–72.

113. Martin, *Sound of Our Voices*, 157.

114. *Proceedings*, 1896, 205.

115. Ibid., 164.

116. Ibid., 158.

117. Martin, *Sound of Our Voices*, 24.

118. Ibid., 18.

119. *Proceedings*, 1896, 169.

120. Ibid.

121. Ibid., 171.

122. Solomon, *Fabric*, 259. This trend was also reflected on a local level, e.g., Ida Cohen Selavan, "The Columbian Council of Pittsburgh, 1894–1909: A Case Study of Adult Immigrant Education" (Ph.D. diss., University of Pittsburgh, 1976), 26; Perry, *Belle Moskowitz*, 29.

123. Mrs. Samuel Alschuler, "The Significance of the National Council of Jewish Women," *Jewish Woman* (January–March 1930), 10. Though NCJW was dominated by Reform Jews, there was a split between those who supported radical and moderate Reform. Also, more than 10 percent of the early leaders identified as traditional (see Appendix A, Chart 16).

124. *Proceedings*, 1896, 99. Also, *NCJW First Annual Report, 1894–1895*, 16.

125. Elwell, "Founding," 114.

126. *NCJW First Annual Report 1894–1895*, 16.

127. Martin, *Sound of Our Voices*, 4.

128. Ibid., 173.

129. Abram S. Isaacs, *Under the Sabbath Lamp: Stories for Old and Young* (Philadelphia: JPS, 1919), 17.

130. Jonathan Sarna, *JPS: The Americanization of Jewish Culture, 1888–1988* (Philadelphia: JPS, 1989), 43, 97.

131. Karp, *Haven and Home*, 74.

132. *Proceedings, 1896*, 209 (attached table). In 1911, the educational director of New York's Kehillah told Council's New York Section that 70,000 of 80,000 Jewish girls received no Jewish education. *American Hebrew*, 6 January 1911, 278.

133. In NCJW's first three years, Sections established schools in 29 communities. Many of these schools, especially in small towns, also served boys. June Sochen, "Some Observations on the Role of American Jewish Women as Communal Volunteers," *American Jewish History* (September 1980), 23–24.

134. Charles S. Bernheimer, *The Russian Jew in the United States* (Philadelphia: John C. Winston, 1905), 180.

135. *CJW Program of Work, 1911–1914*, 29.

136. Rosa Sonneschein in *American Jewess* (August 1895), 260.

137. Rudolf Glanz, *The Jewish Woman in America 1820–1929*, Vol. II (New York: KTAV and NCJW, 1976), 17.

138. *Papers, 1893*, 121.

139. Marcus, *Documents*, 294.

140. Ibid., 186–89.

141. Rosa Sonneschein, "Editor's Desk," *American Jewess* (June 1895), 153.

142. Ibid., November 1895, 112.

143. *Proceedings, 1905*, 15; *NCJW Fiftieth Anniversary Bulletin* (November 1946); Julia A. Sprague, *History of the New England Women's Club, 1868–1893* (Boston: Lee & Shepard, 1894), 17.

144. *Proceedings, 1896*, 209 (table).

145. *Proceedings, 1905*, 42.

146. Minnie D. Louis, "Women in the Synagogue," *Reform Advocate*, 20 February 1897, 7.

147. *1908 Report of the Committee on Religious Schools*, 17.

148. For example, Sophie (Mrs. Julius) Beer, "Women in the Synagogue," *Reform Advocate*, 27 February 1897, 25. Also among Council supporters of the ordination of women were: Sadie American, Louise Mannheimer, Etta Nusbaum, Henrietta Frank, Maud Nathan, and Mary M. Cohen. Also see symposium on women in the synagogue in *American Hebrew*, 14 April 1916, 655ff.

149. *Reform Advocate*, 20 February 1897, 2.

150. Braude, "Jewish Women in the Twentieth Century," 164.

151. Undated, unidentified newspaper clipping, Hannah Solomon Scrapbook.

152. Solomon, *Fabric*, 111–12.

153. *Papers*, 1893, 63. Also *Reform Advocate*, 20 and 27 February 1897 and 21 May 1910; Rosa Sonneschein, "Editor's Desk," *American Jewess* (August 1895), 260.

154. Sklar, *Catharine Beecher*, 135.

155. Douglas, *Feminization*, 9. Also Welter, "Cult of True Womanhood," 112.

156. See, for example, discussions in the *Reform Advocate*, 20 and 27 February 1897, and the *American Hebrew*, 14 April 1916.

157. Douglas, *Feminization*, 8–9.

158. Solomon, *Fabric*, 108–10. Also, for example, Nina Morais Cohen in *Synopsis of Programs with Biographies of Presidents, 1940–1950* (Minneapolis Section, NCJW, n.d.), 193.

159. Solomon, *Fabric*, 108–10.

160. Kohut, *My Portion*, 73.

161. Marcus, *Documents*, 699–700.

162. Cott, *Grounding of Modern Feminism*, 32–33; Martin, *Sound of Our Voices*, 168.

163. Marcus, *Documents*, 390–94; Glanz, *Jewish Woman*, 141.

164. Kohut, *More Yesterdays*, 214.

165. *NCJW Eighth Triennial Convention Proceedings—1917* (New York: NCJW, 1917), 23ff.

166. Annie Nathan Meyer, "The Place of Ideals in Our Daily Life," *American Jewess* (May 1896), 427–28.

167. Annie Nathan Meyer, *It's Been Fun*, 202.

168. "The Jewish Woman and the Suffrage Movement," *American Hebrew*, 5 February 1915, 43.

169. Elinor Lerner, "Jewish Involvement in the New York City Woman Suffrage Movement," *American Jewish Historical Society* 70 (June 1981), 456.

170. Cott, *Grounding of Modern Feminism*, 9.

171. "The New Woman," *American Israelite*, 26 December 1895, 4–5; *Jewish Messenger*, 1 January 1897, 4.

172. Matilda Joslyn Gage, *Woman, Church and State* (n.p., 1893; reprint Watertown, Mass.: Persephone Press, 1980), xxx.

173. Anna Howard Shaw, *Story of a Pioneer* (New York: Harper, 1915; reprint New York: Kraus, 1970), 251.

174. Kohut, *More Yesterdays*, 214.

175. This ambivalence was underscored by Solomon's and Kohut's failure to mention the passage of suffrage in their extensive autobiographies.

176. *Chicago Section Bulletin* (November 1920), 1.

177. *Proceedings, 1923*, 180.

178. "The Lady Behind the Gavel," *Council Woman* (June 1959), 3.

179. Council members opposed the militant wing not only because they objected to its tactics but also because it seemed to focus on suffrage to the exclusion of all other issues. At one suffrage convention, Alice Paul (a leader of the militant wing) opposed working for the legalization of birth control as an unrelated issue. See Cott, *Grounding of Modern Feminism*, 68.

180. *Council Newsletter* (March 1933), 6.

181. *Proceedings, 1923*, 347.

182. Emil G. Hirsch, "Thoughts on the Industrial Emancipation of Woman," *Reform Advocate*, 18 May 1891, 194.

183. Elizabeth Gertrude Stern, "The Job, The Home, and Woman," *Jewish Woman* (March 1925), 8.

184. Rosa Sonneschein, "Editorial," *American Jewess* (July 1896), 554.

185. Mrs. Ben Loewenstein in *Reform Advocate*, 21 May 1910, 685.

3. Jewish Leaders Respond

1. Rose Kohler in *Reform Advocate*, 21 January 1899, 373.

2. James, *Women in American Religion*, 17.

3. *Proceedings, 1896*, 29.

4. Ibid., 43; Solomon, *Sheaf*, 146. Secular women's clubs, for example the New England Women's Club, also accepted men as associate members.

5. *American Jewess* (April 1895), 47.

6. "Special NCJW Issue," *American Hebrew*, 20 November 1896, 67.

7. Ibid., 69.

8. *Menorah* (November 1896), 319.

9. *Jewish Messenger*, 20 October 1893, 4.

10. *American Hebrew*, 31 May 1895, 86 and 20 November 1896, 68; Pauline Rosenberg in *American Israelite*, 3 December 1908, 1; *Reform Advocate*, 23 January 1897, 364; Philip P. Bregstone, *Chicago and Its Jews: A Cultural History* (privately printed, 1933), 46; Wolf, Wolf, and Feibel, *History of Council*, 2. In the 1940s NCJW commissioned Sydney Hook to assess Council's programming with an eye toward future growth. Hook

warned that Council's intellectualism stunted NCJW's growth by over-shadowing the emotional approach to Council's work (which he believed would be more appealing to women). Sydney Hook, *The National Council of Jewish Women on the Present Day Jewish Scene* (NCJW, 1946). In this author's 1987 interviews with current NCJW Board members, many told stories of initially being attracted to the organization because of the high intellectual caliber of the women involved.

11. *American Hebrew*, 16 March 1900, 578.

12. Quoted in "News & Views," *American Israelite*, 12 November 1908, 5.

13. Douglas, *Feminization*, 142.

14. *Proceedings*, 1896, 191. Also confirmed in an address to the same convention by Rabbi S. Greenfield (37).

15. For example, see *American Israelite*, 23 November 1905, 5; Rev. Joseph Silverman, "The Place of Women in Modern Civilization," *Menorah* (December 1896), 405; Berkowitz, *Woman's Part*, 66; Kaufmann Kohler, "Women's Influence on Judaism," *American Hebrew*, 5 January 1900, 304.

16. Julia Richman in *Proceedings*, 1896, 205; Emil Hirsch in *Reform Advocate*, 7 November 1896, 179; Karp, *Haven and Home*, 165.

17. *Reform Advocate*, 7 November 1896, 179.

18. Franklin, "Woman's Noblest Work," 168.

19. Szold cited in Braude, "Jewish Women," 150; *Maccabean* (July 1903), 5–10.

20. *Maccabean* (5 December 1896), 244. Also see, for example, *Menorah* (December 1896), 399.

21. Douglas, *Feminization*, 66.

22. Joseph K. Arnold in *Reform Advocate*, 19 December 1896, 277. For similar attitudes see Emil G. Hirsch, "Editorial," *Reform Advocate*, 9 May 1896, 239–40; Franklin, "Woman's Noblest Work," 168; *American Israelite*, 16 September 1896, 4–5.

23. *Reform Advocate*, 20 February 1897, 7–10; *Proceedings*, 1896, 195; *Proceedings*, 1905, 15.

24. "Decisions of Convention on Recommendations and Resolutions," *Jewish Woman* (January 1927), 19.

25. *Proceedings*, 1896, 31.

26. Solomon, *American Jewess* (April 1895), 31; *Jewish Woman* (October 1924), 11–12; *Proceedings*, 1896, 201.

27. Gotthard Deutsch, "Response to Symposium on Women in the Synagogue," *Reform Advocate*, 6 March 1897, 43.

28. *Proceedings*, 1908, 250.

29. Jennie Franklin Purvin in *Reform Advocate*, 15 December 1914, 528.

30. *American Hebrew*, 13 November 1896, 36.

31. *American Israelite*, 26 December 1895, 4–5.

32. *American Hebrew*, 16 September 1896, 6.

33. *Menorah* (November 1896), 318.

34. Karp, *Haven and Home*, 110.

35. *Jewish Messenger*, 1 January 1897, 5.

36. Emil G. Hirsch in *Reform Advocate*, 7 November 1896, 179.

37. *Jewish Messenger*, 1 January 1897, 5. Similar sentiments were expressed by H. Pereira Mendes in *Reform Advocate*, 2 January 1897, 322–23.

38. Meldola De Sola, *Jewish Ministers: An Arraignment of American Reform Judaism*, reprint from the *Hebrew Standard* (New York, 1905), 27–28.

39. Ibid.

40. For example, Dr. E. Schreiber in *Reform Advocate*, 26 December 1896, 298.

41. Ibid., 2 January 1897, 323–25. Apparently Peres was not the only person to make this argument. A year before Peres made his opinions public, Sadie American's 1896 Triennial speech as Corresponding Secretary made a vague reference to those who opposed NCJW saying "We need none of these . . . you can do nothing here." *Proceedings, 1896*, 138.

42. See especially Rosa Sonneschein in *American Jewess* (February 1897) and subsequent issues.

43. Quoted in *Reform Advocate*, 13 March 1897, 60.

44. For example, Dr. E. Schreiber, *Reform Advocate*, 26 December 1896, 298.

45. "One Lesson," *Reform Advocate*, 24 March 1900, 163.

46. Davis, *Conservative Judaism*, 117; Moore, *B'nai B'rith*, 33.

47. Hannah Solomon, "Modern Judaism," *Reform Advocate*, 10 December 1892, 342.

48. *The National Council of Jewish Women, 1893–1938* (New York: NCJW, 1938); Solomon, *Fabric*, 101; Kohut, "Jewish Women's Organizations," 176.

49. *Proceedings, 1896*, 383.

50. Rose Haas Alschuler in Marcus, *Documents*, 730–31.

51. Kaufmann Kohler, "Women's Influence on Judaism," *American Hebrew*, 5 January 1900, 303–304.

52. Rosa Sonneschein, "Editorial," *American Jewess* (December 1897), 142.

53. *Menorah* (December 1896), 388. Also see Pratt, "Transitions in Judaism," 220.

54. *Proceedings*, 1908, 39.

55. Solomon, *American Jewess* (July 1895), 190.

56. Rev. Dr. Voorsanger quoted in *American Jewess* (April 1896), 380.

4. The Sunday Sabbath Controversy and the End of Council Religion

1. *Proceedings*, 1896, 196.

2. Ibid., 195f.

3. Ruskay, *Hearth and Home Essays*, 8.

4. *Proceedings*, 1896, 22.

5. Among those who opposed Sunday Sabbath observance were Rebekah Kohut, Minnie D. Louis, Maud Nathan, Esther Ruskay, Rosa Sonneschein, Grace Mendes, Hannah Marks, Sarah Lyons, and Mary Cohen.

6. *Proceedings*, 1896, 291–92.

7. Ibid., 349.

8. Ibid., 355.

9. Ibid., 370.

10. Ibid., 379.

11. Ibid., 387.

12. Ibid.

13. Ibid., 391.

14. The *American Israelite* described a gathering to hear American speak at Plum Street Temple as being so large that it was like "a Rosh Hashana congregation" (10 December 1908, 1).

15. Rosa Sonneschein, "Editorial," *American Jewess* (January 1898), 193. Also "Editorial," *American Hebrew*, 9 March 1900, 376.

16. Sonneschein, *American Jewess* (January 1898), 193.

17. Report from *Jewish Chronicle* (London) quoted in *Reform Advocate*, 27 January 1900, 695.

18. Sonneschein, *American Jewess* (January 1898), 191–92.

19. "Council of Jewish Women Triennial Convention," *American Hebrew*, 30 March 1900, 627. Discussion continued in subsequent issues.

20. Ibid.

21. Ibid., 6 April 1900, 675–76.

22. Ibid., 13 April 1900, 697.

23. Ibid., 9 March 1900, 376.

24. Ibid., 14 April 1916, 655ff.

25. *NCJW Sixth Triennial Convention Proceedings—1911* (New York: NCJW, 1911), 34. Studies confirm a similar trend for local sections in Portland (Toll, *Making of an Ethnic Middle Class*, 57) and Pittsburgh (Selavan, "Columbian Council," 26).

26. *Proceedings, 1911*, 34.

27. *Jewish Woman* (October 1923), 23. At this time, "Jewish Studies" generally did not exist on college campuses except in the form of Semitic Studies, so the women were not studying Judaism.

28. Ibid. (December 1926), 29. Reports of competition with sister-hoods can also be found in the NCJW Collection, Manuscript Division, Library of Congress, Boxes 1, 2, 35.

29. Toll, "A Quiet Revolution," 20; Belle Moskowitz, "Jewish Women as Settlement Workers," *Hebrew Standard* 50, 5 April 1907, 9. Moskowitz lists the most important Jewish women working as social workers, almost all of whom were NCJW members.

30. Selavan, "Columbian Council," 4; letter from Sadie American to Felix Warburg, 6 December 1911, Felix Warburg Collection, Box 2, AJA; Bodeck, "Making Do," 162; Presidential Report by Blanche Goldman, Library of Congress, Box 10; Wenger, "Jewish Women of the Club," 318–19; Susan Ware, *Holding Their Own: American Women in the 1930s* (Boston: Twayne, 1982), 81; Charlotte Baum, Paula Hyman, and Sonya Michel, *The Jewish Woman in America* (New York: Dial, 1976), 52–53, 176; Carson, *Settlement Folk*, 182.

31. Emil G. Hirsch, "Editorial," *Reform Advocate*, 9 May 1896, 239–40.

32. "Of Interest to Women," *American Hebrew*, 1 November 1912, 13.

33. James, *Women in American Religion*, 10.

34. Elwell, "Founding," 162f.

35. Jonathan S. Woocher, *Sacred Survival: The Civil Religion of American Jews* (Bloomington: Indiana University Press, 1986).

36. No one objected on the grounds that members could not afford the increase.

37. *Cleveland and the National Council* (pamphlet distributed by the Cleveland Section, 1908).

38. Hannah Solomon, "Why I Refused the Honorary Presidency of the Council of Jewish Women," *Reform Advocate*, 19 December 1908, 522.

39. Emil G. Hirsch, "Reflections of an Outsider on the Cincinnati Triennial," *Reform Advocate*, 26 December 1908, 555.

40. Ibid., 553.

41. Ibid., 579.

42.   Minutes: Special Meeting with Disaffected Sections (1915), Library of Congress, Box 103.

43. *Proceedings, 1911,* 34.

44. Ibid.

45. "Excited Convention of Jewish Women," *American Hebrew,* 15 December 1911, 202.

46. "Council of Jewish Women," *American Hebrew,* 17 November 1911, 71.

47. *Proceedings, 1911,* 34.

48. "Triennial Convention of Jewish Women," *American Hebrew,* 22 December 1911, 235.

49. "The Trouble in the Council of Jewish Women," *American Hebrew,* 26 January 1912, 380.

50. "Convention Votes Against Miss Sadie American," *American Hebrew,* 4 December 1914, 149; *Reform Advocate,* 12 December 1914, 570.

51. Ibid.

52. "Miss Sadie American and the Council of Jewish Women," *American Hebrew,* 11 December 1914, 173.

53. Letter to Jacob Schiff, 9 November 1915, Jacob Schiff Collection, Box 9, Folder 450, AJA.

54. Flora Rothenberg, who never met American, nevertheless remembered her as a "bad girl." Interview by the author, New York City, 2 September 1987.

55. Misch was a respected businesswoman, having taken over her husband's business after his death. She also had a reputation for religious commitment. One story claimed that at age fifteen, having no Jewish school to attend in her hometown, she wrote to a leading rabbi and studied with him through correspondence. Within a year she had organized her own local school. Philip Cowen, *Memories of an American Jew* (New York: International Press, 1932), 70.

56. *Proceedings, 1911, 1914,* in NCJW Collection, Library of Congress, Box 34.

57. Mrs. Ceasar (Marion) Misch, "The Good Fairy," *Jewish Woman,* 2 April 1922, 13.

58. Ibid.

59. *Jewish Woman* (October–December 1927), 11. Other confirming sources include: *Proceedings, 1920,* 263; Ida Cohen Selavan, ed., *My Voice was Heard* (New York: KTAV and Pittsburgh Section, NCJW, 1981), 240; Marcus, *Documents,* 664. Ellen Umansky has suggested that the concern about "non-Jewish affiliations" might have referred to members

who had joined the Christian Science movement, but who still maintained that they were Jews. Christian Science is not mentioned specifically in the documents, but this is certainly a possibility that may be confirmed with more research.

60. Menu in Hannah Solomon scrapbook.

61. For example, *Jewish Woman* (April–June 1924).

62. James Yaffe, in *The American Jews* (New York: Random House, 1968), 204, notes the perception of NCJW as anti-religious still existed in 1968. Interviews with current national board members (2 September 1987) indicate that Council's reputation for irreligiosity still continues. Also confirmed in Moskowitz, "Jewish Women," 29.

63. Madison Section, *Council Bulletin* (September 1958), 3.

64. Woocher, *Sacred Survival*, 80.

65. Ibid., 16.

66. Ibid.

67. Ironically, Woocher's description and analysis of civil religion were not derived from NCJW's experience or that of any women's organizations, but rather were mistakenly attributed *exclusively* to the experience of leaders of Jewish Federations. For example, Woocher writes about post-World War II Federation leaders who repeatedly claimed that philanthropy was not just noblesse oblige, but "a fundamental expression . . . of the essence of Judaism itself" (p. 54) as if this was a new approach when, in fact, Council members had made this a central tenet of their immigrant aid work in the late 1890s. Woocher made this mistake because of the 135 institutions and leaders he analyzed, only one was a female. Scholarship that fails to consider women's experience is not only outdated and sloppy, but inevitably leads to the misconception that American Judaism is primarily a male construction with peripheral contributions from women, when it is more accurately understood as a fusion of male and female experiences.

5. Immigrant Aid Work

1. Michael N. Dobkowski, ed., *Jewish American Voluntary Organizations* (New York: Greenwood Press, 1986), 245f. The National Conference of Jewish Charities, which was created specifically to do "scientific charity," was not founded until 1900.

2. Ida Cohen Selavan, "The Founding of Columbian Council," *AJA* 30, no. 1 (1978), 29.

3. For an excellent summary of the transition, see Toll, "A Quiet Revolution."

4. *Proceedings, 1896*, 236.

5. Quoted in McCarthy, *Noblesse Oblige*, 48.

6. Bertha Rauh in *Jewish Woman* (April 1922), 7. Also Marion Misch in *Proceedings, 1920*, 637ff.; "Public Spirit as Evidenced by the Triennial," *Chicago Section Bulletin* (December 1923), 8.

7. "Public Spirit as Evidenced by the Triennial," 4.

8. Rivka Shpak Lissak, *Pluralism & Progressives: Hull House and the New Immigrants, 1890–1919* (Chicago: University of Chicago Press, 1989), 123; Carson, *Memories*, 53.

9. Solomon, *Fabric*, 18. Also Kohut in *More Yesterdays*, 190.

10. *Proceedings, 1905*, 19.

11. Minutes, National Council of Women of the United States (1895), 241, Gerritson Women's History Collection (microfiche).

12. Kohut, *As I Know Them*, 38.

13. Lissak, *Pluralism & Progressives*, 1.

14. Selma Berrol, "Germans vs. Russians: An Update," *AJA* 73, no. 2 (1983), 155.

15. Ibid.; Annie Nathan Meyer, *It's Been Fun*, 11.

16. Bertha Rauh in *Jewish Woman* (April 1922), 7.

17. Kohut, *As I Know Them*, 45.

18. Lissak, *Pluralism & Progressives*, 22.

19. *CJW Program of Work (1911–1914)*, 26. Also see *Proceedings, 1896*, 239, 368.

20. For a more comprehensive analysis of the shift from female to male dominance in social work, see Judith Ann Rolander, *Professionalism and Social Change* (New York: Columbia University Press, 1987), Chapter 3.

21. Ibid., 47.

22. Buildings that housed both Council's programs and needy immigrants included: Council Home for Jewish Girls (Brooklyn), Martha House (Cleveland), Colfax Settlement House (Denver), Mendelssohn Settlement Home for Girls and Stinson Memorial Industrial School (Los Angeles), South Side Neighborhood House (Minneapolis), Bertha Fensterwald Social Center (Nashville), Council House and Girls' Home Club (New York City), Irene Kaufmann Settlement House (Pittsburgh), Neighborhood House (Portland, Ore.), Council Neighborhood House (Richmond, Va.), Non-Sectarian Free Kindergarten and Neighborhood Center (San Antonio), Marshall Memorial Home (Syracuse), The Educational Center (Seattle), and Community House (Toronto).

23. Lissak, *Pluralism & Progressives*, 61.

24. Selavan, "Columbian Council," 78.

25. Linda Gordon Kuzmack, "The Emergence of the Jewish Women's Movement in England and the United States, 1881–1933: A Comparative Study" (Ph.D. diss., George Washington University, 1986), 334.

26. Ibid.; Edward Bristow, *Prostitution and Prejudice* (New York: Schocken, 1983), 234.

27. Clifford Roe, *The Great War on White Slavery* (n.p., 1911; reprint New York: Garland, 1979), 98.

28. Bristow, *Prostitution and Prejudice*, 219.

29. Ibid., 220, 269.

30. Roe, *Great War on White Slavery*, 148.

31. Bristow, *Prostitution and Prejudice*, 234.

32. Estelle Freedman, *Their Sisters' Keepers: Women's Prison Reform in America, 1830–1930* (Ann Arbor: University of Michigan Press, 1981), 129.

33. *Proceedings, 1908*, 156–57.

34. Alice Menken, "Probation Work Among Jewish Women," *Jewish Woman* (October 1925), 6. Menken's comment was somewhat generous. Though NCJW programs were certainly important, the improvement in the economy in the 1920s also significantly reduced the number of female defendants.

35. Priscilla Fishman, ed., *The Jews of the United States* (New York: Quadrangle and New York Times Book Co., 1973), 130.

36. *CJW Program of Work (1911–1914)*, 21.

37. Ibid., 38.

38. Zosa Szajkowski, "The Yahudi and the Immigrant: A Reappraisal," *PAJHS* 63 (1973), 16.

39. *CJW Program of Work (1911–1914)*, 23.

40. *The Immigrant, Bulletin of the NCJW Department of Immigrant Aid* (December 1924), 7.

41. *CJW Program of Work (1911–1914)*, 22–23.

42. Mrs. Otto Kempner, "Delinquent Girls," *American Hebrew*, 29 December 1911, 285–86; *Proceedings, 1908*, 153; Kohut, *My Portion*, 48.

43. Freedman, *Their Sisters' Keepers*, 109f.

44. Kohut, *My Portion*, 48.

45. Scott, *Making the Invisible Woman Visible*, 284–85.

46. Cott, *Grounding of Modern Feminism*, 97.

47. "The Board Meets in Annual Session," *Jewish Woman* (June 1931), 15; *Council Newsletter* (January 1937), 23ff.

48. Margaret Sanger, *Margaret Sanger: An Autobiography* (n.p., 1938; reprint New York: Dover, 1971), 429.

49. *Jewish Woman* (June 1931), 15.

50. For example, *Cincinnati Section Bulletin* (December 1917), 12.

51. *Proceedings*, 1920, 262.

52. *CJW Program of Work (1911)*, 18.

53. Estelle M. Sternberger, "Institutions Founded by Our Sections," *Jewish Woman* (December 1922), 2.

54. *Proceedings*, 1908, 103.

55. "A History of the Brooklyn Section" in Brooklyn, N.Y., Histories File, AJA.

56. *CJW Program of Work (1911–1914)*, 12.

57. Karp, *Haven and Home*, 101.

58. *Record of Progress, Chicago Section of the Council of Jewish Women* (1908).

59. *Proceedings*, 1926, 206.

60. Mildred G. Welt, "The National Council of Jewish Women," in *American Jewish Yearbook* 46 (Philadelphia: JPS, 1944–45), 66.

61. *Council Woman* (December–January 1940–41), 11.

62. Mrs. Alexander Wolf in *Jewish Woman* (January 1922), 6.

63. Carroll Smith-Rosenberg, "Beauty, The Beast, and the Militant Woman," in *A Heritage of Her Own*, ed. Nancy Cott and Elizabeth H. Pleck (New York: Simon & Schuster, 1979), 207.

64. *CJW Program of Work (1911–1914)*, 109.

65. Roe, *Great War on White Slavery*, 20–21.

66. Smith-Rosenberg, "Beauty, The Beast," 197–221.

67. *CJW Program of Work (1911–1914)*, 107.

68. Ibid., 114.

69. Carroll Smith-Rosenberg, *Disorderly Conduct* (New York: Knopf, 1985), 262–63.

70. *CJW Program of Work (1911–1914)*, 31.

71. Ibid., 41.

72. Letter from Sadie American, 25 September 1913, in the Ida (Mrs. Harry) Davis File, AJA.

73. Ibid.

74. The list of appropriate occupations included: artificial flower and feather, millinery, clothing, confectionery trade, tobacco, bookbinding, button industry. *Summary of Female Employment in New York State, 1905–1915* (CJW Department of Immigrant Aid, 1915).

75. Julie A. Matthaei, *An Economic History of Women in America* (New York: Schocken, 1982), 215.

76. *Proceedings*, 1908, 7.

77. Carson, *Settlement Folk*, 181.

78. For example, Estelle M. Sternberger in Marcus, *Documents*, 745.

79. *Cincinnati Section Bulletin* (February 1918), 11.

80. *Proceedings, 1905*, 4.

81. Ibid.

82. Kuzmack, "Emergence," 516.

83. *Jewish Woman* (April–June 1929), 1.

84. *Chicago Section Bulletin* (November 1920), 1.

85. Welt, "The National Council," 113. Ties to such organizations were often strengthened by leaders who were also Council members. Both Maud Nathan and Sadie American served as officers of the Consumers' League.

86. Nancy Schrom Dye, *As Equals and As Sisters: Feminism, Unionism, and the Women's Trade Union League of New York* (Columbia: University of Missouri Press, 1980), 61.

87. Ibid., 149.

88. Ande Manners, *Poor Cousins* (New York: Coward, McCann & Geoghegan, 1972), 113.

89. Hannah Solomon in *Reform Advocate*, 21 November 1896, 213.

90. Manners, *Poor Cousins*, 113.

91. Handlin, *Adventures*, 157.

92. Oscar Handlin, *The Uprooted* (Boston: Little, Brown & Co., 1951), 71.

93. *Jewish Woman* (February 1924), 19.

94. Elazar, *Community and Polity*, 103.

95. Ailon Shiloh, *By Myself I'm a Book: An Oral History of the Immigrant Jewish Experience in Pittsburgh* (Waltham, Mass.: AJHS and Pittsburgh Section, NCJW, 1972), 66. Also see *Jewish Woman* (December 1924), 37.

96. Selavan, "Founding of Columbian Council," 32.

97. Szajkowski, "The Yahudi," 16.

98. In 1922, NCJW served 17,424 clients at Ellis Island. *Jewish Woman* (October–December 1928), 4.

99. *Proceedings, 1926*, 257.

100. *Jewish Woman* (October–December 1928), 6. For a biographical sketch of one of Council's itinerant rural workers, see Leo Turitz, "Amelia Greenwald: The American Jewish Florence Nightingale," *AJA* (November 1985), 291–92.

101. *CJW Program of Work (1911–1914)*, 65–74.

102. Ibid., 93.

103. NCJW Collection, Manuscript Division, Library of Congress, Box 138.

104. *CJW Program of Work (1911–1914)*, 71.

105. *Proceedings*, 1908, 369.

106. Ibid., 225.

107. *The Immigrant* (December 1924), 14.

108. "Interview With Sadie American," *Jewish Chronicle* (London), quoted in *Reform Advocate*, 23 April 1910, 458.

109. *Jewish Woman* (April 1922), 4.

110. There is no way to estimate the dollar amount that NCJW spent on immigrant aid. Sources such as Council records, Triennial reports, and the *American Jewish Yearbook* present widely conflicting amounts, varying from several thousand dollars per year to several hundred thousand dollars per year. Conflicts seem to arise primarily from inconsistencies on whether to count funds not raised specifically for immigrant aid (such as dues payments), on which projects properly count as immigrant aid, and on whether to include local Section expenditures as well as national expenditures in the reporting of immigrant aid figures.

111. McCarthy has confirmed this for Chicago charities in general (*Noblesse Oblige*, 76).

112. Glanz, *Jewish Woman*, 14.

113. *Toronto Daily Star*, 6 May 1937, 8, clipping in Hannah Solomon Scrapbook, Box X-172, AJA.

114. Martin, *Sound of Our Voices*, 19.

115. Friedman and Shade, *Our American Sisters*, 164.

116. Blair, *Clubwoman as Feminist*, introduction; Martin, *Sound of Our Voices*, 174.

117. Kohut, *My Portion*, 207; also *Proceedings*, 1896, 341.

118. For example, the American Jewish Committee was founded in 1905 in response to pogroms in Eastern Europe.

119. Jennie Franklin Purvin in *Jewish Woman* (April 1922), 4; Mrs. Samuel Alschuler, "Social Welfare," *Jewish Woman* (December 1924), 28; *Chicago Section Bulletin* (1923–24), 4; *Union of American Hebrew Congregations Proceedings, 1907–1911*, Vol. 7, 6238.

120. Bertha Rauh in *Jewish Woman* (April 1922), 7.

121. For example, Jewish Federations did not adopt this attitude until after World War I. Woocher, *Sacred Survival*, 32.

122. Cohen, *Encounter with Emancipation*, 308; Woocher, *Sacred Survival*, 38.

123. NCJW used the terms *charity* and *tzedakah* interchangeably, though a more proper translation of the Hebrew term is "the religious obligation to pursue righteousness by providing for the needy."

124. *Papers*, 1893, 146.

125. Mrs. Samuel Alschuler, "Social Welfare," 28.

126. *Proceedings, 1908,* 12.

127. For example, Rachel Sulzberger chaired the commission responsible for placing trash receptacles in New York City's public parks. See Appendix B for information on individuals who worked on similar projects.

128. Cohen, *Encounter with Emancipation,* 320ff.

129. Karp, *Haven and Home,* 116. Similar suggestions had also been made prior to the Kishineff pogrom by such respected publications as the *Jewish Messenger.* Myron Berman, *The Attitude of American Jewry Toward East European Jewish Immigration, 1881–1914* (New York: Arno Press, 1980), 31–32.

130. Ibid., 173.

131. Historian Naomi Cohen notes that Jewish institutions largely ignored social justice issues until after 1900 and that their eventual attention to such issues was merely following in the footsteps of the Social Gospel movement (*Encounter with Emancipation,* 180). Though the Social Gospel movement was, indeed, an important influence, this explanation ignores Council's work prior to 1900 and fails to recognize that work as an influence on later developments in the Jewish community.

132. Dobkowski, *Jewish American Voluntary Organizations,* 121.

133. Meyer, *It's Been Fun,* 288; David Polish, "The Changing and the Constant in the Reform Rabbinate," in *The American Rabbinate: A Century of Continuity and Change, 1883–1983,* ed. Jacob Rader Marcus and Abraham J. Peck (Hoboken, N.J.: KTAV, 1985), 213.

134. Toll, *Making of an Ethnic Middle Class,* 58.

135. A predominance of advertising in the major Jewish newspapers and periodicals was directed at women, indicating that even articles written by rabbis were conceived with a female readership in mind.

136. Historian Naomi Cohen confirms that Hirsch was untroubled by synagogue attendance figures (*Encounter with Emancipation,* 197). For information on Wise, see Melvin I. Urofsky, *A Voice That Spoke for Justice: The Life and Times of Stephen S. Wise* (Albany: State University of New York Press, 1982), 43.

137. Boris Bogen, *Jewish Philanthropy* (reprint ed., Montclair, N.J.: Patterson Smith, 1969), 35; Bregstone, *Chicago and Its Jews,* 45; Cowen, *Memories,* 169; Maurice Karpf, *Jewish Community Organization in the United States* (New York: Bloch, 1938), 36; Pauline Rosenberg in *American Israelite,* 3 December 1908, 1.

138. *Proceedings, 1908,* 50.

139. Dobkowski, *Jewish American Voluntary Organizations*, 247; Karp, *Haven and Home*, 181.

140. *Summary of Female Employment in New York State*, 1.

141. McCarthy confirms this trend for nonreligious charities in Chicago as well (*Noblesse Oblige*, 173).

142. Scott, *Making the Invisible Woman Visible*, 283–84.

143. *Proceedings*, 1926, 46f.; Reports from NCJW Sixth Triennial in Library of Congress, Box 34.

144. Cohen, *Encounter with Emancipation*, 201.

145. Scott, *Making the Invisible Woman Visible*, 287.

146. Solomon, *Fabric*, 226.

147. Sara Hart's perceptions were validated by Joseph Schaffner's later comments on the strike. As an owner, he was unfamiliar with the problems faced by his workers; he said, "When I found out later of the conditions that had prevailed, I concluded that the strike should have occurred much sooner." Karp, *Haven and Home*, 205.

148. Hart, *Pleasure is Mine*, 137.

149. *American Hebrew*, 29 November 1895, 98–99.

150. Scott, *Making the Invisible Woman Visible*, 288f.

6. The Rest of the Story

1. *American Hebrew*, 30 March 1900, 631. This report incorrectly left off the word "Workers" from the organization's title.

2. Several NCJW sources take credit for the founding of the JFB, but their case is overstated. Council was one among many factors that led to the establishment of the German organization. See Marion Kaplan, *The Jewish Feminist Movement in Germany: The Campaigns of the Jüdischer Frauenbund, 1904–1938* (Westport, Conn.: Greenwood, 1979).

3. Welt, "The National Council," 69.

4. Ibid., 70.

5. Ibid., 69.

6. Carol Ruth Berkin, "Not Separate, Not Equal," in *Women of America*, ed. Carol Ruth Berkin and Mary Beth Norton (Boston: Houghton Mifflin, 1979), 275.

7. *Yearbook*, New York Section, 1919–20, 41.

8. *Jewish Woman* (October 1924), 23.

9. Ibid. (June 1924), 35.

10. *Proceedings*, 1911, 74–75; *Minutes*, Terre Haute Section, 1907.

11. *Proceedings, 1923,* 70–71.

12. Cott, *Grounding of Modern Feminism,* 97.

13. Ware, *Holding Their Own,* 101.

14. Wolf, Wolf, and Feibel, *History of Council,* 14; Ware confirms that the experience of most middle-class women was "making do" or "struggling to get by with less" rather than actual poverty (*Holding Their Own,* 2).

15. Welt, "The National Council," 70.

16. Elazar, *Community and Polity,* 202.

17. Steven M. Lowenstein, *Frankfurt on the Hudson: The German Jewish Community of Washington Heights, 1933–1983* (Detroit: Wayne State University Press, 1989), 103.

18. *Council Newsletter* (Spring 1937), 14.

19. Lyman Cromwell White, *300,000 New Americans* (New York: Harper & Bros., 1957), 296ff. This work provides an excellent, detailed description of how NCJW fit into the framework of immigrant aid organizations during this time period.

20. Ibid., 35.

21. Ibid., 303.

22. "Report on the Survey," *Jewish Woman (1926),* 22–23; Winnie Saltzman, interview by author, 2 September 1987; "Report of Special Meeting on Negotiations, 1946," in Box 10, Library of Congress.

23. White, *300,000 New Americans,* 30.

24. Ruth Gruber, *Haven, The Unknown Story of 1,000 World War II Refugees* (New York: Coward-McCann, 1983), 167, 214, 216.

25. NCJW Collection, Library of Congress, Box 102.

26. *Proceedings, 1920,* 165.

27. Welt, "The National Council," 67.

28. For example, UAHC did not adopt a resolution opposing war until 1925, and leaders like Rabbi Stephen Wise or the CCAR made no public commitment until the 1930s. Michael Meyer, *Response to Modernity,* 313.

29. *Proceedings, 1923,* 155; *Council Newsletter* (October 1935), 22–23.

30. *Report of the Dies Committee* 1 (19 August 1938), 672.

31. *Proceedings, 1920,* 85.

32. "Findings of the Conference on the Cause and Cure of War," *Jewish Woman* (March 1925), 14.

33. Cott, *Grounding of Modern Feminism,* 243.

34. "Judaism and Peace," *Jewish Woman* (March 1925), 18f.

35. *Council Newsletter* (October 1935), 22–23.

36. Cott, *Grounding of Modern Feminism,* 248.

37. NCJW Collection, Manuscript Division, Library of Congress, Box 102.

38. *Council Newsletter* (October 1935), 22–23. Also Gertrude Fiebleman in *Jewish Woman* (January 1922), 8.

39. *Council Newsletter* (October 1935), 22–23.

40. NCJW Collection, Library of Congress, Box 10.

41. *Minutes*, National Committee on International Relations and Peace, 13 December 1945, in NCJW Collection, Library of Congress, Box 94.

42. NCJW Collection, Library of Congress, Box 145.

43. Abraham Cronbach, "Jewish Pioneering in American Social Welfare," in *Critical Studies in American Jewish History*, Vol. I, ed. Jacob Rader Marcus (Cincinnati: AJA, 1971), 217.

44. *Minutes*, Madison, Wisconsin Section (10 May 1954).

45. *Council Woman* (May 1955), 2.

46. FBI file, 100-410898-114, 1–8.

47. *Congressional Record*, 18 January 1962, 364–68.

48. Ibid., 3 November 1958.

49. *Chicago Section Bulletin* (February 1924), 8; Ida B. Wells, *Crusade for Justice: The Autobiography of Ida B. Wells* (Chicago: University of Chicago Press, 1970), 277.

50. FBI file, 61-7559-3598, 1 (1/1/43).

51. Text of resolution can be found in "Guidelines for Council Public Affairs: 1959–1960," *Council Platform* (Summer 1959), 1.

52. Hannah Stein in *Council Platform* (February–March 1962), 1. Also Josephine Wiener, "New Dimensions for Council," *Council Woman* (Summer 1969), 2.

53. Yaffe, *American Jews*, 257.

54. "The Career of Last Resort," *Council Woman* (January 1967), 6–7. Council members were a significant part of the suburban middle class that hired black domestics, but no Council documents comment on the possibility that members, themselves, may have been part of the problem.

55. "NCJW Speaks on Election Issues," *Council Woman* (October 1972), 13f.

56. *NCJW Biennial Report* (1985), 13.

57. *Council Woman* (May 1951), 1.

58. Mrs. Theodore O. Wedel, "Are We Women—or are We Mice?" *Council Woman* (May 1955), 5.

59. *Council Woman* (November 1956), 10.

60. Mrs. Charles [Viola] Hymes, "What Council Means to Me," *Council Woman* (October 1957), 7.

61. Mrs. Alfred Katz, "What Council Means to Me," *Council Woman* (November 1956), 10.

62. Leila J. Rupp and Verta Taylor, *Survival in the Doldrums: The American Women's Rights Movement, 1945 to the 1960s* (New York: Oxford University Press, 1987), 167.

63. *Lilith* 15 (Summer 1990), 26.

64. *NCJW Journal* (Summer 1987), 2.

65. Pearl Water, "Pearl Water on NCJW," *Lilith* (1975), 18.

66. 1987 National Board, interview by author, New York City, 2 September 1987.

67. *CJW Program of Work (1911–1914)*, 12f.

68. *Proceedings*, 1926, 339.

69. *CJW Program of Work (1911–1914)*, 13.

70. Elazar, *Community and Polity*, 177.

71. *National Resolutions, 1987–1990* (NCJW), 12.

72. Council's first resolution urging freedom for Soviet Jews was passed in 1967.

73. From text for "Women in Power," a slide show developed by NCJW for local section use, 1987.

74. *Council Woman* (Special Issue on Voluntarism), (October–December 1977); Water, "Pearl Water on NCJW," 18.

75. *Lilith* 14 (Fall 1989), 10.

76. Aronson, "National Council," 186.

77. Flora Rothenberg, interview by author, New York City, 2 September 1987.

78. Jo Sinclair, *Wasteland* (Philadelphia: JPS, 1987), 281–82.

79. Elazar, *Community and Polity*, 266.

80. Water, "Pearl Water on NCJW," 18.

81. *Council Woman* (May 1956), 8.

82. Does not include funds raised and spent in local Sections and therefore do not pass through the national treasury.

Appendix A

1. Studies of local Sections confirm this trend. See Selavan, "Columbian Council," 19 (Pittsburgh); Toll, *Making of an Ethnic Middle Class*, 57 (Portland); Kohut, *More Yesterdays*, 122 (New York); Gunther Plaut, *The Jews in Minnesota: The First 75 Years* (New York: AJHS, 1959), 296 (Minneapolis); Ida Libert Uchill, *Pioneers, Peddlers, and Tsadikim* (Den-

ver: Sage, 1957), 142 (Denver); Jonathan Rosenbaum and Patricia O'Con-ner-Seger, eds., *Our Story* (Omaha: NCJW, 1981), 70 (Omaha).

2. *Proceedings*, 1896, 193.

3. Carl Degler, *At Odds* (New York: Oxford, 1980), 314.

4. As late as 1959, few single women belonged to NCJW. *Council Woman* (June 1959), 3. Current figures are unavailable.

5. One such example was the Atlanta Section. *Proceedings*, 1923, 269.

6. This was still true in 1968. Yaffe, *American Jews*, 204.

7. For example, Hannah Solomon, Sara Hart, Fanny Brin.

8. For example, the *American Jewess* contained hints on where to find good buys in Europe and articles on proper etiquette for Society parties.

9. Confirmed in Selavan, "Columbian Council," 29.

10. This trend has been true throughout Council's history. In the 1940s and 1950s, all Council presidents had B.A.s. Yaffe confirms the trend for the 1960s (*American Jews*, 204).

11. Degler, *At Odds*, 311.

12. Matthaei, *Economic History*, 178.

13. Ruth Sapinsky, *The Girl at College*. Report for Menorah Movement, 1916, provides only available data. Twice as many Gentile as Jewish women attended college. For every 1,000 Jews who attended college, only 4 were women.

14. Toll, *Making of an Ethnic Middle Class*, 57.

15. Solomon, *Sheaf*, 71.

16. Concurring sources include Yaffe, *American Jews*, 204, Selavan, "Columbian Council," 5.

17. Several sources report similar trends in the 1920s. *Jewish Woman* (December 1924) 37; *Tenth Triennial Program of Work* (1920–1923), 60, 110.

18. Selavan, *My Voice was Heard*, 235–37; *Council Woman* (March 1950).

19. Another policy that contributed to Council networking was the establishment of local Good Will Committees, which visited new members to welcome them into the community and remembered members with notes on important occasions.

20. For example, Chicago Women's Aid, the Pioneers in St. Louis, or the Queen Esther Society of Madison, Wisconsin.

Selected Bibliography

PRIMARY SOURCES

Books and Articles

Adlerblum, Nima H. "Memoirs of Childhood–An Approach to Jewish Philosophy," in *Guardians of Our Heritage, 1724–1953*, ed. Leo Jung, pp. 31–152. New York: Bloch, 1958.

———. "Sara Bayla and Her Times" in *Jewish Leaders, 1750–1940*, ed. Leo Jung, pp. 343–92. New York: Bloch, 1952.

Aguilar, Grace. *Home Influence*. London: George Stoneman, n.d.

Blumauer, Blanche. "The Council of Jewish Women in Portland, 1905." *Jewish Times and Observer* (San Francisco), 17 February 1905; reprinted in *Western States Historical Quarterly* 9:1 (1976), 19–20.

Cowen, Philip. *Memories of an American Jew*. New York: International Press, 1932.

Davis, Isabelle J. *Some Reasons Why the Jew Should Desire Woman Suffrage*. London: Jewish League for Woman Suffrage, 1914 (pamphlet).

De Sola, Meldola. *Jewish Ministers: An Arraignment of American Reform Judaism*. Reprint from the *Hebrew Standard* (N.Y.), 1905.

Ferber, Edna. *Fanny Herself*. New York: Frederick A. Stokes Co., 1917.

Gage, Matilda Joslyn. *Woman, Church and State*. n.p., 1893; reprint Watertown, Mass.: Persephone Press, 1980.

Graziani, Bernice. *Where There's a Woman: 75 Years of History as Lived by the National Council of Jewish Women.* New York: McCall, 1967.

Hart, Sara L. *The Pleasure is Mine: An Autobiography.* Chicago: Valentine-Newman, 1947.

Hirsch, Emil G. *My Religion.* New York: Macmillan, 1925.

Kohler, Kaufmann. *Hebrew Union College and Other Addresses.* Cincinnati: Ark Publishing Co., 1916.

Kohut, Rebekah. *More Yesterdays.* New York: Bloch, 1950.

———. *My Portion.* n.p., 1925; reprint New York: Arno Press, 1975.

———. *As I Know Them.* Garden City, N.Y.: Doubleday, Doran & Co., 1929.

Levinger, Elma Ehrlich. "Jewish Anti-Semitism," in *Jewish Experiences in America: Suggestions For the Study of Jewish Relations with Non-Jews,* ed. Bruno Lasker. New York: The Inquiry, 1930.

Mann, Denise Berg. *The Woman in Judaism.* Hartford, Conn.: Jonathan Publications, 1979.

Marcus, Jacob Rader. *The American Jewish Woman—Documents.* New York: KTAV, 1981.

Meyer, Annie Nathan. *Barnard Beginnings.* Boston: Houghton Mifflin, 1935.

———. *It's Been Fun.* New York: Henry Schuman, 1951.

Miner, Maud E. *Slavery of Prostitution.* New York: Macmillan, 1916.

Proceedings of the Carnegie Hall Celebration of the 250th Anniversary of the Settlement of the Jews in the United States (Thanksgiving Day). New York: New York Cooperative Society, 1906.

Polacheck, Hilda Satt. *I Came A Stranger: The Story of a Hull House Girl.* Chicago: University of Chicago, 1989.

Remy, Nahida Lazarus. *The Jewish Woman.* Trans. Louise Mannheimer. n.p., 1895; reprint New York: Bloch, 1916.

Roe, Clifford. *The Great War on White Slavery.* n.p., 1911; reprint New York: Garland, 1979.

Ruskay, Esther. *Hearth and Home Essays.* Philadelphia: JPS, 1902.

Sachs, Emanie. *Red Damask.* New York: Harper & Bros., 1927.

Sanger, Margaret. *Margaret Sanger: An Autobiography.* n.p., 1938; reprint New York: Dover, 1971.

Schwab, Mrs. Robert. *A Record of Service.* Ft. Wayne: Indiana Jewish Historical Society, 1974.

Shiloh, Ailon. *By Myself I'm a Book: An Oral History of the Immigrant Jewish Experience in Pittsburgh.* Waltham, Mass.: AJHS and Pittsburgh Section, NCJW, 1972.

Solis-Cohen, Emily. "The Jewish Girl's Thoughts on Jewish Life," in

Jewish Experiences in America, ed. Bruno Lasker. New York: The Inquiry, 1930.

Solomon, Hannah. *Fabric of My Life.* New York: Bloch, 1946.

———. *A Sheaf of Leaves.* Chicago: privately printed, 1911.

Stone, Goldie. *My Caravan of Years.* New York: Bloch, 1946.

Wald, Lillian. *The House on Henry Street.* New York: Henry Holt, 1915.

———. *Windows on Henry Street.* Boston: Little, Brown, 1937.

Water, Pearl. "Pearl Water on NCJW," *Lilith* 5 (1975), 18.

Newspapers and Periodicals

American Hebrew. New York. 1886–1931.

American Israelite. Cincinnati. 1893–1920.

American Jewess. St. Louis and Chicago. 1895–1899.

Jewish Messenger. New York. 1893–1897 (then became *American Hebrew*).

The Jewish South. Richmond, Va. 1893.

The Menorah: Official Organ of the Independent Order of B'nai B'rith. 1896.

Reform Advocate. Chicago. 1891–1929.

Council Documents, National

Across the Nation. 1941–1967.

The Branch. 1951–53.

Cohen, Nathan, ed. *The Citizen Volunteer.* New York: NCJW, 1958.

Campbell, Monroe, and William Wirtz. *The First Fifty Years: A History of the National Council of Jewish Women, 1893–1943.* New York: NCJW, 1943.

Constitution of the Council of Jewish Women, 1909.

Council Newsletter (formerly *The Jewish Woman*). 1933–38.

Council of Jewish Women Bulletin. 1908, 1911.

Council Pioneer: A History of the Council in the Vanguard of Social Advance, 1893–1955. New York: NCJW, 1955.

Council Platform: Public Affairs Discussion & Information Bulletin. Vols. 2–10. New York: NCJW, 1956–66.

Council Woman. 1940–77.

A Course of Study on Jewish Prayer. New York: NCJW Committee on Religion, 1923.

Department of Immigrant Aid Programs for Immigrants. 1922.

Fiftieth Anniversary Bulletin. November 1946.

First Annual Report. 1894–95.

Hook, Dr. Sydney. *The National Council of Jewish Women on the Present Day Jewish Scene.* Commissioned by the NCJW, 1946.

Huhner, Leon. *The Jewish Woman in America.* New York: CJW, reprinted from the *American Hebrew,* 1918.

The Immigrant, Bulletin of the NCJW Department of Immigrant Aid. IV:4 (December 1924), V:7 (March 1926).

The Jewish Woman. Vols. 1–11. 1921–31.

Levinger, Elma Ehrlich. *The Tower of David.* New York: NCJW and Bloch, 1924.

Minutes, National Board & Executive Committee. 1914, 1916–17, 1926–31, 1935–50.

Minutes, National Committee on International Relations & Peace. 1940–45.

Minutes, National Committee on Social Legislation. 1943–46.

Minutes, Special Board Meeting with Disaffected Sections. 1915.

The National Council of Jewish Women, 1893–1938. New York: NCJW, 1938.

National Council of Jewish Women: Proceedings of the First Convention, November 15–19, 1896. Philadelphia: JPS, 1897.

Papers of the Jewish Women's Congress, 1893. Philadelphia: JPS, 1894.

Program of Work. 1897–99, 1908–11, 1911–14, 1914–17.

Rosenbaum, Jonathan, and Patricia Rosenbaum, eds. *Our Story.* Omaha: NCJW, 1981.

Spotlight. 1945–53.

Sternberger, Estelle M. *Daily Readings in Human Service: A Handbook of Information on Council Ideals and Activities.* New York: NCJW, 1925.

Summary of Female Employment in New York State, 1905–1915. CJW Department of Immigrant Aid, 1915.

Triennial Proceedings. 1905, 1908, 1911, 1914, 1917, 1920, 1923, 1926, 1930, 1932, 1948.

Council Documents, Local

Albany Section Yearbook. 1912–13.

Baltimore Section Minutes. 1902.

Baltimore Section Program of Work. 1896–1903.

Baltimore Section Yearbook. 1920–21.

Boston Section Fiftieth Anniversary Program. 1943.

Brooklyn Section: A History. Brooklyn Section, 1982.

Cincinnati Section Bulletin. 1916–18.

Cincinnati Section Minutes. 1908–17.

Cincinnati Section Miscellaneous Reports & Correspondence. 1899–1900, 1900–01, 1903–04, 1909–10, 1923–44.

Cincinnati Section Program of Work. 1898–99.

Cincinnati Section Yearbook. 1903–04, 1904–05, 1924–25.

Chicago Section Bulletin. 1921–24.

Chicago Section Calendar & Report, 1915–16.

Cleveland and the National Council. Cleveland Council of Jewish Women, 1908.

Columbia, S.C. Section Minutes. 1919–21.

Hanukkah Service for the Home. Newark Section, CJW, 1912.

Little Daily Helps. New York City Section, 1908.

Madison, Wis. Section Bulletin. 1924–27, 1949–61.

Minneapolis Section Study Circle Program. 1917–18.

Moses, Adolph. *Yahwism and Other Discourses.* Louisville Section, NCJW, 1903.

New York City Section Yearbook. 1904–05.

Plaut, Gunther. *Historical Questionnaire.* St. Paul Section, 1956.

Prayerbook for Jewish Deaf. Philadelphia Section, CJW (Committee on Welfare of the Deaf), 1919.

Record of Progress. Chicago Section of the Council of Jewish Women, 1908.

Report of the Committee of Summer Work for Jewish Girls. Chicago Section, 1894.

St. Louis Section Yearbook. 1926–27.

Savannah, GA Section Minutes. 1895–98.

Skutch, Rachel Frank, and Doris Patz. *Deeds to Live By.* Baltimore: Baltimore Section, NCJW, 1968.

Solomon, Mrs. Henry. *Jews of Illinois in Story and Tableaux.* Chicago Section, CJW, 1919.

Synopsis of Programs with Biographies of Presidents, 1940–1950. Minneapolis Section, NCJW.

Wolf, Rose, Hortense Wolf, and Ruth C. Feibel. *History of the Council (Cincinnati Section), 1895–1965.*

Personal Interviews

(interview by author, audio cassette recording, New York City, 2 September 1987)

Jesse Brilliant

Joan Bronk
Ethel Cohen
Lenore Feldman
Susan Katz
Hannah Levin
Shirley Leviton
Lynn Liss
Barbara Mandel
Diane Marowitz
Ellie Marvin
Helen Powers
Ann Robison
Flora Rothenberg
Winnie Saltzman

Archival Materials, American Jewish Archives

Biographies Files

Barbe, Lizzie
Davis, Dora Cohen
Kahn, Florence Prag (Nearprint Box)
Lasker, Loula D. (Nearprint Box)
Levinger, Elma Ehrlich (Nearprint Box)
Lewi, Alice Bertha
May, Jean Wise

Correspondence Files

Davis, Mrs. Benjamin A.
Mandel, Babette
Ruskay, Esther J.
Szold, Henrietta

Genealogies Files

Adler Family
Mordecai Family
Streng Family

Histories Files

Brooklyn, N.Y.
Kokomo, Ind.

Miscellaneous Files

Davis, Ida (Mrs. Harry)

Microfilm

Kander, Lizzie Black (#1400–1401)
Nathan, Maud—Scrapbook (#488)
Terre Haute, Ind.—Council Minutes 1907 (#2525)

Nearprint Files

Angel, Mrs. Philip—interview with Gerald Kane, 20 April 1970,
    Charleston, W. Va.
Kohut, Rebekah
National Council of Jewish Women, Canada
National Council of Jewish Women—Special Topics
Solomon, Hannah

Boxes and Collections

Engel, Irving (Small Collections)
Felsenthal, Bernard (Box X-12)
Happy Workers minutes, Charleston, S.C. (Box 2094)
Kohut, George Alexander (Box 622)
Gerstley, Mrs. Henry H. (Box 2072)
Mannheimer, Jennie (Box 793)
Jennie Purvin Collection (Box 2278e, g, and l)
Jacob Schiff Collection (Box 9-Folder 450)
Solomon, Hannah (Box X-124, X-172)
Sonneschein, Rosa (Small Collections)
Felix Warburg Collection (Box 1, 2, 3, 23, 28, 85, 93)

Archival Materials, Documents Obtained from the Federal Bureau of
Investigation Under the Freedom of Information Act

Though no file exists on NCJW itself, 46 of 65 pages with cross-references
were released on 2 November 1990 with the following reference numbers:
100-410898-114, 61-3176-1553, 61-6991-334, 61-7559-3598,
61-10498-1042, 100-3-2916, 100-95014-58
One reference number was listed as classified.

Archival Materials, Library of Congress

National Council of Jewish Women Collection

Reports of NCJW U.N. Observer. 1947–1960. Box 145.
Reports of NCJW Statements and Testimony Before the U.S. Congress.
1949–1961. Box 117.
Miscellaneous papers, correspondence, educational materials, program
materials, pamphlets. Box 72, 82, 93–97, 99–103, 107–10, 114–17,
126, 131–35, 141–46, 162.

SECONDARY SOURCES

Though relatively little has been written on the experience of American
Jewish women, several contributions to the field provided a framework for
this study by including general histories. To date, though written too early
in the development of women's history methodology to be definitive, the
most comprehensive and valuable work is Charlotte Baum, Paula Hyman,
and Sonya Michel, *The Jewish Woman in America* (New York: Dial Press,
1976). For a more brief reference, see Ann D. Braude, "Jewish Women in
the Twentieth Century: Building A Life in America," in *Women and
Religion in America*, Vol. 3: *1900–1968*, ed. Rosemary Radford Ruether
and Rosemary Skinner Keller (San Francisco: Harper & Row, 1986),
131–74. The only comprehensive single volume recounting of Jewish
women's multifaceted encounter with modern-day feminism is Susan
Weidman Schneider, *Jewish and Female* (New York: Simon & Schuster,
1984).
Also valuable to this study were articles concentrating on specific sub-

groups of American Jewish women, including Paula Hyman, "Culture and Gender: Women in the Immigrant Jewish Community," in *The Legacy of Jewish Immigration: 1881 and Its Impact*, ed. David Berger (New York: Brooklyn College, 1983), 157–65; Elinor Lerner, "Jewish Involvement in the New York City Woman Suffrage Movement," in *AJHS* 70:4 (June 1981), 442–61; and Corrine Krause, "Jewish Immigrant Women in Pittsburgh, 1865–1890," unpublished paper, 1984. Biographies of specific individuals were also helpful, including Joan Dash, *Summoned to Jerusalem: The Life of Henrietta Szold* (New York: Harper & Row, 1979); and Dianne C. Ashton, "Rebecca Gratz and the Domestication of American Judaism," (Ph.D. diss., Temple University, 1986).

Also important for context, as well as comparison, were works on other Jewish Women's organizations. The most significant were: on Germany, Marion Kaplan, *The Jewish Feminist Movement in Germany: The Campaigns of the Jüdischer Frauenbund, 1904–1938* (Westport, Conn.: Greenwood Press), 1979; and Marion Kaplan, "The Campaign for Woman's Suffrage in the Jewish Community in Germany," #18—Working Papers in Yiddish and Eastern European Jewish Studies (New York: Max Weinreich Center for Advanced Jewish Studies of YIVO Institute for Jewish Research, 1976). On England, see Linda Kuzmack, "The Emergence of the Jewish Women's Movement in England and the United States, 1881–1933: A Comparative Study" (Ph.D. diss., George Washington University, 1986); and Rickie Burman, "Women in Jewish Religious Life: Manchester 1880–1930" in *Disciplines of Faith: Studies in Religion, Politics and Patriarchy*, ed. Jim Obelkevich, Lyndal Roper, Raphael Samuel (London: Routledge & Kegan Paul, 1987), 37–70.

Another obvious framework for this study were academic works analyzing the role of women's clubs in the United States. Particularly helpful was Theodora Penny Martin, *The Sound of Our Own Voices: Women's Study Clubs, 1860–1910* (Boston: Beacon, 1987). Though the history of NCJW contradicts many of its conclusions, also important was Karen Blair, *The Clubwoman as Feminist: True Womanhood Redefined, 1868–1914* (New York: Holmes & Meier, 1980).

Key to developing an understanding of domestic feminism were Ann Douglas, *The Feminization of American Culture* (New York: Knopf, 1977); Daniel Scott Smith, "Family Limitation, Sexual Control, and Domestic Feminism in Victorian America," in *A Heritage of Her Own: Toward a New Social History of American Women*, ed. Nancy F. Cott and Elizabeth H. Pleck (New York: Simon & Schuster, 1979), 222–45; Barbara Welter, "The Feminization of American Religion, 1800–1860," in *Clio's Con-*

sciousness Raised, ed. Mary Hartman and Lois W. Banner (New York: Harper & Row, 1974); and Kathryn Kish Sklar, *Catharine Beecher, A Study in American Domesticity* (New York: Norton, 1976).

One debate that has emerged in the study of women's clubs is over the role and meaning of voluntarism in women's lives. Several scholars have provided valuable insight on this issue, including Arlene Kaplan Daniels, *Invisible Careers: Women Civic Leaders from the Volunteer World* (Chicago: University of Chicago Press, 1988); June Sochen, "Some Observations on the Role of American Jewish Women as Communal Volunteers," in *American Jewish History* 70:1 (September 1980), 23–34; Irene D. Neu, "The Jewish Business Woman in America," in *American Jewish History Quarterly* 66 (1976), 137–54; and Paula Hyman, "The Volunteer Organizations: Vanguard or Rear Guard?" in *Lilith* 5 (1978), 17, 22. Lyman Cromwell White detailed the specific conflicts between NCJW volunteers and professional social workers at Ellis Island (*300,000 New Americans* [New York: Harper & Bros., 1957], 296–309).

At the turn of the century, a vital facet of women's voluntarism was settlement house work. NCJW, especially, modeled many of its programs on Jane Addams' Hull House. Providing essential background on Addams' efforts were two books from University of Chicago Press: Rivka Shpak Lissak, *Pluralism & Progressives: Hull House and the New Immigrants, 1890–1919* (1989) and Mina Carson, *Settlement Folk: Social Thought and the American Settlement Movement, 1885–1930* (1990). Another work from University of Chicago Press important to understanding the community from which NCJW sprang was Kathleen D. McCarthy, *Noblesse Oblige: Charity and Cultural Philanthropy in Chicago, 1849–1929* (1982). Specific to the history of Jews was Selma Berrol, "Germans vs. Russians: An Update," in *American Jewish History* 73:2 (December 1983), 142–56.

Providing the broader context of immigrant aid were histories of the Progressive Era, including Robert Wiebe, *The Search for Order, 1877–1920* (New York: Hill & Wang, 1967); and Richard Hofstadter, *The Age of Reform* (New York: Knopf, 1955).

Of course, also important to context were works on American Jewish history, including Ruth Gruber, *Haven, the Unknown Story of 1,000 World War II Refugees* (New York: Coward-McCann, 1983), which is the only recounting of NCJW's involvement with the Jewish settlement at Oswego, New York. More general works included: Daniel J. Elazar, *Community and Polity: The Organizational Dynamics of American Jewry* (Philadelphia: JPS, 1980); Leon Jick, *The Americanization of the Synagogue, 1820–1870* (Hanover, N.H.: University Press of New England, 1976);

Michael Meyer, *The Origins of the Modern Jew* (Detroit: Wayne State University Press, 1967); Deborah Dash Moore, *B'nai B'rith and the Challenge of Ethnic Leadership* (Albany, N.Y.: SUNY-Albany, 1981); Jonathan Woocher, *Sacred Survival: The Civil Religion of American Jews* (Bloomington: Indiana University Press, 1986); Jonathan Sarna, *JPS: The Americanization of Jewish Culture, 1888–1988* (Philadelphia: JPS, 1989); Naomi Cohen, *Encounter with Emancipation* (Philadelphia: JPS, 1984); and Abraham J. Karp, *Haven and Home: A History of the Jews of America* (New York: Schocken, 1985).

In celebration of several milestone anniversaries NCJW has commissioned popular national histories, but to date, no history of the organization has been published that is national in scope and academic in method. There have, however, been some important unpublished works, the most significant of which is Ellen Sue Levi Elwell, "The Founding and Early Programs of the National Council of Jewish Women: Study and Practice as Jewish Women's Religious Expression" (Ph.D. diss., Indiana University, 1982), which focused on Council's religious development primarily as it affected adult education programs. Although my study is indebted to Elwell's ground-breaking thesis, especially her excellent biographical work, it differs in several significant areas. It broadens Elwell's educational focus to include all Council programming and extends beyond Elwell's 1913 cutoff point to demonstrate how Council's early years affected the formulation of policy in subsequent decades. The most significant departure from Elwell's work is the placement of NCJW in the context of domestic feminism. Where Elwell contends that sexist opposition forced Council to moderate its otherwise radical challenge to traditional Jewish gender roles, I argue that such opposition was minimal because Jews correctly saw NCJW as supporting traditional gender roles rather than challenging them.

Another thesis, Reena Sigman Freedman's "Their Sisters' Keepers: The Response of the National Council of Jewish Women to East European Jewish Women, 1893–1924" (M.A. thesis, Columbia University, 1978), provided important details on the complicated relationship between NCJW and its immigrant clients and recognized that the relationship was not mere paternalism, though Freedman did not adequately explain why NCJW's approach was different from that taken by other Jewish organizations.

Several scholars of American Jewish history have provided valuable close-ups of individual NCJW Sections. Ida Cohen Selavan has chronicled the Pittsburgh Section in "The Columbian Council of Pittsburgh, 1894–1909: A Case Study of Adult Immigrant Education," (Ph.D. diss., University of Pittsburgh, 1976); *My Voice was Heard* (New York: KTAV and Pittsburgh Section, NCJW, 1981); and "The Founding of Columbian Council," in *AJA* 30:1 (1978), 24–42. Other local histories that include material on NCJW include: William Toll, *The Making of an Ethnic Middle Class: Portland Jewry Over Four Generations* (Albany: SUNY, 1982); Selig Adler, *From Ararat to Suburbia: The History of the Jewish Community of Buffalo* (Philadelphia: JPS, 1960); Mark H. Elovitz, *A Century of Jewish Life in Dixie: The Birmingham Experience* (University: University of Alabama Press, 1974); Murray Friedman, ed., *Jewish Life in Philadelphia 1830–1940* (Philadelphia: ISHI Publications, 1983); Steven Hertzberg, *Strangers Within the Gate City: The Jews of Atlanta, 1845–1915* (Philadelphia: JPS, 1978); Gunther Plaut, *The Jews in Minnesota: The First 75 Years* (New York: AJHS, 1959); Marc Lee Raphael, *Jews and Judaism in a Midwestern Community: Columbus, Ohio, 1840–1975* (Columbus: Ohio Historical Society, 1979); Louis J. Swichkow and Lloyd P. Gartner, *The History of the Jews of Milwaukee* (Philadelphia: JPS, 1963); Ida Libert Uchill, *Pioneers, Peddlers, and Tsadikim* (Denver: Sage Books, 1957). Important articles on local Sections include Judith Aronson, "The National Council of Jewish Women: A Study of the Los Angeles Section in Transition," in *Speaking of Faith*, ed. Diana L. Eck and Devaki Jain (London: Women's Press, 1986), 184–89; and Beth Wenger, "Jewish Women of the Club: The Changing Public Role of Atlanta's Jewish Women (1870–1930)," in *AJHS* (March 1987) 311–33;

More general articles on NCJW include: Deborah Grand Golomb, "The 1893 Congress of Jewish Women: Evolution or Revolution in American Jewish Women's History?" in *American Jewish History* 70 (September 1980), 52–67; William Toll, "A Quiet Revolution: Jewish Women's Clubs and the Widening Female Sphere, 1870–1920," in *AJA* (Spring/Summer 1989), 7–26; Evelyn Bodeck, "Making Do: Jewish Women and Philanthropy," in *Jewish Life in Philadelphia, 1830–1940*, ed. Murray Friedman (Philadelphia: ISHI, 1983), 143–162; C.H.L., "The National Council of Jewish Women," *Leslie's Weekly* (19 November 1896), 331; "The National Council of Jewish Women," *Charities and the Commons*, 15 (6 January 1906), 426–28; Rebekah Kohut, "Jewish Women's Organizations in the United States," *American Jewish Yearbook, 1931–32* (Philadelphia: JPS, 1931), 165–201; Michael N. Dobkowski, ed., *Jewish American Voluntary Organizations* (New York: Greenwood Press, 1986).

Biographical information on NCJW members was obtained from several volumes of the *American Jewish Yearbook* and *Who's Who in American Jewry*, Vols. I, II, and III (New York: Jewish Biographical Bureau, 1926, 1928, 1938), as well as from Anita Libman Lebeson, *Recall to Life* (New York: Yoseloff, 1970); Simon Litman, *Ray Frank Litman: A Memoir* (New

York: *AJHS*, 1957); Elisabeth Israels Perry, *Belle Moskowitz* (New York: Oxford, 1987); and Selma C. Berrol, "Julia Richman: Agent of Change in the Urban School," *Review Journal of Philosophy and Social Sciences* 11:2 (Winter 1977), 139–40 and "When Uptown Met Downtown: Julia Richman's Work in the Jewish Community of New York, 1880–1912," *American Jewish History* 70 (September 1980), 35–51; Abram S. Isaacs, "The Jewess in Authorship," *Ladies Home Journal* 9 (October 1892), 17; Jack Nusan Porter, "Rosa Sonneschein and the *American Jewess:* First Independent English Language Jewish Women's Journal in the United States," *American Jewish History* 68:1 (1978), 57–63; and Barbara Stuhler, "Fanny Brin: Woman of Peace," in Barbara Stuhler and Gretchen Kreuter, eds., *Women of Minnesota: 101 Selected Biographical Essays* (St. Paul: Minnesota Historical Society Press, 1977), 284–300.

Index

Page numbers in boldface indicate biographical sketches.

ABOUT THE AUTHOR

AITH ROGOW is Man-
ager of Educational Services, WSKG Public Broadcasting, and
Adjunct Assistant Professor, Women's Studies and School of Education and Human Development, Binghamton, New York. She received her B.A. from Indiana University and her M.A. and Ph.D.
from State University of New York at Binghamton.